uncovered editions

THE CUBAN
MISSILE CRISIS, 1962

SELECTED FOREIGN POLICY
DOCUMENTS FROM THE
ADMINISTRATION OF JOHN F. KENNEDY,
JANUARY 1961–NOVEMBER 1962

∞⧉∞

D0353786

London: The Stationery Office

© The Stationery Office 2001

ISBN 0 11 702745 6
Most of the original documents are from the US Department of State, *Foreign Relations of the United States*, 1961–1963, Volumes X–XI. Others are taken from National Security files and other specialised repositories within the USA.

A CIP catalogue record for this book is available from the British Library.

Cover photograph shows John F. Kennedy on 11 February 1962 giving a speech on the steps of the White House, surrounded by his advisers. © Bettmann/CORBIS.

Maps produced by Sandra Lockwood of Artworks Design, Norwich.

Typeset by J&L Composition Ltd, Filey, North Yorkshire.
Printed in the United Kingdom by The Stationery Office, London.
TJ4363 C30 9/01

Praise for *uncovered editions*

"*The repackaging of classics is a tried and trusted winner, but Tim Coates has come up with something entirely original: the repackaging of history. His* **uncovered editions** *collect papers from the archive of The Stationery Office into verbatim narratives, so, for instance, in* UFOs in the House of Lords *we get a hilarious recreation, directly from Hansard, of a nutty debate that took place in 1979 . . . This is inspired publishing, not only archivally valuable but capable of bringing the past back to life without the usual filter of academic or biographer.*" **Guardian**

"*The Irish Uprising is a little treasure of a book and anyone with an interest in Irish history will really enjoy it. Its structure is extremely unusual as it is compiled from historic official reports published by the British government from 1914 to 1920 . . . For anyone studying this period of history* The Irish Uprising *is a must as the correspondence and accounts within it are extremely illuminating and the subtle nuances of meaning can be teased out of the terms and phrasing to be more revelatory than the actual words themselves.*" **Irish Press, Belfast**

"*Voyeurs of all ages will enjoy the original text of the Denning report on Profumo. It is infinitely superior to the film version of the scandal, containing such gems as: 'One night I was invited to a dinner party at the home of a very, very rich man. After I arrived, I discovered it was rather an unusual dinner party. All the guests had taken off their clothes . . . The most intriguing person was a man with a black mask over his face. At first I thought this was a party gimmick. But the truth was that this man is so well known and holds such a responsible position that he did not want to be associated with anything improper.' *" **Times Higher Education Supplement**

"*Very good to read . . . insight into important things . . . inexorably moving . . . If you want to read about the* Titanic*, you won't read a better thing . . . a revelation.*" **Open Book, BBC Radio 4**

"*Congratulations to The Stationery Office for unearthing and reissuing such an enjoyable vignette*" [*on* Wilfrid Blunt's Egyptian Garden] **The Spectator**

uncovered editions
www.uncovered-editions.co.uk

Series editor: Tim Coates
Managing editor: Michele Staple

New titles in the series
The Assassination of John F. Kennedy, 1963
Attack on Pearl Harbor, 1941
Letters of Henry VIII, 1526–29
Mr Hosie's Journey to Tibet, 1904
The St Valentine's Day Massacre, 1929
Trials of Oscar Wilde
UFOs in America, 1947
The Watergate Affair, 1972

Already published
The Amritsar Massacre: General Dyer in the Punjab, 1919
Bloody Sunday, 1972: Lord Widgery's Report
The Boer War: Ladysmith and Mafeking, 1900
British Battles of World War I, 1914–15
The British Invasion of Tibet: Colonel Younghusband, 1904
Defeat at Gallipoli: the Dardanelles Commission Part II, 1915–16
D Day to VE Day: General Eisenhower's Report, 1944–45
Escape from Germany, 1939–45
Florence Nightingale and the Crimea, 1854–55
The Irish Uprising, 1914–21
John Profumo and Christine Keeler, 1963
The Judgment of Nuremberg, 1946
King Guezo of Dahomey, 1850–52
Lord Kitchener and Winston Churchill: The Dardanelles
    Commission Part I, 1914–15
The Loss of the Titanic, 1912
R.101: the Airship Disaster, 1930
Rillington Place, 1949
The Russian Revolution, 1917
The Siege of Kars, 1855
The Siege of the Peking Embassy, 1900
The Strange Story of Adolf Beck
Tragedy at Bethnal Green
Travels in Mongolia, 1902
UFOs in the House of Lords, 1979
War in the Falklands, 1982
War 1914: Punishing the Serbs
War 1939: Dealing with Adolf Hitler
Wilfrid Blunt's Egyptian Garden: Fox-hunting in Cairo

CONTENTS

About the series

Uncovered editions are historic official papers which have not previously been available in a popular form, and have been chosen for the quality of their story-telling. Some subjects are familiar, but others are less well known. Each is a moment in history.

About the series editor, Tim Coates

Tim Coates studied at University College, Oxford and at the University of Stirling. After working in the theatre for a number of years, he took up bookselling and became managing director, firstly of Sherratt and Hughes bookshops, and then of Waterstone's. He is known for his support for foreign literature, particularly from the Czech Republic. The idea for *uncovered editions* came while searching through the bookshelves of his late father-in-law, Air Commodore Patrick Cave, OBE. He is married to Bridget Cave, has two sons, and lives in London.

Tim Coates welcomes views and ideas on the *uncovered editions* series. He can be e-mailed at
timcoates@theso.co.uk

LIST OF PERSONS

ACHESON, DEAN, Secretary of State under President Truman

ADENAUER, KONRAD, Chancellor of West Germany

ANDERSON, ADMIRAL GEORGE W., USN, Chief of Naval Operations

BALL, GEORGE W., Under Secretary of State

BOHLEN, CHARLES E., Ambassador to France

BUNDY, MCGEORGE, Special Assistant to the President for National Security Affairs

CARTER, LIEUTENANT GENERAL MARSHALL S., USA, Deputy Director of Central Intelligence

CASTRO RUZ, FIDEL, Prime Minister of Cuba

CLEVELAND, J. HARLAN, Assistant Secretary of State for International Organization Affairs

CLINE, RAY S., Deputy Director of Intelligence

DE GAULLE, GENERAL CHARLES, President of France

DENNISON, ADMIRAL ROBERT L., USN, Commander in Chief, Atlantic

DILLON, C. DOUGLAS, Secretary of the Treasury

DONOVAN, JAMES B., New York lawyer; negotiated settlement with Fidel Castro on the release of Cuban captives, after the Bay of Pigs

DOBRYNIN, ANATOLIY F., Soviet Ambassador to the United States

EISENHOWER, DWIGHT D., President of the United States until January 20, 1961

FINLETTER, THOMAS K., Ambassador to the North Atlantic Treaty Organization

FOMIN, ALEKSANDR S., Counselor to Soviet Embassy in the United States

GILPATRIC, ROSWELL L., Deputy Secretary of Defense

GROMYKO, ANDREI, Minister of Foreign Affairs, Union of Soviet Socialist Republics

HARRIMAN, W. AVERELL, Secretary of State for Far Eastern Affairs

JOHNSON, LYNDON B., Vice President of the United States

JOHNSON, U. ALEXIS, Deputy Under Secretary of State for Political Affairs

KATZENBACH, NICHOLAS DE B., Deputy Attorney General

KAYSEN, CARL, Deputy Special Assistant to the President for National Security Affairs

KENNEDY, JOHN F., President of the United States

KENNEDY, ROBERT F., Attorney General of the United States

KENT, SHERMAN, Chairman of the Board of National Estimates, Central Intelligence Agency

KHRUSHCHEV, NIKITA S., Chairman of the Council of Ministers of the Union of Soviet Socialist Republics

KOHLER, FOY D., Ambassador to the Soviet Union

KUZNETSOV, VASILIY V., First Deputy Minister of Foreign Affairs, Union of Soviet Socialist Republics

LANSDALE, MAJOR GENERAL EDWARD G., USAF, Special Assistant to the Secretary of Defense for Special Operations

LEMAY, GENERAL CURTIS, Chief of Staff, US Air Force

LUNDAHL, ARTHUR C., Director, National Photographic Interpretation Center, Central Intelligence Agency

MACMILLAN, HAROLD, British Prime Minister

MARTIN, EDWIN M., Assistant Secretary of State for Inter-American Affairs

MCCLOY, JOHN J., Presidential adviser and Chairman of the Coordinating Committee for US–Soviet Negotiations over Cuba at the United Nations

MCCONE, JOHN A., Director of Central Intelligence

MCNAMARA, ROBERT S., Secretary of Defense

MEEKER, LEONARD C., legal adviser to the State Department

MIKOYAN, ANASTAS I., First Deputy Chairman of the Council of Ministers of the Union of Soviet Socialist Republics

NITZE, PAUL H., Assistant Secretary of Defense for International Security Affairs

ROSTOW, WALT W., Counselor of the Department of State and Chairman of the Policy Planning Council

RUSK, DEAN, Secretary of State

SCALI, JOHN, correspondent, American Broadcasting Company

SCHLESINGER, ARTHUR M., Jr, Special Assistant to the President

SMITH, BROMLEY, Executive Secretary of the National Security Council

SORENSEN, THEODORE C., Special Counsel to the President

STEVENSON, ADLAI E., US Ambassador to the United Nations

TAYLOR, GENERAL MAXWELL D., USA, Chairman of the Joint Chiefs of Staff

THANT, U, Secretary General of the United Nations

THOMPSON, LLEWELLYN E., Ambassador-at-Large, Department of State

TYLER, WILLIAM R., Assistant Secretary of State for European Affairs

WILSON, DONALD, Acting Director of the US Information Agency

ZORIN, VALERIAN, Soviet Ambassador to the United Nations

LIST OF ABBREVIATIONS AND GLOSSARY

AFB	Air Force Base
AG	Attorney General
ARA	Bureau of Inter-American Affairs, Department of State
Bloc countries	Allies of the Soviet Union
Chicadee reports	Surveillance reports
Chiefs	Chiefs of Staff
CI	Counter-intelligence
CIA	Central Intelligence Agency
CINCEUR	Commander in Chief, US Forces, Europe
CINCLANT	Commander in Chief, US Forces, Atlantic
CINCSTRIKE	Commander in Chief, Strike Command
COCOM	Coordinating Committee of the Paris Consultative Group of Nations
CRC	Consejo Revolucionario Cubano (Cuban Revolutionary Council)
DCI	Director of Central Intelligence
Deptel	Department of State telegram
DOD	Department of Defense
Embtel	Embassy telegram
Eyes Only	Document to be read only by individuals with a need-to-know
FBI	Federal Bureau of Investigation
FKR	Russian tactical warhead
FRD	Federal Research Division
FROGS	Free over ground tactical rockets (Soviet Luna rockets)
FYI	For your information

GOT	Government of Turkey
ICBM	Intercontinental ballistic missile
IRBM	Intermediate-range ballistic missile
Ironbark	Special information handling channel for intelligence generated by Colonel Oleg Penkovsky
ISA	Office of International Security Affairs, Department of Defense
JCS	Joint Chiefs of Staff
JFK	John F. Kennedy
JURE	Revolutionary Junta, Cuban revolutionaries
KOMAR	Soviet missile-carrying patrol boats
LCI	Landing craft
LCT	Landing craft transport
LCVP	Troop-carrying landing craft
LOU	Troop-carrying landing craft
MiG	Soviet-made fighter aircraft
MLF	Multilateral force
MRBM	Medium-range ballistic missile
NAC	North Atlantic Council
NATO	North Atlantic Treaty Organization
NEA	Bureau of Near Eastern and South Asian Affairs, Department of State
NIE	National Intelligence Estimate
nm	nautical miles
NORAD	North American Air Defense Command
NPIC	National Photographic Interpretation Center
NRO	National Reconnaissance Office
NSC	National Security Council
OAIP	Russian cruise missile
OAS	Organization of American States
OD	Operating directive

OEP	Office of Emergency Planning
Operation Mongoose	Code name for the covert CIA operation aimed at removing Fidel Castro from power in Cuba. It was approved by President Kennedy in November 1961 and headed by Edward Lansdale.
PM	Prime Minister
POL	Petrol, oil, and lubricants
PRTB	Soviet transport
SAC	Strategic Air Command
SACEUR	Supreme Allied Commander, Europe
SAM	Surface-to-air missile
SCUD	Soviet-made surface-to-surface missile
SHAPE	Supreme Headquarters Allied Powers Europe
SNIE	Special National Intelligence Estimate
SYG	Secretary General of the United Nations
TASS	Telegraphnoye Agentstvo Sovyetskogo Soyuza (Telegraph Agency of the Soviet Union; Soviet news agency)
UN[O]	United Nations [Organization]
UNMIS	United Nations Mission
US[A]	United States [of America]
USIA	United States Information Agency
USIB	United States Intelligence Board
USN	United States Navy
USRO	United States Mission to European Regional Organizations in Paris
USSR	Union of Soviet Socialist Republics

*In 1961, the balance of power in the world was held by the
Soviet Union and the United States. One represented the
communist world, the other the capitalist. In 1945 the United
States had used two atom bombs to defeat and end the war with
Japan. Since that time, while both the Soviets and the Americans
had created and tested vast arsenals of nuclear weapons, neither
had ever again used them in conflict. The threat that either
country might initiate such a conflagration that would effectively
end life on the planet hung over the whole world. This was a
daily anxiety. It became known as the Cold War.*

*The symbolic dividing line between the powers was known as
the Iron Curtain, which was a heavily guarded and patrolled
frontier that lay across Europe. The city of Berlin, occupied by
armies of both Eastern and Western powers, lay inside the Soviet
alliance, in East Germany, as a consequence of treaties made at
the end of World War II.*

*Each power strove to enlarge its influence by alliances with
countries sympathetic to its ideology. In this way Cuba, an island
that lies just south of Florida in the United States, became,
through its revolutionary government, an ally of the Soviet
Union. It was this close geographical proximity, in an age when
far-ranging missile attack could be devastating, that caused so
much anxiety in the United States. America's first response to
Fidel Castro's Communist regime in Cuba was to attempt to
discredit it and have it overthrown, which culminated in the
ill-fated Bay of Pigs incident on 17 April 1961. The second*

response was precipitated by the Soviets sending intermediate-range nuclear missiles to Cuba, at Castro's invitation, which led to the Cuban Missile Crisis of October 1962.

John F. Kennedy had become the youngest-ever president of the United States in the elections of 1960, while Nikita Khrushchev had been leader of the Soviet Union since the death of Josef Stalin in 1953. During the crisis, the two sides exchanges many letters and other communications, a selection of which have been released under the Freedom of Information Act (along with other pertinent documents) and are presented in this book. The papers begin in January 1961, four months before the Bay of Pigs invasion, and conclude in November 1962, after the Kennedy–Krushchev "agreement" of 28 October 1962.

The Bay of Pigs, 1961

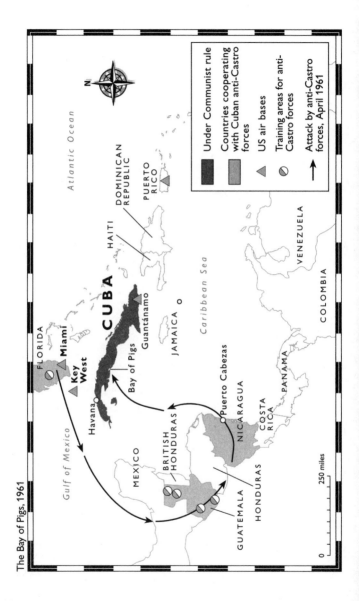

PART I

❦

THE BAY OF PIGS
1961

Memorandum from the Chief of WH/4/PM, Central Intelligence Agency (Hawkins) to the Chief of WH/4 of the Directorate for Plans (Esterline)
Washington, January 4, 1961

Policy decisions required for conduct of strike operations against Government of Cuba

Purpose: The purpose of this memorandum is to outline the current status of our preparations for the conduct of amphibious/airborne and tactical air operations against the Government of Cuba and to set forth certain requirements for policy decisions which must be reached and implemented if these operations are to be carried out.

Concept: As a basis for the policy requirements to be presented below, it would appear appropriate to review briefly the concept of the strike operations contemplated and outline the objectives which these operations are designed to accomplish.

The concept envisages the seizure of a small lodgement on Cuban soil by an all-Cuban amphibious/airborne force of about 750 men. The landings in Cuba will be preceded by a tactical air preparation, beginning at dawn of $D-1$ Day. The primary purpose of the air preparation will be to destroy or neutralize all Cuban military aircraft and naval vessels constituting a threat to the invasion force. When this task is accomplished, attacks will then be directed against other military targets, including artillery parks, tank parks, military vehicles, supply dumps, etc. Close air support will be provided to the invasion force on D Day and thereafter as long as the force is engaged in combat. The primary targets during this time will be opposing military formations in the field. Particular efforts will be made to interdict opposing troop movements against the lodgement.

The initial mission of the invasion force will be to seize and defend a small area, which under ideal conditions will include an airfield and access to the sea for logistic support. Plans must provide, however, for the eventuality that the force will be driven into a tight defensive formation which will preclude supply by sea or control of an airfield. Under such circumstances supply would have to be provided entirely by air drop. The primary objective of the force will be to survive and maintain its integrity on Cuban soil. There will be no early attempt to break out of the lodgement for further offensive operations unless and until there is a general uprising against the Castro regime or overt military intervention by United States forces has taken place.

It is expected that these operations will precipitate a general uprising throughout Cuba and cause the revolt of large segments of the Cuban Army and Militia. The lodgement, it is hoped, will serve as a rallying point for the thousands who are ready for overt resistance to Castro but who hesitate to act until they can feel some assurance of success. A general revolt in Cuba, if one is successfully triggered by our operations, may serve to topple the Castro regime within a period of weeks.

If matters do not eventuate as predicted above, the lodgement established by our force can be used as the site for establishment of a provisional government which can be recognized by the United States, and hopefully by other American states, and given overt military assistance. The way will then be paved for United States military intervention aimed at pacification of Cuba, and this will result in the prompt overthrow of the Castro Government.

While this paper is directed to the subject of strike operations, it should not be presumed that other paramilitary programs will be suspended or abandoned. These are being intensified and accelerated. They include the supply by air and sea of guerrilla elements in Cuba, the conduct of sabotage operations, the introduction of specially trained paramilitary teams, and the expansion of our agent networks throughout the island.

Status of forces

(a) Air. The Project tactical air force includes ten B-28 aircraft currently based in Guatemala and at Eglin Air Force

Base. However, there are only five Cuban B-26 pilots available at this time who are considered to be of highly
technical competence. Six additional Cuban pilots are
available, but their proficiency is questionable.

It is planned that seven C-54 and four C-46 transports
will be available for strike operations. Here again, the
number of qualified Cuban crews is insufficient. There is
one qualified C-54 crew on hand at this time, and three
C-46 crews.

Aviation ordnance for conduct of strike operations is yet
to be positioned at the strike base in Nicaragua. Necessary
construction and repairs at this base are now scheduled to
commence, and there appears to be no obstacle to placing
this facility in a state of readiness in time for operations as
planned.

Conclusions:
(1) The number of qualified Cuban B-26 crews avail-
     able is inadequate for conduct of strike operations.
(2) The number of qualified Cuban transport crews is
     grossly inadequate for supply operations which will
     be required in support of the invasion forces and
     other friendly forces which are expected to join or
     operate in conjunction with it in many parts of
     Cuba. It is anticipated that multiple sorties will be
     required on a daily basis.

(b) Maritime. Amphibious craft for the operation, including
three LOUs and four LCVPs are now at Viaques, Puerto
Rico, where Cuban crew training is progressing satisfactorily. These craft with their crews will soon be ready for
operations.

The *Barbara J* (LCI), now en route to the United States
from Puerto Rico, requires repairs which may take up to
two weeks for completion. The sister ship, the *Blagar*, is
outfitting in Miami, and its crew is being assembled. It is

expected that both vessels will be fully operational by mid-January at the latest.

In view of the difficulty and delay encountered in purchasing, outfitting and readying for sea the two LCIs, the decision has been reached to purchase no more major vessels, but to charter them instead. The motor ship, *Rio Escondido* (converted LCT), will be chartered this week and one additional steam ship, somewhat larger, will be chartered early in February. Both ships belong to a Panamanian Corporation controlled by the Garcia family of Cuba, who are actively cooperating with this Project. These two ships will provide sufficient lift for troops and supplies in the invasion operation.

Conclusion: Maritime assets required will be available in ample time for strike operations in late February.

(c) Ground. There are approximately 500 Cuban personnel now in training in Guatemala. Results being achieved in the FRD recruiting drive now underway in Miami indicate that extraordinary measures may be required if the ranks of the Assault Brigade are to be filled to its planned strength of 750 by mid-January. Special recruiting teams comprised of members of the Assault Brigade are being brought to Miami to assist in recruiting efforts in that city and possibly in other countries, [*less than one line of source text not declassified*]. All recruits should be available by mid-January to allow at least four to six weeks of training prior to commitment.

The Assault Brigade has been formed into its basic organization (a quadrangular infantry battalion, including four rifle companies, and a weapons company). Training is proceeding to the extent possible with the limited number of military instructors available. This force cannot be adequately trained for combat unless additional military trainers are provided.

Conclusions:

(1) It is probable that the Assault Brigade can reach its planned strength of 750 prior to commitment, but it is possible that upward of 100 of these men will be recruited too late for adequate training.

(2) Unless US Army Special Forces training teams as requested are sent promptly to Guatemala, the Assault Brigade cannot be readied for combat by late February as planned and desired.

(3) The Assault Brigade should not be committed to action until it has received at least four and preferably six weeks of training under supervision of the US Army team. This means that the latter half of February is the earliest satisfactory time for the strike operation.

Major policy questions requiring resolution

In order that planning and preparation for the strike operation may proceed in an orderly manner and correct positioning of hundreds of tons of supplies and equipment can be effected, a number of firm decisions concerning major questions of policy are required. These are discussed below.

(a) The concept itself

Discussion. The question of whether the incoming administration of President-Elect Kennedy will concur in the conduct of the strike operations outlined above needs to be resolved at the earliest possible time. If these operations are not to be conducted, then preparations for them should cease forthwith in order to avoid the needless waste of great human effort and many millions of dollars. Recruitment of additional Cuban personnel should be stopped, for every new recruit who is not employed in operations as intended presents an additional problem of eventual disposition.

Recommendation. That the Director of Central Intelligence attempt to determine the position of the President-Elect and his Secretary of State-Designate in regard to this question as soon as possible.

(b) Timing of the operation

If Army Special Forces training teams are made available and dispatched to Guatemala by mid-January, the Assault Brigade can achieve acceptable readiness for combat during the latter half of February, 1961. All other required preparations can be made by that same time. The operation should be launched during this period. Any delay beyond March 1, 1961, would be inadvisable for the following reasons:

(1) It is doubtful that Cuban forces can be maintained at our Guatemalan training base beyond March 1, 1961. Pressures upon the Government of Guatemala may become unmanageable if Cuban ground troops are not removed by that date.

(2) Cuban trainees cannot be held in training for much longer. Many have been in the camp for months under most austere and restrictive conditions. They are becoming restive and if not committed to action soon there will probably be a general lowering of morale. Large-scale desertions could occur with attendant possibilities of surfacing the entire program.

(3) While the support of the Castro Government by the Cuban populace is deteriorating rapidly and time is working in our favor in that sense, it is working to our disadvantage in a military sense. Cuban jet pilots are being trained in Czechoslovakia and the

appearance of modern radar throughout Cuba indicates a strong possibility that Castro may soon have an all-weather jet intercept capability. His ground forces have received vast quantities of military equipment from the Bloc countries, including medium and heavy tanks, field artillery, heavy mortars, and antiaircraft artillery. Bloc technicians are training his forces in the use of this formidable equipment. Undoubtedly, within the near future Castro's hard core of loyal armed forces will achieve technical proficiency in the use of available modern weapons.

(4) Castro is making rapid progress in establishing a Communist-style police state which will be difficult to unseat by any means short of overt intervention by US military forces.

Recommendation. That the strike operation be conducted in the latter half of February, and not later than March 1, 1961.

(c) Air strike
The question has been raised in some quarters as to whether an amphibious/airborne operation could not be mounted without tactical air preparation or support or with minimal air support. It is axiomatic in amphibious operations that control of air and sea in the objective area is absolutely required. The Cuban Air Force and naval vessels capable of opposing our landing must be knocked out or neutralized before our amphibious shipping makes its final run into the beach. If this is not done, we will be courting disaster. Also, since our invasion force is very small in comparison to forces which may be thrown against it, we must compensate for numerical inferiority by effective tactical air support not only during the land-

ing but thereafter as long as the force remains in combat. It is essential that opposing military targets such as artillery parks, tank parks, supply dumps, military convoys, and troops in the field be brought under effective and continuing air attack. Psychological considerations also make such attacks essential. The spectacular aspects of air operations will go far toward producing the uprising in Cuba that we seek.

Recommendations
(1) That the air preparation commence not later than dawn of D−1 Day.
(2) That any move to curtail the number of aircraft to be employed from those available be firmly resisted.
(3) That the operation be abandoned if policy does not provide for use of adequate tactical air support.

(d) Use of American contract pilots
The paragraph above outlines the requirement for precise and effective air strikes, while an earlier paragraph points up the shortage of qualified Cuban pilots. It is very questionable that the limited number of Cuban B-26 pilots available to us can produce the desired results unless augmented by highly skillful American contract pilots to serve as section and flight leaders in attacks against the more critical targets. The Cuban pilots are inexperienced in war and of limited technical competence in navigation and gunnery. There is reason also to suspect that they may lack the motivation to take the stern measures required against targets in their own country. It is considered that the success of the operation will be jeopardized unless a few American contract B-26 pilots are employed.

With regard to logistical air operations, the shortage of Cuban crews has already been mentioned. There is no prospect of producing sufficient Cuban C-54 crews to run the seven C-54 aircraft to be used in the operation. Our experience to date with the Cuban transport crews has left much to be desired. It is concluded that the only satisfactory solution to the problem of air logistical support of the strike force and other forces joining it will be to employ a number of American contract crews.

Recommendation. That policy approval be obtained for use of American contract crews for tactical and transport aircraft in augmentation of the inadequate number of Cuban crews available.

(e) Use of Puerto Cabezas, Nicaragua

The airfield at Puerto Cabezas is essential for conduct of the air strike operation unless a base is made available in the United States. Our air base in Guatemala is 800 miles from central Cuba—too distant for B-26 operations and for air supply operations of the magnitude required, using the C-46 and C-54 aircraft. Puerto Cabezas is only 500 miles from central Cuba—acceptable, although too distant to be completely desirable, for B-26 and transport operations.

Puerto Cabezas will also serve as the staging area for loading assault troops into transports much more satisfactorily than Puerto Barrios, Guatemala which is exposed to hostile observation and lacks security. It is planned that troops will be flown in from Guatemala to Puerto Cabezas, placed in covered trucks, loaded over the docks at night into amphibious shipping, which will then immediately retire to sea.

Conclusion. The strike operation cannot be conducted unless the Puerto Cabezas air facility is available for our use, or unless an air base in the United States is made available.

Recommendation. That firm policy be obtained for use of Puerto Cabezas as an air strike base and staging area.

(f) Use of US air base for logistical flights

An air base in southern Florida would be roughly twice as close to central Cuba as Puerto Cabezas. This means that the logistical capability of our limited number of transport aircraft would be almost doubled if operated from Florida rather than Puerto Cabezas. Logistical support of the strike force in the target would be much more certain and efficient if flown from Florida.

There is also a possibility that once the strike operations commence, conditions would develop which would force us out of the Nicaraguan air base. Without some flexibility of an air base with pre-positioned supplies in the United States, we could conceivably be confronted with a situation wherein the Assault Brigade would be left entirely without logistical air support. Supply by sea cannot be relied upon, for the Brigade may be driven by superior forces from the beach area. Such a situation could lead to complete defeat of the Brigade and failure of the mission.

It seems obvious that the only real estate which the United States can, without question, continue to employ once the operation commences is its own soil. Therefore, an air base for logistical support should be provided in the United States. This will offer the possibility of continued, flexible operations, if one or both of our bases in Guatemala and/or Nicaragua are lost to our use.

Recommendation. That policy be established to permit use of an air base in southern Florida (preferably Opa Locka which is now available to us and has storage facilities for supplies) for logistical support flights to Cuba.

J. HAWKINS
Colonel, US Marine Corps

Memorandum of Conference with President Kennedy
Washington, January 25, 1961, 10:15 a.m.

OTHERS PRESENT: General Lemnitzer, General Decker, Admiral Burke, General White, General Shoup, General Clifton, General Goodpaster

The President asked what the Chiefs think should be done regarding Cuba. General Lemnitzer replied, recalling that the initial plans were for clandestine operations. However, with the shipment in of heavy new military equipment from Czechoslovakia—30,000 tons or more—the clandestine forces are not strong enough. We must increase the size of this force and this creates very difficult problems. What is required is a basic expansion of plans. He noted that time is working against us—although living conditions in Cuba are deteriorating, Castro is tightening police state controls within the area. He is also sending agents and arms into other countries of Latin America. General Lemnitzer thought that the hope is to get a government in exile, then put some troops ashore, and have guerrilla groups start their activities. At that point we would come in and support them. He noted that plans are ready for such action. General Decker added that this action should be taken under a recognized Cuban leader, and, unfortunately, we do not have one at present. General Lemnitzer confirmed that there are a multitude of splinter groups. The President commented that Castro has been able to develop a great and striking personality throughout Latin America and this gives him a great advantage. Admiral Burke agreed that there is a lack of a leader to rally around, and that we need somebody to fill this role.

Memorandum of discussion on Cuba
Washington, January 28, 1961

PRESENT: The President, The Vice President, the Secretary of State, the Secretary of Defense, the Director of Central Intelligence, the Chairman of the Joint Chiefs of Staff, Assistant Secretary Mann, Assistant Secretary Nitze, Mr Tracy Barnes, Mr McGeorge Bundy

The meeting began with a description of the present situation in Cuba by the Director of Central Intelligence. The judgment expressed without dissent was that Cuba is now for practical purposes a Communist-controlled state. The two basic elements in the present situation are a rapid and continuing build-up of Castro's military power, and a great increase also in popular opposition to his regime.

The United States has undertaken a number of covert measures against Castro, including propaganda, sabotage, political action, and direct assistance to anti-Castro Cubans in military training. A particularly urgent question is the use to be made of a group of such Cubans now in training in Guatemala, who cannot remain indefinitely where they are.

The present estimate of the Department of Defense is that no course of action currently authorized by the United States Government will be effective in reaching the agreed national goal of overthrowing the Castro regime. Meanwhile, the Department of State sees grave political dangers to our position throughout the Western Hemisphere in any overt military action not authorized and supported by the Organization of American States [OAS].

After considerable discussion, the following proceedings were authorized by the President:

(1) A continuation and accentuation of current activities of the Central Intelligence Agency, including

increased propaganda, increased political action, and increased sabotage. Continued overflights for these purposes were specifically authorized.

(2) The Defense Department, with CIA, will review proposals for the active deployment of anti-Castro Cuban forces on Cuban territory, and the results of this analysis will be promptly reported to the President.

(3) The Department of State will prepare a concrete proposal for action with other Latin American countries to isolate the Castro regime and to bring against it the judgment of the Organization of American States. It is expected that this proposal may involve a commitment of the President's personal authority behind a special mission or missions to such Latin American leaders as Lleras, Betancourt, and Quadros.

Finally, it was agreed that the United States must make entirely clear that its position with respect to the Cuban Government is currently governed by its firm opposition to Communist penetration of the American Republics, and not by any hostility to democratic social revolution and economic reform. The President intends to deal with this matter himself in the State of the Union Address.

The President particularly desires that no hint of these discussions reach any personnel beyond those most immediately concerned within the Executive Branch.

McGeorge Bundy

MARCH, 1961

Memorandum from the Under Secretary of State (Bowles) to Secretary of State Rusk
Washington, March 31, 1961

On Tuesday, April 4th, a meeting will be held at the White House at which a decision will be reached on the Cuban adventure.

During your absence I have had an opportunity to become better acquainted with the proposal, and I find it profoundly disturbing. Let me frankly say, however, that I am not a wholly objective judge of the practical aspects.

In considerable degree, my concern stems from a deep personal conviction that our national interests are poorly served by a covert operation of this kind at a time when our new President is effectively appealing to world opinion on the basis of high principle. Even in our imperfect world, the differences which distinguish us from the Russians are of vital importance. This is true not only in a moral sense but in the practical effect of these differences on our capacity to rally the non-Communist world in behalf of our traditional democratic objectives.

In saying this, I do not overlook the ruthless nature of the struggle in which we are involved, nor do I ignore the need on occasion for action which is expedient and distasteful. Yet I cannot persuade myself that means can be wholly divorced from ends—even within the context of the Cold War. Against this background, let me suggest several points which I earnestly hope will be fully taken into account in reaching the final decision.

1. In sponsoring the Cuban operation, for instance, we would be deliberately violating the fundamental obligations we assumed in the Act of Bogota establishing the Organization of American States. The Act provides:

> No State or group of States has the right to intervene,
> directly or indirectly, for any reason whatever, in the
> internal or external affairs of any other State. The
> foregoing principle prohibits not only armed force but also
> any other form of interference or attempted threat against
> the personality of the State or against its political,
> economic and cultural elements.
>
> No State may use or encourage the use of coercive
> measures of an economic or political character in order to
> force the sovereign will of another State and obtain from it
> advantages of any kind.

> The territory of a State is inviolable; it may not be the object, even temporarily, of military occupation or of other measures of force taken by another State, directly or indirectly, on any grounds whatever ...

I think it fair to say that these articles, signalling an end of US unilateralism, comprise the central features of the OAS from the point of view of the Latin American countries.

To act deliberately in defiance of these obligations would deal a blow to the Inter-American System from which I doubt it would soon recover. The suggestion that Cuba has somehow "removed itself" from the System is a transparent rationalization for the exercise of our own will.

More generally, the United States is the leading force in and substantial beneficiary of a network of treaties and alliances stretching around the world. That these treaty obligations should be recognized as binding in law and conscience is the condition not only of a lawful and orderly world, but of the mobilization of our own power. We cannot expect the benefits of this regime of treaties if we are unwilling to accept the limitations it imposes upon our freedom to act.

2. Those most familiar with the Cuban operation seem to agree that as the venture is now planned, the chances of success are not greater than one out of three. This makes it a highly risky operation. If it fails, Castro's prestige and strength will be greatly enhanced.

The one way we can reduce the risk is by a sharply increased commitment of direct American support. In talking to Bob McNamara and Ros Gilpatric at lunch Tuesday at the Pentagon, I gathered that this is precisely what the military people feel we should do.

3. Under the very best of circumstances, I believe this operation will have a much more adverse effect on world

opinion than most people contemplate. It is admitted that there will be riots and a new wave of anti-Americanism throughout Latin America. It is also assumed that there will be many who quietly wish us well and, if the operation succeeds, will heave a sigh of relief.

Moreover, even if the reaction in Latin America is less damaging than we expect, I believe that in Europe, Asia, and Africa, the reaction against the United States will be angry and the fresh, favorable image of the Kennedy Administration will be correspondingly dimmed. It would be a grave mistake for us to minimize this factor and its impact on our capacity to operate effectively in cooperation with other nations in other parts of the world.

4. If the operation appears to be a failure in its early stages, the pressure on us to scrap our self-imposed restriction on direct American involvement will be difficult to resist, and our own responsibility correspondingly increased.

5. A pertinent question, of course, is what will happen in Cuba if this operation is cancelled and we limit ourselves to small and scattered operations?

There is the possibility that the Castro effort will be a failure without any further intervention from us. It is not easy to create a viable Communist state on an island, totally dependent upon open sea lanes, with a large population, and inadequate resources. As Castro applies more and more pressure, the spirit of rebellion is likely to grow.

6. It appears more likely that Castro will succeed in solidifying his political position. Although this would be sharply contrary to our national interest, it does not mean that we would be impotent to deal with him.

If the Soviets should attempt to provide Castro with substantially larger amounts of arms, including naval vessels, we have the power to throw a blockade around Cuba and to extend it, if necessary, to petroleum supplies. This could bring the Cuban economy to a grinding halt within a few months.

Technically, this would be an act of war. However, I believe we would find it vastly easier to live with direct action of this kind in the face of what we could fairly describe as an open Soviet move to establish Cuba as a military base than with the covert operation now under consideration.

7. Another possibility is that Castro, once he has created sufficient military power, will move against a neighboring area, such as Haiti, the Dominican Republic, or perhaps into Central America. If this occurs, we can move to block him with whatever force is required, presumably through the Organization of American States and with the full support of the people in Latin America and elsewhere.

Since January 20th our position has been dramatically improved in the eyes of the world vis-à-vis the Soviet Union.

The Kennedy Administration has been doing particularly well in Africa and Latin America, and with a little luck in Laos and more affirmative policies, we may soon be able to improve our position in East Asia, South Asia, and the Middle East. Within the next few months we can also begin to strengthen our relations with Western Europe.

I believe it would be a grave mistake for us to jeopardize the favorable position we have steadily developed in most of the non-Communist world, by the responsible and restrained policies which are now associated with the President, by embarking on a major covert adventure with such very heavy built-in risks.

I realize that this operation has been put together over a period of months. A great deal of time and money has been put into it, and many able and dedicated people have become emotionally involved in its success. We should not, however, proceed with this adventure simply because we are wound up and cannot stop.

I believe that it is important for you to discuss this venture with people who can bring to it a fresh and objective view; for instance, Ed Murrow, Abe Chayes, Harlan Cleveland, Phillips Talbot, George McGhee, Soapy Williams, or Phil Coombs.

If you agree after careful thought that this operation would be a mistake, I suggest that you personally and privately communicate your views to the President. It is my guess that your voice will be decisive. In that event he may decide to call off tomorrow's meeting and transmit his decision directly to Allen Dulles, Bob McNamara, and other interested people.

APRIL, 1961

Telegram from the Embassy in the Soviet Union to the Department of State
Moscow, April 18, 1961, 2:00 p.m.

Following letter to President Kennedy from Khrushchev handed me by Acting Foreign Minister Semenov at 12:15 today.

Begin text.

Mr President, I send you this message in an hour of alarm, fraught with danger for the peace of the whole world. Armed aggression has begun against Cuba. It is a secret to no one that the armed bands invading this country were trained, equipped and armed in the United States of America. The planes which are bombing Cuban cities belong to the United States of America, the bombs they are dropping are being supplied by the American Government. All of this evokes here in the Soviet Union an understandable feeling of indignation on the part of the Soviet Government and the Soviet people.

Only recently, in exchanging opinions through our respective representatives, we talked with you about the mutual desire of both sides to put forward joint efforts directed toward improving relations between our countries and eliminating the danger of war. Your statement a few days ago, that the USA would not participate in military activities against Cuba, created the impression that the top leaders of the United States were taking into account the consequences for general peace, and for the USA itself, which aggression against Cuba could have. How can what is being done by the United States in reality be understood, when an attack on Cuba has now become a fact?

It is still not too late to avoid the irreparable. The Government of the USA still has the possibility of not allowing the flame of war ignited by interventions in Cuba to grow into an incomparable conflagration. I approach you, Mr President, with an urgent call to put an end to aggression against the Republic of Cuba. Military armament and the world political situation are such at this time that any so-called "little war" can touch off a chain reaction in all parts of the globe.

As far as the Soviet Union is concerned, there should be no mistake about our position: We will render the Cuban people and their government all necessary help to repel an armed attack on Cuba. We are sincerely interested in a relaxation of international tension, but if others proceed toward sharpening it, we will answer them in full measure. And in general it is hardly possible so to conduct matters that the situation is settled in one area and conflagration extinguished, while a new conflagration is ignited in another area.

I hope that the Government of the USA will consider our views dictated by the sole concern not to allow steps which could lead the world to military catastrophe.
End text.

FREERS

Memorandum from the President's Special Assistant for National Security Affairs (Bundy) to President Kennedy
Washington, April 18, 1961

TOP SECRET

I think you will find at noon that the situation in Cuba is not a bit good. The Cuban armed forces are stronger, the popular response is weaker, and our tactical position is feebler that we had hoped. Tanks have done in one beachhead, and the position is precarious at the others.

The CIA will press hard for further air help—this time by Navy cover to B-26s attacking the tanks. But I think we can expect other pleas in rapid crescendo, because we are up against a formidable enemy, who is reacting with military know-how and vigor.

The immediate request I would grant (because it cannot easily be proven against us and because men are in need), but the real question is whether to reopen the possibility of further intervention and support or to accept the high probability that our people, at best, will go into the mountains in defeat.

In my own judgment the right course now is to eliminate the Castro air force, by neutrally-painted US planes if necessary, and then let the battle go its way.

McG. B

Letter from President Kennedy to Chairman Khrushchev
Washington, April 18, 1961

Mr Chairman: You are under a serious misapprehension in regard to events in Cuba. For months there has been evident and growing resistance to the Castro dictatorship. More than 100,000 refugees have recently fled from Cuba into neighboring countries. Their urgent hope is naturally to assist their fellow Cubans in their struggle for freedom. Many of these refugees fought alongside Dr Castro against the Batista dictatorship; among them are prominent leaders of his own original movement and government.

These are unmistakable signs that Cubans find intolerable the denial of democratic liberties and the subversion of the 26th of July Movement by an alien-dominated regime. It cannot be surprising that, as resistance within Cuba grows, refugees have been using whatever means are available to return and support their countrymen in the continuing struggle for freedom. Where people are denied the right of choice, recourse to such struggle is the only means of achieving their liberties.

I have previously stated, and I repeat now, that the United States intends no military intervention in Cuba. In the event of any military intervention by outside force we will immediately honor our obligations under the Inter-American System to protect this Hemisphere against external aggression. While refraining from military intervention in Cuba, the people of the United States do not conceal their admiration for Cuban patriots who wish to see a democratic system in an independent Cuba. The United States Government can take no action to stifle the spirit of liberty.

I have taken careful note of your statement that the events in Cuba might affect peace in all parts of the world. I trust that this does not mean that the Soviet

Government, using the situation in Cuba as a pretext, is planning to inflame other areas of the world. I would like to think that your government has too great a sense of responsibility to embark upon any enterprise so dangerous to general peace.

I agree with you as to the desirability of steps to improve the international atmosphere. I continue to hope that you will cooperate in opportunities now available to this end. A prompt cease-fire and peaceful settlement of the dangerous situation in Laos, cooperation with the United Nations in the Congo, and a speedy conclusion of an acceptable treaty for the banning of nuclear tests would be constructive steps in this direction. The regime in Cuba could make a similar contribution by permitting the Cuban people freely to determine their own future by democratic processes and freely to cooperate with their Latin American neighbors.

I believe, Mr Chairman, that you should recognize that free peoples in all parts of the world do not accept the claim of historical inevitability for Communist revolution. What your government believes is its own business; what it does in the world is the world's business. The great revolution in the history of man, past, present and future, is the revolution of those determined to be free.

JOHN F. KENNEDY

Notes on Cuban crisis, Cabinet meeting, Chester Bowles
Washington, April 20, 1961

The Cabinet meeting took place on the first day immediately after the collapse of the Cuban expedition became known.

I attended the Cabinet meeting in Rusk's absence and it was about as grim as any meeting I can remember in all my experience in government, which is saying a good deal. The President was really quite shattered, and understandably so. Almost without exception, his public career had been a long series of successes, without any noteworthy setbacks. Those disappointments which had come his way, such as his failure to get the nomination for Vice President in 1956, were clearly attributable to religion.

Here for the first time he faced a situation where his judgment had been mistaken, in spite of the fact that week after week of conferences had taken place before he gave the green light.

It was not a pleasant experience. Reactions around the table were almost savage, as everyone appeared to be jumping on everyone else. The only really coherent statement was by Arthur Goldberg, who said that while it was doubtful that the expedition was wise in the first place, the Administration should not have undertaken it unless it was prepared to see it through with United States troops if necessary.

At least his remarks had an inherent logic to them, although I could not agree under any circumstances to sending troops into Cuba—violating every treaty obligation we have.

The most angry response of all came from Bob Kennedy and also, strangely enough, from Dave Bell, who I had always assumed was a very reasonable individual.

The discussion simply rambled in circles with no real coherent thought. Finally after three-quarters of an hour the President got up and walked toward his office. I was so distressed at what I felt was a dangerous mood that I walked after him, stopped him, and told him I would like an opportunity to come into his office and talk the whole thing out.

Lyndon Johnson, Bob McNamara, and Bob Kennedy joined us. Bobby continued his tough, savage comments, most of them directed against the Department of State for reasons which are difficult for me to understand. When I took exception to some of the more extreme things he said by suggesting that the way to get out of our present jam was not to simply double up on everything we had done, he turned on me savagely.

What worries me is that two of the most powerful people in this administration—Lyndon Johnson and Bob Kennedy—have no experience in foreign affairs, and they both realize that this is the central question of this period and are determined to be experts at it.

The problems of foreign affairs are complex, involving politics, economics, and social questions that require both understanding of history and various world cultures. When a newcomer enters the field and finds himself confronted by the nuances of international questions, he becomes an easy target for the military–CIA–paramilitary type answers which are often in specific logistical terms which can be added, subtracted, multiplied, or divided.

This kind of thinking was almost dominant in the conference and I found it most alarming. The President appeared the most calm, yet it was clear to see that he had been suffering an acute shock and it was an open question in my mind as to what his reaction would be.

All through the meeting which took place in the President's office and which lasted almost a half hour, there was an almost frantic reaction for an action program which people would grab onto.

From "The Inspector General's Survey of the Cuban Operation," an internal inquiry into the CIA's Bay of Pigs invasion in 1961

The agency committed at least four extremely serious mistakes in planning:

(a) Failure to subject the project, especially in its latter frenzied stages, to a cold and objective appraisal by the best operating talent available, particularly by those not involved in the operation, such as the Chief of Operations and the chiefs of the Senior Staffs. Had this been done, the two following mistakes (b and c, below) might have been avoided.

(b) Failure to advise the President, at an appropriate time, that success had become dubious and to recommend that the operation be therefore canceled and that the problem of unseating Castro be restudied.

(c) Failure to recognize that the project had become overt and that the military effort had become too large to be handled by the agency alone.

(d) Failure to reduce successive project plans to formal papers and to leave copies of them with the President and his advisers and to request specific written approval and confirmation thereof.

Timely and objective scrutiny of the operation in the months before the invasion, including study of all available intelligence, would have demonstrated to agency officials that the clandestine paramilitary operations had almost totally failed, that there was no controlled and responsive underground movement ready to rally to the invasion force, and that Castro's ability both to fight back and to roll up the internal opposition must be very considerably upgraded.

It would also have raised the question of why the United States should contemplate pitting 1,500 soldiers, however well trained and armed, against an enemy vastly superior in number and armament on a terrain which offered nothing but vague hope of significant local support. It might also have suggested that the agency's responsibility in the operation should be drastically revised and would certainly have revealed that there was no real plan for the post-invasion period...

Cancellation would have been embarrassing. The Brigade could not have been held any longer in a ready status, probably could not have been held at all. Its members would have spread their disappointment far and wide. Because of multiple security leaks in this huge operation, the world already knew about the preparations, and the government's and the agency's embarrassment would have been public.

However, cancellation would have averted failure, which brought even more embarrassment, carried death and misery to hundreds, destroyed millions of dollars' worth of US property, and seriously damaged US prestige...

It is beyond the scope of this report to suggest what US action might have been taken to consolidate victory, but we can confidently assert that the agency had no intelligence evidence that Cubans in significant numbers could or would join the invaders or that there was any kind of an effective and cohesive resistance movement under anybody's control, let alone the agency's, that could have furnished internal leadership for an uprising in support of the invasion. The consequences of a successful lodgment, unless overtly supported by US armed forces, were dubious ...

The choice was between retreat without honor and a gamble between ignominious defeat and dubious victory. The agency chose to gamble, at rapidly decreasing odds.

The project had lost its covert nature by November 1960. As it continued to grow, operational security became more and more diluted. For more than three months before the invasion the American press was reporting, often with some accuracy, on the recruiting and training of Cubans. Such massive preparations could only be laid to the US. The agency's name was freely linked with these activities. Plausible denial was a pathetic illusion.

JANUARY–MARCH, 1962

Program review of the Cuba Project by the Chief of Operations,
Operation Mongoose (Lansdale)

Washington, January 18, 1962

I. Objective
The US objective is to help the Cubans overthrow the Communist regime from within Cuba and institute a new government with which the United States can live in peace.

II. Concept of operation
Basically, the operation is to bring about the revolt of the Cuban people. The revolt will overthrow the Communist

regime and institute a new government with which the United States can live in peace.

The revolt requires a strongly motivated political action movement established within Cuba, to generate the revolt, to give it direction toward the object, and to capitalize on the climactic moment. The political actions will be assisted by economic warfare to induce failure of the Communist regime to supply Cuba's economic needs, psychological operations to turn the people's resentment increasingly against the regime, and military-type groups to give the popular movement an action arm for sabotage and armed resistance in support of political objectives.

The failure of the US-sponsored operation in April 1961 so shook the faith of Cuban patriots in US competence and intentions in supporting a revolt against Castro that a new effort to generate a revolt against the regime in Cuba must have active support from key Latin American countries. Further, the foreignness (Soviet Union and Bloc) of the tyranny imposed on the Cuban people must be made clear to the people of the Western Hemisphere to the point of their deep anger and open actions to defend the Western Hemisphere against such foreign invasion. Such an anger will be generated, in part, by appeals from the popular movement within Cuba to other Latin Americans especially.

The preparation phase must result in a political action organization in being in key localities inside Cuba, with its own means for internal communications, its own voice for psychological operations, and its own action arm (small guerrilla bands, sabotage squads, etc.). It must have the sympathetic support of the majority of the Cuban people, and make this fact known to the outside world. (It is reported that the majority of Cubans are not for the present regime, but are growing apathetic toward what appears to be a hopeless future or the futility of their status.)

The climactic moment of revolt will come from an angry reaction of the people to a government action (sparked by an incident), or from a fracturing of the leadership cadre within the regime, or both. (A major goal of the Project must be to bring this about.) The popular movement will capitalize on this climactic moment by initiating an open revolt. Areas will be taken and held. If necessary, the popular movement will appeal for help to the free nations of the Western Hemisphere. The United States, if possible in concert with other Western Hemisphere nations, will then give open support to the Cuban people's revolt. Such support will include military force, as necessary.

III. Estimate of the situation

Our planning requires sound intelligence estimates of the situation re Cuba. The latest Special National Intelligence Estimate (SNIE 85-61) of November 28, 1961 contains operational conclusions not based on hard fact, in addition to its intelligence conclusions; this is a repetition of an error in the planning for the unsuccessful operation of last April.

The planning indicated herein will be revised, as necessary, based on the hard intelligence estimate of the situation by the US Intelligence community. A new National Intelligence Estimate (NIE 85-62 on Cuba), due on January 23, apparently has been postponed until February 7.

It is recognized that one result of the Project, so far, has been to start the collection of Intelligence on Cuba in depth, to provide facts on which to base firm estimates and operations.

IV. Initial phase (30 November 61 to 31 January 62)

A. Establish a US mechanism for the project

Status: The President's directive of 30 November 1961 was implemented by creating a US operations team, with Brig.

Gen. Lansdale as Chief of Operations, and with tasks promptly assigned. His immediate staff are Mr Hand and Major Patchell. Representatives of Secretaries and Agency Directors are: State—Woodward (Goodwin, Hurwitch); CIA—Helms; Defense—Brig. Gen. Craig; USIA—Wilson.

B. Intelligence support

Status: CIA made a special survey of US capabilities to interrogate Cuban refugees in the USA (1,700–2,000 arriving per month) and on 16 January approved a program increasing the staff at the Opa Locka Interrogation Center in Florida from the present two people to 34. CIA will build up agent assets (positive intelligence assets inside Cuba are very limited and it has no counter-intelligence assets inside). Special intelligence assets will be exploited more fully. The Cuba Project needs far more hard intelligence in depth than is presently available. CIA will require further assistance from Defense and other US organizations in this intelligence effort, and is submitting specific qualifications for personnel on 19 January.

C. Political platform for people's movement inside Cuba

Status: State has sketched in a broad outline. CIA is to produce the firm platform statement of aims for which the Cubans who will operate inside Cuba are willing to risk their lives, and upon which popular support can be generated.

D. Nucleus for popular movement

Status: To date, CIA has been unable to produce the necessary political action agents for this purpose. Upon re-evaluation of its capabilities, CIA now hopes to complete spotting and assessing eight to ten Cuban political action agents by 15 February, from among Cubans available in the United States. The minimum need for the Project to be effective is 30 such political action Cubans and CIA is tasked to make a priority search for them among Cubans in the US and Caribbean area.

E. Deployment of nucleus

Status: CIA is tasked to select 20 localities within Cuba where political action groups can be established. Initial selection and plans for establishing these action groups are now due 1 February. Havana, and localities in the provinces of Camaguey and Las Villas, will receive priority consideration, according to present intelligence. Planning on this must be adjusted as firmer intelligence is acquired.

F. Diplomatic actions

Status: State is concentrating on the OAS Meeting of Foreign Ministers, which opens 22 January, hoping to get wide Western Hemisphere support for OAS resolutions condemning Cuba and isolating it from the rest of the Hemisphere. A companion resolution, to offer OAS relief directly to the suffering Cuban people (similar to US relief to Russia, 1919–20), is being considered, as a means to reach the Cuban people sympathetically without going through their Communist government. The OAS meeting is to be supported by public demonstrations in Latin America, generated by CIA, and a psychological campaign assisted by USIA.

The major task for our diplomatic capability is to encourage Latin American leaders to develop independent operations similar to this Project, seeking an internal revolt of the Cuban people against the Communist regime. This is yet to be initiated by State and must be vigorously pressed.

G. Economic warfare

Status: This critical key to our political action Project is still in the planning stage under State leadership. State is basing future economic actions, including plans for an embargo on Cuban trade, on the outcome of the forth-coming OAS meeting. Meanwhile, State has chaired an economic action group, which agreed on developing 13 actions. 15 February is set for a report on implementing plans, so that actions can be initiated. CIA was unable to undertake action to sabotage the sugar harvest, which commences about 15 January, and upon which Cuba's one-crop sugar economy depends. (Sabotage of transport, mills, sugar sacking, and cane fields were explored.)

H. TV intrusion

Status: Equipment to enable TV intrusion of Havana TV broadcasts has been reactivated on a small vessel under CIA control. CIA plans to attempt intrusion on 22 January during Castro's forthcoming speech and parade demon-strations.

I. Special sabotage support

Status: State has explored, with negative results, the fea-sibility of pre-emptive action with respect to tanker charters (most Bloc shipments to Cuba are carried in Western bottoms). CIA has initiated action to contaminate POL supplies for Cuba, although visible results (stoppage of some Cuban transport) are not expected until mid-1962. [*five lines of source text not declassified*]

J. Military actions

Status: Defense has been tasked with preparing a contin-gency plan for US military action, in case the Cuban people request US help when their revolt starts making headway. This contingency plan will permit obtaining a policy decision on the major point of US intentions, and is looked upon as a positive political–psychological factor in a people's revolt, even more than as a possible military action. Defense also has been tasked with fully assisting State and CIA, as commitments of Defense men, money, and materiel are required.

K. Major elements of the population

Status: Both State and CIA are continuing to explore their capabilities (with results largely negative to date) for mounting special group operations inside Cuba focused upon dynamic elements of the population, particularly [*one line of source text not declassified*] through Labor contacts to reach the workers. Other elements include enlistment of the youth and professional groupings. Special consideration is to be given to doing this through Latin American operational contacts. This is vital to the success of our political action nucleus when CIA can put it into place.

L. Outlook

Status: As reported to the Special Group last week, there has been a period of a realistic second look at CIA capabilities to mount the required clandestine operations against Cuba, and a subsequent start in "tooling up." After this second look, CIA has concluded that its realistic role should be to create at least the illusion of a popular movement, to win external support for it, to improve CIA operational capability, and to help create a climate which will permit provocative actions in support of a shift to overt action. This outlook, although arrived at thoughtfully within CIA, is far short of the Cuba Project's goals. CIA must take yet another hard look at its potential capabilities, in the light of the following tasking, to determine if it cannot make the greater effort required.

V. Target schedule

A. Intelligence

Task 1: NIE 85-62 on Cuba due 7 February (CIA).

Task 2: By 15 February, Opa Locka Interrogation Center to be made an effective operation for collection and processing of intelligence (CIA with support of Defense, State, I&NS, FBI).

Task 3: Intelligence collection from Cuban refugees elsewhere than Miami area. CIA to survey other refugee points (etc.) and on a priority basis to ensure maximum coverage of all such source points. 15 February target date.

Task 4: CIA to continue its re-examination of intelligence assets, with priority on agents inside Cuba, and report on capability by 15 February. Also included is coverage of intelligence through third country sources, particularly those having diplomatic relations with Cuba.

B. Political

Task 5: CIA to submit plan by 1 February for defection of top Cuban government officials, to fracture the regime from within. The effort must be imaginative and bold enough to consider a "name" defector to be worth at least a million US dollars. This can be the key to our political action goal and must be mounted without delay as a major CIA project.

Task 6: CIA to complete plans by 1 February for Cover and Deception actions, to help fracture the Communist regime in Cuba. Defense, State, and FBI are to collaborate on this.

Task 7: By 1 February, CIA to submit operations schedule for initiating popular movement within Cuba. This must include localities selected inside Cuba, assessment of selected Cubans, their infiltration, activity assignments, and political platform. One section must deal with the "underground," assess its true status and plans to use it.

Task 8: State to follow up the OAS meeting by having US embassies in Latin America exploit all opportunities to enlist local sympathy for the Cuban people and to increase hostility toward the Communist regime in Cuba. State to submit report on results of this assignment by 13 February, so further planning can be programmed.

Task 9: By 15 February, State to submit an inventory of operational assets in the Caribbean area, including capabilities of local governments or groups to mount operations on their own, to help achieve the Project's goals. Plans for early use of such capabilities are due by 19 February.

Task 10: CIA to submit operational schedule for using assets in the Caribbean area to achieve the Project's political action goals. The objective of working on dynamic elements of the Cuban population (such as workers, farmers) is underscored. Due 19 February.

C. Economic

Task 11: State to prepare recommendations to the President on US trade with Cuba, as follow-up to OAS meeting. (If the minimum result of the meeting is an agreement to condemn Cuba as an accomplice of the Sino–Soviet Bloc and adoption of a general statement that Cuba presents a threat to the peace and security of the Hemisphere, State is prepared to recommend to the President that remaining trade between the US and Cuba be barred.)

Task 12: State to plan, with Commerce and other US agencies, on how to halt the diversion of vital items in the Cuban trade. Due date 15 February. Cooperation of other OAS nations, particularly Canada and Mexico, is to be explored by State.

Task 13: State with Commerce and others involved, to plan on how to make "positive list" items to Latin America be subject to the same licensing procedures as applied to such shipments to other parts of the free world. Due 15 February.

Task 14: State to obtain from Commerce proposal to amend present export controls of technical data (petrochemical, communications equipment) so that Cuba is treated the same as the Sino–Soviet Bloc. Due 15 February.

Task 15: State by 15 February to submit recommendations on issuance of transportation order (T-3) under authority of the Defense Production Act of 1950 forbidding US-owned vessels to engage in trade with Cuba.

Task 16: State plan due 15 February on feasible extension of US port treatment now given to Bloc and Cuban vessels to charter vessels of Bloc and Cuba (Treasury to advise on this).

Task 17: State to report by 15 February on feasibility of harassing Bloc shipping by refusing entry into US ports (statedly for security reasons), if vessels have called or will call at Cuban ports.

Task 18: [*source text not declassified*]

Task 19: State to report by 15 February on possibilities for obtaining the discreet cooperation of the National Foreign Trade Council to urge US shippers to refuse to ship on vessels which call at Cuban ports. (Commerce to assist on this.)

Task 20: State to report by 15 February on possibilities to obtain the discreet cooperation of the US Chamber of

Commerce and the National Association of Manufacturers to influence US firms having subsidiaries abroad to adhere to the spirit of US economic sanctions. (Commerce to assist on this.)

Task 21: CIA to submit plan by 15 February for inducing failures in food crops in Cuba.

Task 22: State to report by 15 February on status of plans to gain cooperation of NATO allies (bilaterally and in the NATO forum, as appropriate). Objective is to persuade these nations to take steps to isolate Cuba from the West.

Task 23: State to report by 15 February on status of actions undertaken with Japan, which has comparatively significant trade with Cuba, along lines similar to those with NATO nations.

Task 24: CIA to submit plan by 15 February on disruption of the supply of Cuban nickel to the Soviet Union.

D. Psychological

Task 25: USIA to submit plan by 15 February for the most effective psychological exploitation of actions undertaken in the Project, toward the end result of awakening world sympathy for the Cuban people (as a David) battling against the Communist regime (as a Goliath) and toward stimulating Cubans inside Cuba to join "the cause."

Task 26: CIA to submit by 15 February its operational schedule for a psychological campaign to provoke a relaxing of police state control within Cuba. This is to include effective means of publicly indicting "people's criminals" for justice after liberation of Cuba (not only individual top officials, but members of the Vigilancia, etc.).

Task 27: CIA and USIA will report on progress as of 15 February in developing identification of the popular movement inside Cuba, as with songs, symbols, propaganda themes.

Task 28: By 15 February CIA will report on plans and actions for propaganda support of the popular movement inside Cuba. Included will be exactly what is planned for use by the movement inside Cuba, and feasibility of using smuggled food packets (such as the "I Shall Return" cigarette packets to Philippine guerrillas in World War II) as morale boosters in generating the popular movement.

E. Military action

Task 29: Defense to submit contingency plan for use of US military force to support the Cuban popular movement, including a statement of conditions under which Defense believes such action would be required to win the Project's goal and believes such action would not necessarily lead to general war. Due 28 February.

Task 30: CIA to submit by 15 February its operational schedule for sabotage actions inside Cuba, including timing proposed for the actions and how they affect the generation and support of a popular movement, to achieve the Project goals.

Task 31: CIA to submit specific requests to Defense for required support by Defense as early as possible after its plans firm up. Requests for all major needs are expected by 23 February.

Task 32: Defense will submit plan for "special operations" use of Cubans enlisted in the US armed forces. Due 28 February.

VI. Future plans

By 20 February, it is expected that sufficient realistic plans for individual tasks will have been received, and initial actions started, to permit a firm timetable to be constructed. Since the President directed that the Chief of Operations conduct the Project through the appropriate organizations and Departments of the Government, and since these US organizations are mainly in the initial inventory and development of capabilities phase concerning assigned tasks, a precise operations timetable as of today would be too speculative to be useful.

CIA has alerted Defense that it will require considerable military support (including two submarines, PT boats, Coast Guard type cutters, Special Forces trainers, C-54 aircraft, F-86 aircraft, amphibian aircraft, helio-couriers, Army leaflet battalion, and Guantánamo as a base for submarine operations). Also, CIA apparently believes that its role should be to create and expand a popular movement, illusory and actual, which will create a political climate which can provide a framework of plausible excuse for armed intervention. This is not in conformity with the Presidential directive now governing Project tasking. Actually, the role of creating the political climate and plausible excuse for armed intervention would be more properly that of State and Defense, if such an objective becomes desirable.

National Intelligence Estimate on the situation and prospects in Cuba, NIE 85-62
Washington, March 21, 1962

The problem

To analyze the situation in Cuba and the relationships of the Castro regime with both the Soviet Bloc and the Latin

American Republics, and to estimate the prospects over the next year or so.

Foreword

Cuba is now, in effect, surrounded by an iron curtain. Our information on internal developments is not as complete or as reliable as we could wish. On some important matters, it is seriously inadequate. The estimate will be under continuing review as additional information is obtained.

Summary and conclusions

1. The pattern of events in Cuba clearly reveals the historical step by step Communist procedure for attaining complete control of a country. During the past year Cuba has, in effect, gone behind an iron curtain. The regime has thoroughly reorganized its political, economic, police, and military systems in the classic Communist ideological fashion. It has also sought to identify itself with the Soviet Bloc in terms that would obligate the USSR to protect it. The Bloc, however, has avoided any explicit military commitment to defend Cuba.

2. In Cuba there is in process of development a single party organization essentially Communist in character. It is designed to be the means of directing and controlling the operations of the government, the economy, and the mass organizations through which revolutionary indoctrination and leadership are transmitted to the people. Fidel Castro will presumably be the titular head of this organization, but the real political power in Cuba is likely to be vested in a collective leadership including Castro but dominated by a group of veteran Communists. Some degree of friction is probable in this relationship, but an open conflict is highly unlikely.

3. The regime has sought to commit the Cuban people to positive personal identification with it through propaganda,

indoctrination, and mass organizations. At the same time, it has developed a pervasive system of surveillance and police control.

4. The forces available to the regime to suppress insurrection or repel invasion have been and are being greatly improved, with substantial Bloc assistance through the provision of materiel and instruction. Cuban military capabilities, however, are essentially defensive. We believe it unlikely that the Bloc will provide Cuba with strategic weapon systems or with air and naval capabilities suitable for major independent military operations overseas. We also believe it unlikely that the Bloc will station in Cuba combat units of any description, at least for the period of this estimate. This attitude would not preclude the liberal provision of Bloc advisers, instructors, and service personnel, the provision of such defensive weapons and equipment as surface-to-air missiles and radars, and such improvement of Cuban naval and air facilities as would enable them to service Soviet units.

5. The state has taken over the direct control of all important economic activities in Cuba, and has developed a more elaborate organization for economic management.

6. Cuba is now faced with an economic crisis attributable in large part to an acute shortage of the convertible foreign exchange required to finance greatly needed imports of foodstuffs and of replacement parts for machinery and equipment of US origin. The Bloc provides a guaranteed market for Cuban sugar and minerals, and supplies foodstuffs, other consumers' goods, and industrial raw materials in return, but not in sufficient quantity to meet Cuba's needs. The Bloc has also extended credits for Cuban industrial development, but the actual implementation of these projects is slow. Castro has now told the Cuban people that they face years of privation.

7. The initial popular enthusiasm for the Revolution has steadily waned. Many men who fought against Batista have been alienated by the even more dictatorial character of the Castro regime and its increasingly Communist complexion. The vaunted agrarian reform has done little to improve the lot of the peasants. Moreover, people are becoming fed up with the privations, exactions, and regimentation that characterize life in Castro's Cuba.

8. Nevertheless, Fidel Castro and the Revolution retain the positive support of at least a quarter of the population. The hard core of this support consists principally of those who now have a vested interest in the regime: the new managerial class and the Communists. These are reinforced by the substantial numbers of Cubans, especially those in the mass organizations, who are still under the spell of Castro's charismatic leadership or are convinced the Revolution has been to their advantage.

9. There is active resistance in Cuba, but it is limited, uncoordinated, unsupported, and desperate. The regime, with all the power of repression at its disposal, has shown that it can contain the present level of resistance activity.

10. The majority of the Cuban people neither support the regime nor resist it, in any active sense. They are grumbling and resentful, but apparently hopeless and passive, resigned to acceptance of the present regime as the effective government in being with which they must learn to live for lack of a feasible alternative.

11. The next year or two will be a critical period for the Castro regime. The 1962 sugar crop will be the smallest in years; the difficulty of acquiring convertible foreign exchange will be greater than ever. Want of convertible exchange will limit Cuba's ability to purchase foodstuffs and other needed supplies in the Free World. No substan-

tial increase in the supplies provided by the Bloc is likely during 1962. In these circumstances it is unlikely that the total output of the Cuban economy in 1962 can rise above the 1961 level. Under consequent privations, the Cuban people are likely to become more restive. Much will depend on whether the regime succeeds in directing their resentment toward the US, or whether it comes to focus on the regime.

12. The regime's apparatus for surveillance and repression should be able to cope with any popular tendency toward active resistance. Any impulse toward widespread revolt is inhibited by the fear which this apparatus inspires, and also by the lack of dynamic leadership and of any expectation of liberation within the foreseeable future. In these circumstances, increasing antagonism toward the regime is likely to produce only a manageable increase in isolated acts of sabotage or of open defiance on the part of a few desperate men. A sequence of disaffection–repression–resistance could conceivably be set in motion, but would be unlikely to cause major difficulties for the regime in the absence of considerable external support.

13. The overriding concern of Cuban foreign policy is to obtain external support and protection against the hostility of the US. The USSR and other Bloc states will continue to render such aid and support to the Castro regime as they consider necessary. If the overthrow of the regime should be seriously threatened by either external or internal forces, the USSR would almost certainly not intervene directly with its own forces. However, interpreting even an internal threat as US intervention, the USSR would seek to deter the US by vigorous political action, including threats of retaliation on the periphery of the Bloc as well as ambiguous references to Soviet nuclear power. Nevertheless, the USSR would almost certainly

never intend to hazard its own safety for the sake of Cuba.

14. By the end of 1960, Castro had few admirers left among politically active Latin Americans, except the Communists, extremist splinter groups broken off from the established social revolutionary parties, and certain student and labor elements.

15. At Punta del Este the OAS unanimously condemned Communism in Cuba as incompatible with the Inter-American System and laid the groundwork for increased efforts to combat Castro-Communist subversion. However, Mexico, Brazil, Argentina, Chile, Bolivia, and Ecuador abstained on the operative resolution excluding the Castro regime from the organs of the OAS. The Castro regime will seek to cultivate those Latin American governments which have shown reluctance to support measures against it and will probably refrain from flagrant acts which could provide the occasion for US or OAS intervention in Cuba.

16. The Castro-Communist threat in Latin America results from the ability of a well-organized subversive movement centered in Cuba to exploit the natural tendency of entrenched oligarchies to resist the growing demand for radical social reform. What is seen by radical revolutionary elements in Latin America is that, while others have talked of social reform, Fidel Castro has actually accomplished a radical social revolution in Cuba, and has done so in defiance of the Yankees with the support of an apparently more powerful patron. Relatively moderate reformist regimes are now ascendant in most Latin American countries, but, if the Alliance for Progress should fail to produce its intended social reforms in time to meet rising popular demands, the conviction will grow that Castro's way is the

only way to get timely and positive results. Thus, despite Castro's alienation of the moderate reformists, there remains a danger that the Cuban example will set the pattern of the impending social revolution in Latin America.

PART II

THE CUBAN MISSILE CRISIS
1962

MAY, 1962

Memorandum from the General Staff to Comrade
N. S. Khrushchev

May 24, 1962

TOP SECRET
SPECIAL IMPORTANCE
ONE COPY

In accordance with your instructions the Ministry of
Defense proposes:

1. To deploy on the island of Cuba a Group of Soviet
Forces comprising all branches of the Armed Forces, under

Island of Cuba, 1962

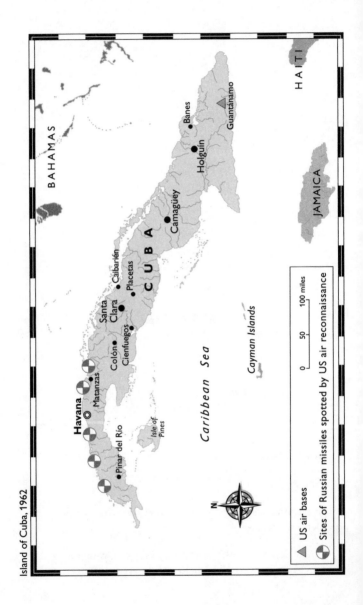

▲ US air bases

◉ Sites of Russian missiles spotted by US air reconnaissance

a single integrated staff of the Group of Forces headed by a Commander in Chief of Soviet forces in Cuba.

2. To send to Cuba the 43rd Missile Division (commander of the division Major General Statsenko) comprising five missile regiments:

- The 79th, 181st and 664th R-12 [SS-4] missile regiments with eight launchers each, in all 24 launchers.
- The 665th and 668th R-14 [SS-5] missile regiments with eight launchers each, in all 16 launchers.

In all, 40 R-12 and R-14 launchers.

With the missile units to send 1.5 missiles and 1.5 warheads per each launcher (in all 60 missiles and 60 warheads), with one field missile technical base (PRTB) per regiment for equipping the warheads and rocket fuel in mobile tanks with 1.75 loadings per R-12 missile and 1.5 per R-14 missile at each launcher.

Deployment of the R-12 missiles is planned in the [*illegible*] variant with the use of SP-6. Prepared assembly-disassembly elements of the SP-6 for equipping the missile pads will be prepared at construction enterprises of the Ministry of Defense by 20 June and shipped together with the regiments. Upon arrival at the designated locations, personnel of the missile regiments will within 10 days equip the launch positions by their own efforts, and will be ready to launch missiles.

For deployment of the missile units armed with R-14 missiles, construction on site will last about four months. This work can be handled by the personnel of the units, but it will be necessary to augment them with a group of 25 engineer-construction personnel and 100 construction personnel of basic specialties and up to 100 construction fitters from State Committees of the Council of Ministers of the USSR for defense technology and radioelectronics.

For accomplishing the work it is necessary to send:

- 16 complete sets of earth equipment for the R-14 produced by [*the machine*] industry in the current year;
- machinery and vehicles: mobile cranes (5 ton) – 10; bulldozers – 20; mobile graders – 10; excavators – 10; dump trucks – 120; cement mixers (GVSU) – 6

Special technical equipment for [*illegible*] and testing apparatuses:

- basic materials: cement – 2,000 tons; reinforced concrete – 15,000 sq meters (not counting access roads); metal – 2,000 tons; SP-6 sets – 30; GR-2 barracks – 20; prefabricated wooden houses – 10; cable, equipment and other materials.

Further accumulation of missile fuel, missiles, and warheads for the units is possible depending on the creation of reserve space and storage in Cuba, inasmuch as it would be possible to include in each missile regiment a third battalion with four launchers.

The staff of the Group and of the missile division can expediently be sent from the Soviet Union in the first days of July 1962 in two echelons: the 1st echelon (R-12 regiments) and the 2nd (R-14 regiments).

3. For air defense of the island of Cuba and protection of the Group of Forces to send two antiaircraft divisions, including in their composition six antiaircraft missile regiments (24 battalions), six technical battalions, one fighter air regiment with MiG-21 F-13 (three squadrons—40 aircraft), and two radar battalions.

With the divisions to ship four missiles per launcher, in all 576 [SAM] missiles.

To send the antiaircraft divisions: one in July, and one in August, 1962.

4. For defense of coasts and bases in the sectors of probable enemy attack on the island of Cuba to send one regiment of *Sopka* ["little volcano"] comprising three battalions (six launchers) with three missiles per launcher

- on the coast in the vicinity of Havana, one regiment (four launchers)
- on the coast in the vicinity of Banes, one battalion (two launchers)

On the southern coast in the vicinity of Cienfuegos to locate one battalion (two launchers), [already] planned for delivery to Cuba in 1962.

The *Sopka* complex is capable of destroying surface ships at a range of up to 80 km.

5. To send to Cuba as part of the Group of Forces:

- a brigade of missile patrol boats of the class Project 183-R, comprising two units with six patrol boats in each (in all 12 patrol boats), each armed with two P-15 [trans: NATO SS-N-2 *Styx*] missiles with a range up to 40 km;
- a detachment of support ships comprising: one tanker, two dry cargo transports, and four repair afloat ships;
- fuel for missiles: fuel for the R-13 [trans: NATO SS-N-4 *Sark*] and P-15 – 70 tons; oxidizer for the R-13 – 180 tons; oxidizer for the P-15 – 20 tons; kerosene for the S-2 and KSShCh [trans: probably NATO SA-N-1 *Goa*] – 60 tons;
- two combat sets of the P-15 missile (24 missiles) and one for the R-13 (21 missiles).

Shipment of the missile patrol boats Project 183-R class, the battalions of *Sopka*, technical equipment for the missile patrol boats and technical batteries for the *Sopka* battalions, and also the missiles, missile fuel, and other equipment for communications to be carried on ships of the Ministry of the Maritime Fleet.

Shipment of the warheads, in readiness state 4, will be handled by ships of the Navy.

6. To send as part of the Group of Forces in Cuba in July–August:

- Two regiments of FKR (16 launchers) with PRTB, with their missiles and five special [trans: nuclear] warheads for each launcher. Range of the FKR is up to 180 km;
- A mine-torpedo aviation regiment with IL-28 air-craft, comprising three squadrons (33 aircraft) with RAT-52 jet torpedoes (150 torpedoes), and air dropped mines (150 mines) for destruction of surface ships;
- An Mi-4 helicopter regiment, two squadrons, 33 helicopters;
- A separate communications [liaison] air squadron (two IL-14, five Li-2, four Yak-12, and two An-2 air-craft).

7. With the objective of combat security of our technical troops, to send to Cuba four separate motorized rifle regi-ments, with a tank battalion in each, at the expense of the 64th Guards Motorized Rifle Division in the Leningrad Military District, with an overall personnel strength of 7,300. The regiments to be sent in June–July 1962.

8. Upon completion of the concentration of Soviet troops planned for Cuba, or in case of necessity, to send to Cuba on a friendly visit, tentatively in September:

A. A squadron of surface ships of the Navy under the command of Vice Admiral G. S. Abashvili (deputy commander of the Red Banner Baltic Fleet) comprising:

- two cruisers, *Mikhail Kutuzov* (Black Sea Fleet) and *Sverdlov* (Red Banner Baltic Fleet);
- two missile destroyers of the Project 57-bis class, the *Boikii* and *Gnevny* (Black Sea Fleet);
- two destroyers of the Project 76 class, the *Skromnyi* and *Svedushchii* (Northern Fleet);

Along with the squadron to send one refueling tanker. On the ships to send one full combat set of standard ammunition (including one combat set of KSShCh missiles – 24 missiles) and standard equipment. Sailing time of the ships 15 days.

B. A squadron of submarines, comprising:

- 18th Division of missile submarines of the Project 629 class [trans: NATO *Golf* or G-class] (seven submarines each with 3 R-13 [SS-N-4] missiles with range of 540 km);
- a brigade of torpedo submarines of Project 641 class [NATO: *Foxtrot* or F-class] (four submarines with torpedo armament);
- two submarine tenders.

Sailing time for the submarines, 20–22 days. If necessary, the squadrons can be sent separately. Time for preparation to depart, after 1 July, is 10 days. Upon arrival of the squadrons in Cuba, they would be incorporated into the Group of Soviet Forces.

9. For rear area security of the Group of Forces in Cuba to send:

- three hospitals (200 beds each);
- one anti-epidemic sanitary detachment;
- seven warehouses (two for food, one for general storage,

four for fuel, including two for automotive and
aviation fuel, and two for liquid fuel for the Navy);
- one company for servicing a trans-shipping base;
- one field bakery factory.

Create reserves:

- in the Group – fuel and provisions for routine maintenance of the troops for three months;
- in the troops – mobile (fuel, ammunition, provisions)
by established norms;
- for follow-up secure provisions for 25 days.

10. The overall number of the Group of Soviet Forces in
Cuba will be about 44,000 military personnel and 1,300
workers and civilians. For transport of the troops and combat equipment in summertime a simultaneous lift of about
70–80 ships of the Ministry of the Maritime Fleet of the
USSR will be required.

11. To establish a staff of the Group of Soviet Forces in
Cuba to command the Soviet troops. To form the staff of
the Group convert the staff of the 49th Missile Army from
Vinnitsa, which has a well qualified integrated apparatus
with support and service elements. To incorporate into the
staff of the Group a naval section, an air force section, and
an air defense section. The Commander in Chief of the
Group to have four deputies—one for general matters, one
for the Navy (VMF), one for Air Defense (PVO), and one
for the Air Force (VVS).

12. The form of dress envisioned for the troops sent to
Cuba, except for the Navy, is one set of civilian clothes and
one tropical uniform (as for troops in the Turkestan
Military District).

13. Food for the personnel of the Group of Soviet Forces
in Cuba will be arranged from the USSR.

14. Financial support will be paid on the same general basis as for other troops located abroad.

15. Measures for creation of the Group of Soviet Forces in Cuba will proceed under the codename *Anadyr*.

We request your review.

R. MALINOVSKY
M. ZAKHAROV
24 May 1962

Prepared in one copy on seven pages, no draft.
Attested COLONEL GENERAL S. P. IVANOV

SEPTEMBER, 1962

Statement by President John F. Kennedy on Cuba
September 4, 1962

All Americans, as well as all of our friends in this Hemisphere, have been concerned over the recent moves of the Soviet Union to bolster the military power of the Castro regime in Cuba. Information has reached this Government in the last four days from a variety of sources which establishes without doubt that the Soviets have provided the Cuban Government with a number of antiaircraft defense missiles with a slant range of 25 miles which are similar to early models of our Nike. Along with these missiles, the Soviets are apparently providing the extensive radar and other electronic equipment which is required for their operation. We can also confirm the presence of several Soviet-made motor torpedo boats carrying ship-to-ship guided missiles having a range of 15 miles. The number of Soviet military technicians now known to be in Cuba or en route—approximately 8,500—is consistent with assistance in setting up and learning to use this equipment. As I stated last week, we shall continue to make information available as fast as it is obtained and properly verified.

There is no evidence of any organized combat force in Cuba from any Soviet Bloc country; of military bases provided to Russia; of a violation of the 1984 treaty relating to Guantánamo; of the presence of offensive ground-to-ground missiles; or of other significant offensive capability either in Cuban hands or under Soviet direction and guidance. Were it to be otherwise, the gravest issues would arise.

The Cuban question must be considered as a part of the worldwide challenge posed by Communist threats to the peace. It must be dealt with as a part of that larger issue as well as in the context of the special relationships which have long characterized the Inter-American System.

It continues to be the policy of the United States that the Castro regime will not be allowed to export its aggressive purposes by force or the threat of force. It will be prevented by whatever means may be necessary from taking action against any part of the Western Hemisphere. The United States, in conjunction with other Hemisphere countries, will make sure that while increased Cuban armaments will be a heavy burden to the unhappy people of Cuba themselves, they will be nothing more.

*Memorandum from R. Malinovsky to the Chairman of the
Defense Council of the USSR, Comrade N. S. Khrushchev*
6 September 1962

TOP SECRET
SPECIAL IMPORTANCE
SOLE COPY

I am reporting:

I. On the possibility of reinforcing Cuba by air

1. About the transport by air of special warheads [*spetsial=nye boevye chasti*; nuclear warheads] for the Luna [FROG] and R-11M [SCUD-B] missiles.

Tests have been conducted at the test range and practical instructions have been worked out for the transportation of special warheads for R-11M missiles, two on AN-8 aircraft, and four on AN-12 aircraft. The alternatives for transport of warheads for the Luna missile are analogous to those for the R-11M. The transport of special warheads by Tu-114 is not possible owing to the absence of a freight hatch and fasteners.

2. About the transport by air of R-11M and Luna missiles. Practice loading, securing and transport of training R-11M and Luna missiles has been carried out on AN-8 and AN-12 aircraft, with two Luna or one R-11M missiles on AN-8 or AN-12 aircraft.

3. The size of the freight hold and carrying-capacity of AN-8 (5–8 tons) and AN-12 (7–16 tons) do not permit air transport of launchers, special earth moving machines, and field missile-technical bases (PRTB) for the R-11M and Luna missiles.

The Tu-114 aircraft, notwithstanding its large loading capacity (up to 30 tons) and long range (up to 8,000 km), is not suitable for transport of missile equipment as it is not adapted in a transport mode.

II. Proposals of the Ministry of Defense for reinforcing Group of Forces in Cuba

In order to reinforce the Group of Forces in Cuba, send:

1.* One squadron of IL-28 bombers, comprising 10–12 aircraft including delivery and countermeasures aircraft, with a mobile PRTB and six atomic bombs (407N), each of 8–12 kilotons;

2. One R–11M missile brigade made up of three battalions (total: 1,221 men, 18 R–11M missiles) with PRTB (324 men) and 18 special warheads, which the PRTB is capable of storing;

3. Two to three battalions[†] of Luna for inclusion in separate motorized infantry regiments in Cuba. Each Luna battalion will have two launchers and 102 men.

With the Luna battalions, send 8–12 missiles and 8–12 special warheads.

For the preparation and custody of special warheads for the Luna missiles, send one PRTB (150 men).

The indicated squadron of IL-28s, one R–11M missile brigade with PRTB, and two to three Luna battalions with PRTB, and the missiles are to be sent to Cuba in the first half of October. Atom bombs (six), special warheads for the R–11M missiles (18) and for the Luna missiles (8–12) are to be sent on the transport *Indigirka* on 15 September.

The Defense Ministry has just conducted successful firing tests of the S-75 antiaircraft system against surface

---

* [In Khrushchev's handwriting on top of "II.1" above]: Send to Cuba six IL-28s with atomic warheads N. S. Khrushchev 7.IX.1962.
† [Overwritten]: Three Luna battalions. N. S. Khrushchev 7.IX.62

targets on level terrain. At distances of 24 kilometers, accuracy of plus or minus 100–120 meters was achieved. The results of computer calculations indicate the possibility also of successful use against naval targets.

In order to fire against land or sea targets using S-75 complexes with the troops [in Cuba], small modifications in the missile guidance stations will be required by factory brigades together with some additional equipment prepared by industry.

R. MALINOVSKY
Marshal of the Soviet Union
6 September 1962

Memorandum, personally, to the Commander of the Group of Soviet Forces in Cuba
September 8, 1962

TOP SECRET
SPECIAL IMPORTANCE
COPY #1

The temporary deployment of Soviet Armed Forces on the island of Cuba is necessary to insure joint defense against possible aggression toward the USSR and the Republic of Cuba.

A decision on employment of the Soviet Armed Forces in combat actions in order to repel aggression and reinstatement will be undertaken by the Soviet Government.

1. The task of the Group of Soviet Forces in Cuba is not to permit an enemy landing on Cuban territory from the sea or from the air. The island of Cuba must be turned into an impenetrable fortress.

Forces and means: Soviet troops together with the Cuban Armed Forces.

2. In carrying out this task, the Commander of the Group of Soviet Forces on the island of Cuba will be guided by the following considerations:

(a) With respect to missile forces
The missile forces, constituting the backbone for the defense of the Soviet Union and Cuba, must be prepared, upon signal from Moscow, to deal a nuclear missile strike on the most important targets in the United States of America.

Upon arrival of the missile division in Cuba, two R-12 [SS-4] regiments (539th and 546th) and one R-14 [SS-5] regiment (564th) will deploy in the western region, and one R-12 regiment (the 514th) and one R-14 regiment (the 657th) in the central region of Cuba.

The missile units will deploy to the positional areas and take up their launch positions; with the establishment of launchers on combat duty, regiments will maintain Readiness No. 4.

(b) With respect to air defense (PVO) forces
PVO forces of the Group will not permit incursion of foreign aircraft into the air space of the Republic of Cuba and strikes by enemy air against the Group, the most important administrative political centers, naval bases, ports.

Combat use of PVO forces will be activated by the Commander of the Group of Forces. The PVO divisions will be deployed:

- 12th Division [surface-to-air missiles] – the western region of Cuban territory
- 27th Division [surface-to-air missiles] – the eastern region of Cuban territory
- 213th Fighter Air Division will be deployed at Santa Clara airfield

After unloading in Cuba of the surface-to-air missiles, fighter aviation will be deployed [*illegible*] and organization of combat readiness.

(c) With respect to the ground forces

Ground forces troops will protect the missile and other technical troops and the Group command center, and be prepared to provide assistance to the Cuban Armed Forces in liquidating enemy landings and counterrevolutionary groups on the territory of the Republic of Cuba.

The independent motorized rifle regiments (OMSP) will deploy:

- The 74th OMSP, with a battalion of Lunas, in the western part of Cuba in readiness to protect the Missile Forces [trans: in the San Cristobal and Guanajay areas] and to operate in the sectors Havana and Pinar del Río;
- The 43rd OMSP, with a battalion of Lunas, in the vicinity of Santiago de las Vegas in readiness to protect the Command of the Group of Forces and to operate in the sectors Havana, Artemisa, Batabanó, and Matanzas;
- The 146th OMSP, with a battalion of Lunas, in the area Camajuaní, Placetas, Sulu ... in readiness to protect the Missile Forces and to operate in the sectors: Caibarién, Colón, Cienfuegos, Fomento;
- The 106th OMSP in the eastern part of Cuba in the vicinity of Holguín in readiness to operate in the sectors Banes, Victoria de las Tunas, Manzanillo, and Santiago de Cuba.

(d) With respect to the Navy

The naval element of the Group must not permit combat ships and transports of the enemy to approach the island of

Cuba and carry out naval landings on the coast. They must be prepared to blockade from the sea the US naval base in Guantánamo, and provide cover for our transport ships along lines of communication in close proximity to the island.

Missile-equipped submarines should be prepared to launch, upon signal from Moscow, nuclear missile strikes on the most important coastal targets in the USA.

The main forces of the fleet should be based in the region around Havana and in ports to the west of Havana. One detachment of the brigade of missile patrol boats should be located in the vicinity of Banes.

The battalions of *Sopka* [coastal defense cruise missiles] should be deployed on the coast:

- One battalion east of Havana in the region of Santa Cruz del Norte;
- One battalion southeast of Cienfuegos in the vicinity of Gavilan;
- One battalion northeast of Banes in the vicinity of Cape Mulas;
- One battalion on the Isle of Pines in the vicinity of Cape Buenavista.

The torpedo-mine air regiment will deploy at the airfield San Julián Asiento, and plan and instruct in destroying combat ships and enemy landings from the sea.

(e) With respect to the Air Force
The squadron of IL-28 delivery aircraft will be based on Santa Clara airfield in readiness to operate in the directions of Havana, Guantánamo, and the Isle of Pines. [Trans. note: This deployment was later changed to Holguín airfield.]

The independent aviation engineering regiments [OAIP] (FKR) [cruise missiles] will deploy:

- 231st OAIP – in the western region of Cuba, designated as the main means to fire on the coast in the northeastern and northern sectors, and as a secondary mission in the direction of the Isle of Pines.
- 222nd OAIP – in the eastern part of the island. This regiment must be prepared, upon signal from the General Staff, in the main sector of the southeastern direction, to strike the US naval base at Guantánamo. Secondary firing sectors in the northeastern and southwestern directions. The fighter aviation regiment armed with MiG-21 [F-13] aircraft is included as a PVO [air defense] division, but crews of all fighters will train also for operations in support of the Ground Forces and Navy.

3. Organize security and economy of missiles, warheads, and special technical equipment, and all combat equipment in the armament of the Group of Soviet Forces in Cuba.

4. Carry out daily cooperation and combat collaboration with the armed forces of the Republic of Cuba, and work together in instructing the personnel of the Cuban armed forces in maintaining the arms and combat equipment being transferred by the Soviet Union to the Republic of Cuba.

5. Deploy the rear units and offices and organize all-round material, technical, and medical support of the troops.
   Rear area bases will be located in the regions as follows:

- Main Base – comprising: the 758th command base, separate service companies, the 3rd automotive platoon, 784th POL fuel station, the 860th food supply depot, the 964th warehouse, the 71st bakery factory, the 176th field technical medical detachment – Mariel, Artemisa, Güira de Melena, Rincón;

- Separate rear base – comprising: 782nd POL station, 883rd food supply depot, a detachment of the 964th warehouse, [the 1st] field medical detachment, a detachment of the 71st bakery factory—Caibarién, Camajuaní, Placetas;
- Separate rear base – comprising: separate detachments of the 784th POL station, the 883rd food supply depot, the 964th warehouse, [the 71st bakery unit], and the 1st field medical detachment – Gibara, Holguín, Camasan.

Fuel stocks for the Navy will be:

- Depot No. 4472 – Mariel, a branch at Guanabacoa;
- Depot No. 4465 – vicinity of Banes.

Hospitals will be set up in the regions: Field hospitals No. 965 with blood transfusion unit – Guanajay; No. 121 – Camajuaní, Placetas; No. 50 – Holguín.

The transport of material to be organized by troop transport means, and also do not use local rail or water transport.

6. The operational plan for the employment of the Group of Soviet Forces in Cuba should be worked out by 01 November 1962.

R. MALINOVSKY
USSR Minister of Defense
Marshal of the Soviet Union

M. ZAKHAROV
Chief of the General Staff
Marshal of the Soviet Union

OCTOBER 1–5, 1962

Analysis of SAM sites
Washington, October 1, 1962

1. The intelligence community has now identified and confirmed a total of 15 SA-2 SAM sites. From the location of these sites, a discernible pattern is developing:

(a) In the Oriente Province, the identified sites (three) form a triangular pattern around the new military airfield at Holguín. This field is probably not yet operational, but soon could be. At the present time, there are no MiG-type aircraft stationed at this field. The MiGs believed to be assigned to the operational control of the Commander, Eastern Army, are stationed at the airfield at Camagüey, in the Central Army area. When Holguín becomes operational, these aircraft will probably be moved to that location. There are no SA-2 sites identified in the vicinity of Camagüey.

(b) In the Central Army area, four SA-2 sites form a rectangular pattern around the military airfield near Santa Clara. This airfield has had MiGs for several months and is also the field upon which the first MiG-21 was identified.

(c) In the Western Army area, there are three and possibly four SA-2 sites forming a linear pattern to provide defense for the military airfield at San Antonio de los Banos and coincidentally for the defense of the Havana–Mariel complex. San Antonio de los Banos is the headquarters for the Cuban revolutionary Air Force and the assembly point for all MiGs, except the MiG-21s, which have previously been received in Cuba.

2. Further west in the Pinar del Río Province a triangular pattern of three SA-2 sites cannot be connected with any significant military installation. The only known installation within this triangle are two underground facilities whose use and purpose are unknown. The only other military installation in this particular area is the military air base at San Julian near the western tip of Cuba. However, one of the three SA-2 sites is located at or very near this military airfield, a most unlikely spot to place SA-2s for the defense of this particular air base. Therefore, curiosity is immediately aroused to the purpose of this triangular pattern on the far western tip of Cuba.

3. In the north central portion of the Pinar del Río Province is a large trapezoid-shaped restricted area controlled by the Soviet military personnel recently introduced into Cuba, measuring 15–20 miles on each side. There are no known military installations in this rough and sparsely populated area. According to reports from refugees arriving in Miami, all Cubans have been evacuated from this restricted area. The purpose of this restricted area is not currently known.

4. Information concerning the deployment of Soviet military personnel and "technicians" recently arriving in Cuba is derived from unevaluated refugee sources; however, an attempt has been made to plot all reported locations to determine whether there is any correlation between the location of Soviet personnel and missiles or missile activity. So far, the pattern indicates that there is a definite correlation, but significantly the greatest concentration of Soviet personnel, activity, and camps is in the western end of the Island of Cuba. This would indicate a greater interest on the part of the Soviets in Pinar del Río than in the other provinces.

5. A single unevaluated report states that the Soviet "SS-4 Shyster" missile may have been delivered to Cuba on or about 11 September. Some confusion is apparent in this report. The SS-4 missile is nicknamed "Sandal," while the "Shyster" carriers a designation of SS-3. This confusion was caused by the interrogators of the source using a recognition manual which designated the SS-4 as the Shyster. However, the description of the missiles reportedly observed by the source could have applied equally to either the Shyster or the Sandal. Both missiles have essentially the same outward appearance except that the Sandal is about 5 feet longer. In all other respects, including the missile carrier, the two appear identical. The source of this report

stated that on 12 September he had personally seen some 20 such missiles in the vicinity of Campo Libertad, a small airfield on the western edge of Havana. While this report is still unconfirmed and there are no other reports concerning the presence of either SS-3 or SS-4 missiles, it is significant to note that by using the approximate center of the restricted area referred to above as a point of origin and with a radius of 1,100 nm, the accepted range of the SS-4 missile, the arc includes the cities of Philadelphia, Pittsburgh, St Louis, Oklahoma City, Fort Worth–Dallas, Houston, San Antonio, Mexico City, all of the capitals of the Central American nations, the Panama Canal, and the oil fields in Maricaibo, Venezuela. The presence of operational SS-4 missiles in this location would give the Soviets a great military asset.

Memorandum from Acting Secretary of State Ball to
President Kennedy
Washington, October 2, 1962

Policy toward non-Bloc ships in Cuban trade

A. Recommended action

1. The President should make a public statement dealing with this topic.

2. The President should close all US ports to all ships of any country if any ship under the flag of that country hereafter carries arms to Cuba.

3. The President should direct that no government cargo shall be carried on a foreign flag ship if any ship of the same owners is used hereafter in Bloc–Cuba trade.

4. The President should direct that no United States flag ship and no United States owned ship shall carry goods to or from Cuba.

5. *Alternative I:* The President should close all United States ports to any ship on a continuous voyage to or from Cuba.
   Alternative II: The President should close all United States ports to any ship that on the same continuous voyage carried or carries to Cuba items on the COCOM list.
   Alternative III: The President should close all United States ports to any ship that on the same continuous voyage carried or carries to Cuba items on the positive list under Regulation T-1.
   Alternative IV: The President should close all United States ports to any ship that on the same continuous voyage was used or is being used in Bloc–Cuba trade.

6. The President should instruct the Secretary of State to explore every avenue to obtain cooperation from other countries in restricting the use of their ships in Bloc–Cuba trade.

B. Legal authority
The President has all the necessary legal authority to carry out the above recommendations without new legislation. A small supplemental appropriation for the Department of Agriculture might have to be included in the budget to pay for shipping in US bottoms.

C. Action not recommended
The President has adequate legal powers to adopt more restrictive policies than those recommended above. There has been some talk, for example, of closing US ports to the ships of any country which permits its ships to go to Cuba.

Others have mentioned the possibility of closing territorial waters of the US to such ships, or denying them use of the Panama Canal.

These proposals are not recommended.

Printed from an unsigned copy.

National Security Action Memorandum No. 194
Washington, October 2, 1962

To: The Secretary of State, The Secretary of Defense, The Secretary of the Treasury, The Secretary of Commerce, The Secretary of Labor, The Administrator, Maritime Commission, The Director, Agency for International Development, The Director, Bureau of the Budget, The Director of Central Intelligence, The President, Commodity Credit Corporation

Policy toward non-Bloc ships in Cuban trade (State memo of 10/2/62)

The President has approved the memorandum we discussed at the meeting this morning, including Alternative IV, under point 5. A group will be formed to do what is necessary to put these recommendations into effect. Mr Abram Chayes, Legal Adviser of the State Department, will lead it. Will you arrange for your department to put an appropriate person in touch with Mr Chayes?

CARL KAYSEN

*Memorandum from Secretary of Defense McNamara to the
Chairman of the Joint Chiefs of Staff (Taylor)
Washington, October 2, 1962*

During my meeting with the Joint Chiefs of Staff on
October 1, 1962, the question arose as to the contingencies under which military action against Cuba may be
necessary and toward which our military planning should
be oriented. The following categories would appear to
cover the likely possibilities:

(a) Soviet action against Western rights in Berlin calling
    for a Western response including among other
    actions a blockade of Communist or other shipping
    en route to Cuba.
(b) Evidence that the Castro regime has permitted the
    positioning of Bloc offensive weapon systems on
    Cuban soil or in Cuban harbors.
(c) An attack against the Guantánamo base, or against
    US planes or vessels outside Cuban territorial air
    space or waters.
(d) A substantial popular uprising in Cuba, the leaders of
    which request assistance in recovering Cuban inde-
    pendence from the Castro Soviet puppet regime.
(e) Cuban armed assistance to subversion in other parts
    of the Western Hemisphere.
(f) A decision by the President that affairs in Cuba have
    reached a point inconsistent with continuing US
    national security.

May I have the views of the Chiefs as to the appropriate-
ness of the above list of contingencies and answers to the
following three sets of questions:

(a) The operational plans considered appropriate for
    each contingency.

(b) The preparatory actions which should now and pro-
gressively in the future be undertaken to improve
US readiness to execute these plans.
(c) The consequences of the actions on the availability
of forces and on our logistics posture to deal with
threats in other areas, i.e. Berlin, Southeast Asia, etc.

We can assume that the political objective in any of these
contingencies may be either:

(a) the removal of the threat to US security of Soviet
weapon systems in Cuba, or
(b) the removal of the Castro regime and the securing
in the island of a new regime responsive to Cuban
national desires.

Inasmuch as the second objective is the more difficult
objective and may be required if the first is to be permanently achieved, attention should be focused upon a
capability to assure the second objective.

I have asked ISA to initiate discussion with State as to
the political actions which should precede or accompany
the various military actions being planned.

ROBERT S. MCNAMARA

*Memorandum from the Director of Intelligence and Research
(Hilsman) to the Under Secretary of State (Ball)*
Washington, October 2, 1962

Summary of recent Soviet military assistance to Cuba

Since July, when the volume of Soviet military shipments
to Cuba suddenly increased very substantially, 85 shiploads
of various military items, supplies, and personnel have
arrived. More ships are en route.

In part the Soviet shipments have consisted of types of weapons previously delivered to the Cuban Armed Forces including more tanks, self-propelled guns, and other Ground Force equipment. The major tonnage however has been devoted to supplying SA-2 surface-to-air missiles (SAMs) together with all of the related gear and equipment necessary for their installation and operation. To date 15 SAM sites have been established in the island. We estimate the total may eventually reach 25.

In addition three (possibly four) missile sites of a different type have been identified. These sites are similar to known coastal defense missile sites and are believed to accommodate Soviet anti-shipping missiles with a range of 20–35 miles. We expect that several more such sites will be installed.

Cuba is now estimated to have 60 older type MiG jet aircraft plus at least one advanced jet interceptor (MiG-21) recently received and probably several more in process of assembly. The MiG-21 is usually equipped with infrared air-to-air missiles. We estimate that the total of MIG-21s in Cuba may eventually reach 25–30.

Sixteen "Komar" class guided-missile patrol boats which carry two short-range missiles (11–17 miles) were included in the new shipments.

About 4,500 Soviet military specialists have arrived including construction men and technicians.

If the SAM sites are to be operated solely by Cuban personnel six months to a year of training will be required.

There is a considerable amount of other new equipment which has not been precisely identified but it is believed to include a large quantity of electronic gear.

*Memorandum from Secretary of Defense McNamara to
President Kennedy
Washington, October 4, 1962*

Presidential interest in SA-2 missile system and contingency planning for Cuba

1. In your memorandum of 21 September 1962, you noted an apparent lack of unanimity between General LeMay and Admiral Anderson with respect to aircraft losses that might occur in attacking an SA-2 site. You further requested assurance as to the currency of contingency planning for Cuba.

2. I have discussed with General LeMay and Admiral Anderson their estimate of aircraft losses in attacking SA-2 missile sites. Admiral Anderson agrees with General LeMay's point that no losses would be suffered from the SA-2 missile since the attacking aircraft would fly below the effective minimum altitude of the SA-2. General LeMay shares Admiral Anderson's estimate that attacking aircraft might suffer some loss to antiaircraft artillery defenses of the SA-2 site. The National Intelligence Estimate credits the SA-2 missile system with a minimum effective altitude of 3,000 feet due to inherent radar limitations.

3. If antiaircraft artillery is employed in direct support of the missile site, losses may be expected. World War II and Korean experience, updated to reflect current antiaircraft artillery capabilities against modern aircraft, indicates that low-level attack forces would incur some combat losses from antiaircraft artillery fire; however, numbers cannot be predicted accurately. There are currently no known anti-aircraft artillery defenses of SA-2 sites in Cuba. Attack plans can be amended to take the antiaircraft weapons under fire during the attack if reconnaissance shows such

defenses and if analysis shows such fire suppression necessary. Korean experience proved that such fire suppression
was unnecessary when surprise could be achieved.

4. In my opinion, and that of the Joint Chiefs, it is not
necessary to build a model of an SA-2 site for training purposes. However, the aircraft revetment of the type found at
Santa Clara and Camagüey is a more difficult target than
the SA-2 site. Therefore, the Air Force has found it desirable to reproduce that type of aircraft revetment to aid in
the selection of weapons, method of delivery, and to assist
in training crews. The target was completed at Nellis AFB,
Nevada, on 30 September 1962, at an approximate cost of
$28,000. Initial tests indicate that the GAM 83, 20 mm
cannon, and napalm is the most effective weapons mix
against aircraft in such revetments.

5. I have taken steps to insure that our contingency plans
for Cuba are kept up to date.

6. The Navy plans to attack SA-2 targets at low level
using four divisions of A-4Ds (four aircraft per division)
armed with 250#, 500#, and 2000# low drag bombs and
napalm. All crews are proficient in the delivery techniques
planned. Similarly, the Air Force plans primary use of
napalm and 20 mm cannon delivered at low level, and
crews are proficient. Both have made detailed target studies; target folders are in the hands of crews; and crews are
familiar with their assigned targets. As new missile sites are
located, they are picked up in the target and attack plans
within a few hours of receipt of photographs.

ROBERT S. MCNAMARA

Memorandum of Mongoose meeting
Washington, Thursday, October 4, 1962

CHAIRED by the Attorney General.
ATTENDED BY: Gilpatric, Johnson, General Taylor, General
Carter, McCone, Scoville, General Lansdale and Colonel
Steakley (part of the time)

The Attorney General reported on discussions with the
President on Cuba; dissatisfied with lack of action in the
sabotage field, went on to stress that nothing was moving
forward, commented that one effort attempted had failed,
expressed general concern over developing situation.

General Lansdale reviewed operations, pointing out that
no sabotage had been attempted and gave general impression that things were all right.

McCone then stated that phase one was principally
intelligence gathering, organizing, and training, that no
sabotage was authorized, that one operation against a pow-
erhouse had been contemplated but was discouraged by
group, that he had called a meeting to review matters this
morning, and that he had observed a lack of forward
motion due principally to "hesitancy" in government circles to engage in any activities which would involve
attribution to the United States.

AG took sharp exception stating the Special Group had
not withheld approval on any specified actions to his
knowledge, but to the contrary had urged and insisted
upon action by the Lansdale operating organization.

There followed a sharp exchange which finally was clarifying inasmuch as it resulted in a reaffirmation of a
determination to move forward. In effect it seemed to be
the consensus that phase two as approved on September 6
was now outmoded, that more dynamic action was indicated, that hesitancy about overflights must be

reconsidered (this to be commented on later in this memorandum), that actions which could be attributed to indigenous Cubans would not be important or very effective, and that a very considerable amount of attribution and "noise" must be expected.

As a result, General Lansdale was instructed to give consideration to new and more dynamic approaches, the specific items of sabotage should be brought forward immediately and new ones conceived, that a plan for mining harbors should be developed and presented, and the possibility of capturing Castro forces for interrogation should be studied.

With respect to overflights, the NRO and Colonel Steakley were instructed to prepare and present to the Special Group on next Tuesday at a special meeting alternate recommendations for overflights. These to include the use of U-2s on complete sweeps (as contrasted with peripheral or limited missions), the use of firefly drones, the use of 101s or other reconnaissance planes on low level, intermediate level, and high level missions, and other possible reconnaissance operations.

Consideration was given to stating publicly that we propose to overfly Cuba in the interest of our own security and the security of the Western Hemisphere, and then to proceed even though doing so involved risk.

It was the consensus that we could not accept restrictions which would foreclose gaining all reasonable knowledge of military installations in Cuba.

During the meeting McCone reviewed the earlier meeting with General Lansdale, and pointed out to the group that this meeting clarified General Lansdale's authority over the entire Mongoose operation and that the CIA organization was responsive to his policy and operational guidance, and this was thoroughly understood.

Consideration was given to the existing guidelines and it was the consensus that the August 1st guidelines for phase two were inadequate and new guidelines must be considered.

JOHN A. MCCONE
Director
CIA

Memorandum of discussion with the President's Special Assistant for National Security Affairs (Bundy) Washington, October 5, 1962, 5:15 p.m.

McCone reviewed details of the Donovan negotiations, discussions with the President, Attorney General, Eisenhower, the decisions not to approach Congressional leadership, the discussion with Senator Javits, and the final report from Donovan. Bundy expressed general agreement.

At the October 4th meeting of the Special Group, Mongoose was discussed in some detail as was the meeting with Carter, Lansdale *et al.* in DCI's office on that day. McCone stated there was a feeling in CIA and Defense that the "activist policy" which founded the Mongoose operation was gone and that while no specific operational activities had been (refused) the amount of "noise" from minor incidents such as the sugar, the students firing on the Havana Hotel and other matters, and the extreme caution expressed by State, had led to this conclusion. More importantly, however, the decisions to restrict U-2 flights had placed the United States Intelligence Community in a position where it could not report with assurance the development of offensive capabilities in Cuba. McCone stated he felt it most probable that Soviet–Castro operations would end up with an established offensive capability in Cuba including MRBMs. McCone stated he thought this a probability rather than a mere possibility. Bundy took issue stating that he felt the Soviets would not go that far, that he was satisfied that no offensive capability would be installed in Cuba because of its worldwide effects, and therefore seemed relaxed over the fact that the Intelligence Community cannot produce hard information on this important subject. McCone said that Bundy's viewpoint was reflected by many in the Intelligence Community, perhaps a majority, but he just did not agree and furthermore did not think the United States could afford to take such a risk.

Bundy then philosophized on Cuba stating that he felt that our policy was not clear, our objectives not determined and therefore our efforts were not productive. He discussed both the Mongoose operations and the Rostow "Track Two." Bundy was not critical of either or of the Lansdale operations. It was obvious that he was not in sympathy with a more active role such as those discussed at [Special Groups] 5412 on Thursday as he felt none of them would bring Castro down nor would they particularly enhance the US position of world leadership. Bundy seemed inclined to support the Track Two idea and also inclined (though he was not specific) to play down the more active Lansdale operation.

Bundy had not talked to Lansdale but obviously had received some of the "static" that is being passed around in Washington. (Before) McCone in reporting on the discussions at Thursday's 5412 meeting repeated the views of the President and expressed by the Attorney General it was agreed that the whole Government policy with reference to Cuba must be resolved promptly as basic to further actions on our part. In general, Bundy's views were that we should either make a judgment that we would have to go in militarily (which seemed to him intolerable) or alternatively we would have to learn to live with Castro, and his Cuba, and adjust our policies accordingly.

McCone then elaborated on his views of the evolution of Soviet–Castro military capability stating he felt defense was just phase one, phase two would be followed by various offensive capabilities and indeed the existing defensive capabilities such as the (MiG) 21s a very definite offensive capability against nearby American cities and installations. McCone stated that he thought that the establishment of a very expensive defensive mechanism could not be the ultimate objective of the Soviets or Castro and therefore the objective was (a) to establish an offensive base or (b) to insert sufficient Soviet specialists and military leaders to take Cuba away from Castro and establish it as a true Soviet controlled satellite. McCone stated that he felt there were only two courses open—one was to take military action at the appropriate time or secondly to pursue an effort to split Castro off from the Communists and for this reason he, McCone, had vigorously supported the Donovan mission as it is the only link that we have to the Castro hierarchy at the present time. Note in this connection it might be well to study the evolution of the Touré experience in Guinea when the Communists moved in and captured all elements of the Government and economy and forced Touré to expel the ambassador and try to rectify the situation. There may be a parallel here.

McCone reviewed the Eisenhower discussions. Bundy read the memorandum covering these discussions. Bundy stated that Adenauer did not express the concern of the US policy reflected by Eisenhower and reported in the memorandum.

Bundy rejected the idea of regular NSC meetings, stating that every President has to organize his Government as he desires, and that the Eisenhower pattern was not necessarily adaptable to the Kennedy type of administration. McCone stated that if this is the case he intended to request occasional NSC meetings to review specific estimates or other intelligence situations and the next one would be a report and discussion of the estimate of Soviet air defense capabilities. Bundy agreed.

Bundy rejected the idea (calling) the several Special Groups 5412, CIA, Mongoose, and North Vietnam together feeling it was better to keep them separated. He also rejected the idea that the visiting commissions such as the Byroade Team and the Draper Team should report back to the Special Group (CI) feeling it was appropriate that they report to the President, (through) the Secretary of State, with consultation with the Special Group (CI). It was agreed that we would have a further discussion over the weekend.

JOHN A. MCCONE
Director
CIA

Handwritten note for the record by Colonel General S. P. Ivanov
17:20 hours, October 5, 1962

N. S. Khrushchev telephoned from [*illegible*] and inquired how the shipment [of nuclear weapons] was going.

Ivanov reported: The *Indigirka* arrived 4 October. No overflights [by US surveillance aircraft]. [*word illegible*] shipment 22 [? *unclear reference*]. In transit 20 [days].

Transport with special [nuclear] munitions *Aleksandrovsk* is loaded and ready for dispatch. Permission requested to send it.

N. S. Khrushchev: Send the *Aleksandrovsk*. Where are the Lunas and IL-28s?

I responded: en route.

[*NSK:*] Everything is clear. Thanks. [*two words illegible*]

Written by S. P. IVANOV
By VCh [secure telephone]
executed in one copy, on one sheet, without a draft
Major General G. Yeliseyev [*later stamped:*]
4 [sic; should be 5] October 1962 TOP SECRET
No. 746-1 Yeliseyev

*Memorandum from the Central Intelligence Agency Project
Officer for Operation Mongoose (Harvey) to the Chief of
Operations, Operation Mongoose (Lansdale)*
Washington, October 8, 1962

Sabotage of Cuban-owned ship

1. It is requested that you present the following proposal to the Special Group (Augmented) for policy approval.

2. Policy approval is requested to permit the sabotage of Cuban-owned vessels wherever and whenever secure access to them can be attained; normally this will be in non-Bloc ports. Attacks against the Cuban-owned ships must be considered essentially as attacks against targets of opportunity in the sense that, in most cases, there will be little advance information prior to the arrival of the ship in a non-Bloc port and the duration of the port call will be limited.

3. The following specific types of action are contemplated:
   [*13 paragraphs (40 lines of source text) not declassified*]

6. It is necessary to submit the request for policy approval in a somewhat more general form than usual to permit us to take advantage of targets of opportunity as they occur. In most cases we will not have sufficient advance notice of

the arrival of the ship or have sufficient access to the ship to permit the preparation and submission of detailed individual approval requests in advance. In every case where time and circumstance permit, specific proposals will be submitted to the Special Group (Augmented) for approval. Any case involving unusual operational or security risks will be submitted in advance for Special Group (Augmented) approval.

7. Later we will submit requests for policy approval of actions against other ships supplying Cuba.

WILLIAM K. HARVEY

OCTOBER 11–13, 1962

Memorandum on Donovan Project meeting (10 Oct 62)
by Director of Central Intelligence McCone
Washington, October 11, 1962

Immediately after my discussion with the Cannon Committee (including Taber, Ford and Mahon), I went to the White House and explained to the President and McGeorge Bundy the positions taken by Ford and Mahon, as covered in a separate memorandum prepared by Mr Warner. The President made the judgment that we should proceed with the negotiations, recognizing there would be some political consequences and criticisms, but he, the President, was willing to accept this as a fact.

I then showed the President photographs of the crates which presumably would carry, or were carrying, IL-28s, Soviet medium bombers, and were deck loaded on a ship which had arrived in Havana in the early days of October. The President requested that such information be withheld at least until after the elections as, if the information got into the press, a new and more violent Cuban issue would be injected into the campaign and this would seriously affect his independence of action.

McCone stated that these particular photographs could not be restricted as they had been disseminated to the Intelligence Community and several joint and specified commands, such as CINCLANT, SAC, NORAD, and others and would be reported in the CIA Bulletin on Thursday morning. The President then requested that the report be worded to indicate a probability rather than an actuality because in the final analysis we only saw crates, not the bombers themselves. DCI agreed. The President further requested that all future information be suppressed. DCI stated that this was extremely dangerous.

It was then agreed that future information would be disseminated to members of USIB, with appropriate instructions that only those responsible for giving the President advice be given the information. Furthermore, that within CIA circles a minimum number of experts be informed. McCone stated there was no problem in CIA, that it was secure. It was therefore agreed that the USIB members would be instructed to restrict the information to their personal offices and fully and currently inform the Chiefs of Staff, the Chairman, the Service Secretaries, and the Secretary of Defense. Similar restrictive action would be taken in State. Therefore all those involved in "giving advice to the President" would be fully informed.

However operational divisions and the joint and specified commands would not be informed at this time, except at the direction of the above people who are receiving the information.

At this point the President mentioned that "we'll have to do something drastic about Cuba" and I am anxiously looking forward to the JCS operational plan which is to be presented to me next week.

McCone effected the above instructions by calling Mr Cline, who was unavailable, and then Mr Sheldon who agreed to prepare a procedure for review on Thursday morning.

McCone then called the Attorney General and advised him of his talk with the Cannon Committee. The Attorney General had no particular comment.

At six o'clock McCone received a report from Houston that Donovan had gone into a meeting at five o'clock. At eleven o'clock Houston reported the meeting was still in progress. At seven o'clock on Thursday morning Donovan still had no report.

At 11:15 General Eisenhower called McCone stating he was sorry a meeting could not be arranged, he was leaving very early the following morning for Gettysburg. McCone reported that negotiations were in progress and he also reported objections stated by several members of Congress. Eisenhower advised that the negotiations be pursued, indicating his support of it and further-more stated that if the negotiations were satisfactorily con-cluded the complaints and objections would, in his words, disappear.

McCone told General Eisenhower there were some defendable evidences of shipments of twin-engined light jet bombers. Eisenhower responded the situation must be watched very carefully. Positive action might be indicated and then he said there had been two instances where action was warranted but had not been taken. Eisenhower did not elaborate; however, I know from previous discussions he feels that when Castro embraced Communism publicly and announced publicly his allegiance to Moscow, we had then a reason to act militarily and if we had chosen to so act, such action would have been defendable.

On Thursday morning McCone reported by telephone to Mr Kennedy, reviewing the Eisenhower discussion and stating that he, McCone, was concerned over Donovan's safety in view of the rash of publicity, most particularly the *Herald Tribune* article, and that he had instructed that contact be made with Donovan and that if things were not proceeding satisfactorily and a conclusion to the negotiations along the lines agreed in sight, then Donovan should come out. The Attorney General stated that he had no concern over Donovan's personal safety, that "they will not do anything to him." McCone stated he was not so sure and that he therefore concluded to bring Donovan out unless things were going well.

With reference to the political implications, McCone recalled that he had told the President and the AG that he would take all, or his full share of responsibility, that he wished the AG to bear this in mind as the position taken in this respect by Mr McCone in the first conversation after his return from Europe still stood. AG expressed appreciation for this statement.

JOHN A. McCONE

*Memorandum from the Director for the Operations of the Joint
Staff (Unger) to the Assistant Secretary of Defense for
International Security Affairs (Nitze)*
Washington, October 12, 1962

Political actions/military actions concerning Cuba
1. In furtherance of our discussion of last evening concerning the project included in the reference, we are having a meeting at 1300 hours today of operational and logistical planners from CINCLANT and CINCSTRIKE for the purpose of developing our responses to the contingencies and other matters requested by the SecDef.

2. Pending completion of the requirement given us by the SecDef, a general picture of each of our military contingency plans for Cuba is tabulated below as a basis for your initial discussions with State. On the other hand, it may be better to delay discussions with State until we have completed our part of the requirement and have submitted it to the SecDef and the JCS on Monday, 15 October.

(a) Blockade Plan: employs 24 to 36 destroyers, a carrier task force, etc., which can marshal significant strength to blockade Cuba, both air and maritime.
(b) Air Strike Plan: currently being revised, but employs between 450 and 500 aircraft. In the event of any execution of this plan steps would be taken to alert all forces allocated to the other assault plans.
(c) Fast Reaction Assault Plan: employs both airborne and amphibious assault with about 32,000 troops in initial phase, with balance of assault forces arriving in increments as they become available. Ultimately builds up to about 80,000 troops in Cuba around D+18 days.
(d) Full-Scale Deliberate Assault Plan: employs simultaneous airborne and amphibious assault with around

49,000 troops engaged on D Day, building to about 60,000 by D+5 days, and again to 80,000 by D+16 days.

3. For your consideration, following are some of the political actions which might be undertaken in connection with the implementation of one or more of the foregoing plans: final arrangements for the tactical use of Mayaguana Island in the Bahamas; perhaps a request for token participation by Latin American military forces; in the case of blockade, notification of "neutral" shipping and publication of US intent; in all cases, possibly, the preliminary political arrangements attendant to a state of war; and, of course, coordination with international organizations, such as the OAS and the UN during the execution of military action.

Memorandum from the Assistant Secretary for Inter-American Affairs (Martin) to the Deputy Under Secretary of State for Political Affairs (Johnson)
Washington, October 12, 1962

Track Two
The following is the pertinent portion of Mr Rostow's paper:

> I believe we should consider the possibility of a Two-Track covert operation.
>
> Track One would consist of a heightened effort to move along the present Mongoose lines. The minimum objective here would be harassment: the maximum objective would be the triggering of a situation where there might be conflict at the top of the Cuban regime leading, hopefully, to its change or overthrow by some group within Cuba commanding arms.

Track Two would consist of an effort to engage Cubans more deeply, both within Cuba and abroad, in efforts of their own liberation. This requires an operation with the following characteristics:

(a) Authentic Cuban leadership with a considerable range of freedom to implement ideas and to assume risk.

(b) Minimal US direct participation: ideally, one truly wise US adviser—available, but laying back; equipped to provide finance, but not monitoring every move; capable of earning their respect rather than commanding it by his control over money or equipment.

(c) Basing outside the United States.

(d) A link-up with the scattered and sporadic groups and operations now going forward of their own momentum in Cuba.

(e) A plan of operation which aims at the overthrow of Castro primarily from within rather than by invasion from without.

(f) A long enough time horizon to build the operation carefully and soundly.

In suggesting that Track Two be studied—and sharply distinguished from Track One—I am, of course, wholly conscious of our failure of last year. But, as I read that failure in retrospect, its root lay in: US bureaucratic domination; the lack of a Cuban political and organizational base; and a plan of operation that hinged on a type of overt invasion by a fixed date rather than the patient build-up of a true movement of national liberation. I'm sure it would be easy to argue that such a movement could not be generated against a Communist control system; that the Cuban refugees lack the capacity to play their part in such an enterprise with skill and minimal security; etc. And I am in no position to reply with confidence to such argument. On the other hand, Cuba is not located in Eastern Europe; and, presumably, some Cubans have learned something from last year's failure, too.

On the balance, I am prepared to recommend that Track Two be sympathetically studied and that General Lansdale be asked to formulate a design for it.

The underlying philosophy is one which we have felt for some time merited exploration.

There is attached (Tab A) as you have requested, a paper describing the more important policy considerations bearing on this course of action.

The ARA memorandum (Tab B), previously forwarded to you, described some of the political thinking which led us to the conclusion that we should experiment with this course of action.

Tab A: Track Two

A program of "giving the Cubans their heads" in an effort to effect the downfall of the Castro regime from within involves embarking upon uncharted waters as far as the US is concerned. Grandiose US plans based upon a substantially unified exile community would be unrealistic. Nearly all Cuban exile leaders, of whatever political persuasion, are convinced that only overt US military action can remove the Castro regime. While we could probably force a semblance of unity based upon the "downfall from within" thesis, despite the sharp political rivalry among the exile leaders, our purposes would not be served. While "accepting" our thesis, most of the waking hours of these exiles would be devoted to devising ways of involving the US militarily, rather than building the internal base of opposition we seek. We could thereby lose initiative and control over the situation and find ourselves in an untenable position from the international, and, perhaps, domestic, standpoint.

If the above judgment is accepted, two alternatives are available. We could cooperate with all anti-Castro–Batista exile groups which we have reason to believe have a following inside Cuba, or we could, on an experimental basis, work with one such group. By cooperating with all such groups we run the serious risk of accentuating rivalries among the exile leaders which would be inevitably reflected within Cuba. Rather than achieving a broad base of political opposition within Cuba, we may only be instrumental in fomenting splinter groups. In attempting to administer such a program, the US would probably find itself in the midst of the crossfire of exile politics, very likely satisfying no one inside or outside Cuba.

Working with one group, on an experimental basis, would provide us with experience which could guide our future thinking and at the same time probably prevent problems of unmanageable proportions. Selection of the right group is of paramount importance. Even then, if we saw no progress in Cuba, we could not be certain that the thesis was impractical or the selection of the group erroneous.

Of all the exile groups the only one which has publicly adopted the thesis of "downfall from within" is that known as JURE, formed in September 1962 by Manolo Ray and based in Puerto Rico. (Since Ray has some friends within the US Government and is presently employed by the Puerto Rican Government, it is reasonable to suppose that some of the recent official interest in the "downfall from within" thesis has been generated by him.) Ray was former Minister of Public Works under Castro, broke with Castro and formed an important underground movement which has since been badly smashed by Castro. Ray is a nationalist and left of center. The political program of JURE is one with which the US can live.

The other feasible possibility is the CRC with which we have had a long standing relationship. Apart from Dr Miro and some of the organizations that form an integral part of the Council, the CRC is not a very effective organization for what we have in mind. Its background is associated with the Bay of Pigs and its outlook is essentially one of military action.

Advantages of working with JURE would appear to be:

(1) A new organization which, as such, has no past relationship with the US.
(2) Commitment to the "downfall from within" thesis.
(3) Base outside the US.
(4) Political ideology which may be attuned to the desires of the Cuban people.
(5) Ray is experienced in underground activities and an independent thinker.

Disadvantages of working with JURE are:

(1) Little, if any, assets known within Cuba today.
(2) Opposed by most of the established exile groups, particularly Dr Miro.
(3) Ray is a complex personality, sometimes difficult to handle.

On balance it is worth trying. Although we would try to maintain security, Dr Miro may discover our assistance to Ray and resign. The CRC is useful to us, but its disappearance would be bearable.

If we embark upon these unchartered waters, and it is recommended that we do so, we must be prepared for increased noise level and press inquiry. We must be prepared for a comparatively high rate of loss, failures and cries of anguish from JURE for assistance we may not be able to give it. It is essential that we recognize this and not be permitted to be stampeded into regrettable public postures or actions. A further important consideration is that Track Two operations may compromise Track One operations. Coordination would be essential.

Another conflict arises from the President's desire that a Cuban Brigade be formed. While this would not necessarily be a serious conflict with the program envisaged, for there are probably enough exiles for both programs, it should be recognized that a number of young men qualified for infiltration activities will probably join the Brigade.

If we attempt our program on a large scale, or with more than one group, the immediately above-mentioned problems would multiply.

The program we would visualize is one of providing the selected exile group with funds, arms, sabotage equipment, transport and communications equipment for infiltration operations in order to build a political base of opposition inside Cuba. We would provide the best technical advice we could. Our role would essentially be that of advisers and purveyors of material goods—it would be the exile group's show. We would insist that hit and run raids or similar harassing activities that clearly originate from outside Cuba and do not reflect internal activity not be engaged in.

In sum, we should be cautious about grandiose schemes, a "major" US effort, and deep commitments to the exiles. We should experiment in this new venture on a small scale with patience and tolerance for high noise levels and mistakes.

Memorandum from the Ambassador at Large (Bowles)
to President Kennedy
Washington, October 13, 1962

Report of conversation with Ambassador Dobrynin on Saturday, October 13th, regarding Cuba and other subjects

A week ago Ambassador Dobrynin called my office to say that he understood I was leaving for Africa and would like to have our "long postponed luncheon" before my departure. I met him at the USSR Embassy on 16th Street at 1 p.m. on October 13th. With the exception of an occasional exchange of courtesies at diplomatic functions, this was the first time I had talked with him.

It was a frank, free-wheeling discussion, lasting more than an hour and a half. Dobrynin's manner was pleasant, with a show of reasonableness and concern about the current drift in Soviet–American relations.

At my first opportunity, I expressed deep disappointment that no more progress had been made in reducing tensions, and concern over the consequences of a further decline. I said that since I was speaking wholly unofficially, he should not attempt to read anything into my remarks. I would like to be utterly frank with him. Almost immediately Dobrynin brought up the question of Cuba and expressed worry and surprise at the intensity of US public reaction.

In response to his question as to why we attached such importance to a relatively small island, I outlined the history of US–Cuban relations and drew a parallel to the situation in 1898, the presence of Spanish misrule, and the US public agitation that abetted the outbreak of war.

When he protested that the Soviet presence in Cuba was no greater provocation than the US presence in Turkey, I pointed out that the present Administration had inherited a status quo that had grown up since the war. In some areas the advantage in this status quo had been with us, in others with Moscow; in still others it was a stand-off.

Our presence in Greece and Turkey, for instance, represented our reaction to Stalin's military and political pressures against these two countries following the war. It had become part of a status quo which in all its complexity could safely be changed only by negotiation with reciprocal benefits to each side. The Kennedy Administration had hoped and expected that we could in fact negotiate a more rational set of relationships, easing the various danger points on a basis of reciprocal action to everyone's benefit.

However, in Cuba the USSR had unilaterally altered this status quo by introducing a wholly new element. Our reaction, in these circumstances, should have been foreseeable.

Moreover, many US students of Soviet affairs were soberly convinced that the USSR had made this move deliberately to provoke a US military response against Cuba on the theory that this would divert our energies from Berlin, and elsewhere, and enable Soviet spokesmen to charge us with aggression in the UN.

If this kind of thinking had in fact played a part in the Soviet analysis, it was extremely dangerous. If we did move into Cuba in response to some overt act or offensive build-up by the USSR, a global chain of events might be set in motion which could have catastrophic consequences.

For instance, the Soviets might then be tempted to take what they would term "counter-action" in Berlin and perhaps Turkey; and the United States, by that time in an extremely tense mood, would react with vigor. The USSR, in turn, would feel pressed by the Chinese and other extremists to counter our moves, and we would be on our way together down the long slippery slide.

I asked Dobrynin if he had read *The Guns of August*. [Barbara Tuchman, *The Guns of August*, New York, 1962] He said "only a three-page summary." I urged him to read at least the first few chapters in which he would see a pattern of politico-military action and counter-action that could be repeated in the next six months.

In July 1914, men of intelligence in Russia, Germany, Austria-Hungary, France, and England, all quite conscious of the forces which were feeding the approaching holocaust, found themselves enmeshed in internal pressures, commitments, and precedents which left them powerless to avoid the inevitable. It would be the greatest folly in history if we were to repeat this insane process in the nuclear age.

Dobrynin asked me what, in the circumstances, I thought could be done in regard to Cuba. Stressing that I was speaking solely as an individual, I suggested three moves that the USSR could sponsor to ease the situation.

1. Dobrynin should remind his government of President Kennedy's sharp distinction between defensive and offensive weapons in his recent statement. I was particularly concerned on this point because current reports indicated that Soviet shipments were in fact beginning to include weapons which had a clearly offensive capacity.

If this continued, it could produce—with the help of some incident perpetrated perhaps by individuals striving to provoke another "Remember the Maine" incident*— the very conflict which the Administration is anxious to avoid. President Kennedy had committed himself to act under certain specific circumstances. This was a clear commitment, and the USSR should not take it lightly.

2. From many reports, Castro now had ample defensive arms with which to protect himself from casual landings. The USSR should tell him that under present circumstances no more arms will be shipped. The USSR should then ask Castro himself to make a statement announcing that the defense of Cuba was assured and that no more arms were needed. Moscow could then inform us that no more arms would be shipped.

* A brief conflict in 1898, when the US intervened in Cuba's struggle to gain independence from Spain. The blowing up of the US battleship *Maine* in Havana propelled the US into war with Spain (and ultimately victory for the US).

3. Castro should be asked by Moscow to state that he has no design on his neighbors, that his entire energies would henceforth be devoted to the economic development of Cuba, and that he sought only peaceful competition with other Latin American nations. His decision not to indulge in further subversion, propaganda, and expansion in neighboring Latin American countries would, of course, have to be confirmed by deeds. However, Soviet assurances on this point would serve to reduce some of the current tensions and give us all a breathing spell.

If some progress along these lines were not possible, I had deep forebodings about the weeks ahead. To all of this Dobrynin appeared to listen intently. I believe he was impressed.

He answered that in spite of our worries, the USSR was not shipping offensive weapons and well understood the dangers of doing so. Moreover, it was unreasonable for the US, as a major power, to expect a small, weak country such as Cuba to make such public concessions to US public opinion even though both the USSR and Cuba might accept all three points in principle.

Why, he asked repeatedly, do we get so excited about so small a nation? Although the USSR could not let Cuba down, they had no desire to complicate the situation further. Was it not possible for us to negotiate a modus vivendi with Castro directly?

I commented that Cuba had initiated the current conflict. Indeed, in 1959, most Americans had strongly applauded Castro's revolution. If Dobrynin were misinformed about the types of weapons now arriving in Cuba, it would not be the first time in diplomatic history that this had occurred. As long as Soviet weapons flowed into Cuba and Cuban money was used to subvert Latin American countries which we were striving to assist into the 20th century, the situation would remain dangerously explosive. I hoped that his government would see the danger and act accordingly to help ease the tensions.

Without directly responding to my remarks, Dobrynin referred to Max Frankel's story in the morning *Times* which cited agitation by various private agencies, Cuban and American, to provoke a "Maine incident" with the connivance of US official groups. I replied that our government would have no part in such an operation, that we were genuinely worried, and that his government should view the situation with serious concern.

Telegram from the Embassy in the Soviet Union to the Department of State
Moscow, October 16, 1962, 7:00 p.m.

Khrushchev said he wanted to express his disappointment at one thing that adds fuel to fire of the cold war, namely, that US now is trying to stop Soviet airplanes from flying to Cuba. After I interjected confirmation, he said they regard this as unfriendly act. This is not wartime. We should be developing trade and culture between our countries. He could not understand why we were acting this way. Perhaps we were frightened and our leaders' nerves were bad. If we were going to start a war, then he could understand it. US was boycotting trade with Cuba and appealing to all countries to stop their ships from going there. US is great country with population 183 million, while Cuba has only seven million. Could it really be that US was afraid of Cuba? Who would believe that Cuba was a nightmare for US? It was too small; even if it wanted to gobble up US, it couldn't. (There followed some good-natured byplay about census figures.)

Khrushchev said that what US was doing complicated life of simple people and did not simplify it. Result was to make Cuban people go hungry. What did US want? To start war? If not, what was happening? "Are you too afraid? Do you want to commit suicide?" When last war started in USSR, on third or fourth day, a certain general came to him, where he was serving as member of military council of front, and said everything was lost, just as in France. General said command must be changed. General went to sleep that night and next morning came into peasant hut in which Khrushchev was staying and shot himself. He was a coward, lost his self-control, and let his nerves dominate his mind. Had US become a coward? Such people end by shooting themselves. Did US want to commit suicide? Is this the state in which American imperialism now finds itself?

I said I should of course report his remarks to President. At Vienna, President had spoken very frankly to him about Cuba. Chairman was misinterpreting Castro regime. Not only US, but all Western Hemisphere countries, feel Castro has let Cuban people down. US and other Western Hemisphere states are not going to help Cuba. We are certainly not afraid of them but we don't intend to help them. Of course, we have different views than Chairman about situation. Speaking as frankly as he had, I felt I must add that size of Soviet shipments to Cuba has increased feeling in US on this problem.

Khrushchev said we must be responsible, since our countries are great powers. We cannot demand that other countries live as we like or there would be war. US has bases in countries neighboring USSR, such as Turkey, as well as in Greece, Italy, France, West Germany, and Pakistan. But USSR does not attack these countries. If US thinks it has right to do as it likes about Cuba, why hasn't USSR right to do as it likes about these countries? If we acted that way, might would make right. UN Charter would lose its force. That would be policy of banditry. Cuba is small; US is big. "You are so afraid of Cuba, you almost lost your pants." US is located in Western Hemisphere; what is it doing in Eastern Hemisphere? USSR does not recognize right of US to be everywhere in world and to rule everywhere. It was one thing when US was very powerful, but now there is a force as great as yours. We will never agree to your capitalistic way of thinking. Our policy is, let us live in peace. Let us have our socialism and you can have your capitalism. Let's respect internal affairs of other countries and not interfere with life of other countries. Take, for example, Shah of Iran, whom we don't like. But we have no intention of attacking him. Or take Afghanistan, country with monarchical government. Its King recently visited me here and I entertained him. He is a nice fellow. We have good relations with him and this is the way it should be.

I said I took note of Chairman's remarks. President has made it clear we are not going to interfere in Cuba by force. But we are not going to help Cuba, which does not mean we intend to interfere there.

Khrushchev accepted this, saying he also understood President that way but must still express his disappointment about blockade, which is inimical action. Let the people choose their own system. As a result of blockade, Cuban people are suffering and will become more embittered against US. You should trade with Cuba, as we do with Turkey and others of your allies. Why are you not trading with us? You want to strangle us. But you've lost any real understanding of history.

OCTOBER 16, 1962

Off the record meeting on Cuba
October 16, 1962, 6:30–7:55 p.m.

JFK: Anything in 'em?

Carter: Nothing on the additional film, sir. We have a much better read-out on what we had initially. There's good evidence of their back-up missiles for each of the four launchers at each of the three sites, so that there would be twice the number for a total of eight which could eventually be erected. This would mean a capability of from 16 or possibly 24 missiles. We feel, on the basis of information that we presently have, that these are solid propellant, inertial guidance missiles with 1,100-mile range rather than the oxygen propellant, radar-controlled. Primarily because we have no indication of any radar or any indication of any oxygen equipment. And it would appear to be logical from an intelligence estimate view-point that if they are going to this much trouble that they would go ahead and put in the 1,100 miles because of the tremendously increased threat coverage. Let me see that [*words unintelligible*].★

JFK: What is this map?

Carter: That's, shows the circular range...

JFK: When was this drawn?

Carter: ...capability.

JFK: Is this drawn in relation to this information?

Carter: No, sir. It was drawn in some time ago, I believe, but the ranges there are the nominal ranges of the missiles rather than the maximum.

Speaker ?: The circles [around, or are added?] ...

Carter: That's a ten hundred and twenty circle, as against eleven hundred.

JFK: Well, I was just wondering whether San Diego de los Banos is where these missiles are?

Carter: Yes, sir. Well, the...

JFK: Well, I wonder how many of these have been printed out.

★ All brackets except those citing declassification excisions and unrelated material are in the source text.

Bundy: Yeah, well, the circle is drawn in red ink on the map, Mr President.

Carter: The circle is...

JFK: Oh, I see. It was never printed?

Carter: No, that's on top.

JFK: I see. It isn't printed.

Carter: It would appear that with this type of missile, with the solid propellant and inertial guidance system, that they could well be operational within two weeks as we look at the pictures now. And once operational they could fire on very little notice. They'll have a refire rate of from four to six hours over each launcher.

JFK: What about the vulnerability of such a missile to bullets?

Speaker ?: Highly vulnerable, [Mr President?].

Carter: They're vulnerable. They're not nearly as vulnerable as the oxygen propellant, but they are vulnerable to ordinary rifle fire. We have no evidence whatsoever of any nuclear warhead storage near the field launchers. However, ever since last February we have been observing an unusual facility which now has automatic antiaircraft weapon protection. This is at [Bahu?]. There are some similarities, but also many points of dissimilarity between this particular facility and the national storage sites in the Soviet Union. It's the best candidate for a site, and we have that marked for further surveillance. However, there is really totally inadequate evidence to say that there is a nuclear storage capability now. These are field-type launchers. They have mobile support, erection and check-out equipment. And they have a four-in-line deployment pattern in launchers which is identical—complexes about five miles apart—representative of the deployments that we note in the Soviet Union for similar missiles.

JFK: General, how long would you say we had before these—at least to the best of your ability for the ones we now know—will be ready to fire?

Carter: Well, our people estimate that these could be fully operational within two weeks. This would be the total complex. If they're the oxygen type we have no. . . It would be considerably longer since we don't have any indication of oxygen refueling there nor any radars.

Speaker ?: This wouldn't rule out the possibility that one of them might be operational very much sooner.

Carter: [Well, or No?], one of 'em, one of them could be operational much sooner. Our people feel that this has been, being put in since probably early September. We have had two visits of a Soviet ship that has an eight-foot-hold capacity sideways. And this about, so far, is the only delivery vehicle that we would have any suspicion that they came in on. And that came in late August, and one in early September.

Speaker ?: Why would they have to be sideways [though?]?

Carter: Well, it's just easier to get 'em in, I guess.

Speaker ?: [Well?], this way it sets down on [words unintelligible].

Speaker ?: Well, all right.

Speaker ?: Fine.

Rusk: The total readout on the flights yesterday will be ready tonight, you think?

Carter: It should be finished pretty well by midnight.

JFK: Now what, that was supposed to have covered the whole island, was it?

Carter: Yes, sir.

JFK: Except for...

Carter: In two throws. But part of the central and, in fact, much of the central and part of the eastern was cloud covering. The western half was in real good shape.

JFK: I see. Now what have we got laying on for tomorrow?

Carter: There are seven, six or seven...

McNamara: I just left [*word unintelligible*] [equipment?]. We're having ready seven U-2 aircraft, two high-altitude U-2s, five lesser-altitude U-2s; six equipped with an old type film, one equipped with a new type, experimental film which hopefully will increase the resolution. We only need two aircraft flying tomorrow if the weather is good. We will put up only two if the weather is good. If the weather is not good, we'll start off with two and we'll have the others ready to go during the day as the weather improves. We have weather aircraft surrounding the periphery of Cuba, and we'll be able to keep track of the weather during the day over all parts of the island. Hopefully, this will give us complete coverage tomorrow. We are planning to do this, or have the capability to do this, every day thereafter for an indefinite period.

Carter: This is a field-type missile, and from collateral evidence, not direct, that we have with the Soviet Union, it's designed to be fielded, placed, and fired in six hours. It would appear that we have caught this in a very early stage of deployment. It would also appear that there does not seem to be the degree of urgency in getting them immediately into position. This could be because they have not been surveyed. Or it could be because it is the shorter-range missile and the radars and the oxygen has not yet arrived.

JFK: There isn't any question in your mind, however, that it is an intermediate-range missile?

Carter: No, there's no question in our minds at all. These are...

JFK: Just [*word unintelligible*]...

Carter: ...all the characteristics that we have seen, [live ones?].

Rusk: You've seen actual missiles themselves and not just the boxes have you?

Carter: No, we've seen ... In the picture there is an actual missile.

Rusk: Yeah. Sure there is.

Carter: Yes. There's no question in our mind, sir. And they are genuine. They are not a camouflage or covert attempt to fool us.

Bundy: How much do we know, uh, [Pat?]? I don't mean to go behind your judgment here, except that there's one thing that would be really catastrophic would be to make a judgment here on, on a bad guess as to whether these things are. We mustn't do that.

Carter: Well ...

Bundy: How do we really know what these missiles are and what their range is?

Carter: Only that from the read-out that we have now and in the judgment of our analysts and of the guided missile and astronautics committee, which has been convening all afternoon, these signatures are identical with those that we have clearly earmarked in the Soviet Union, and have fully verified.

Bundy: What [made?] the verification? That's really my question. How do we know what a given Soviet missile will do?

Carter: We know something from the range firings that we have vetted for the past two years. And we know also from comparison with the characteristics of our own missiles as to size and length and diameter. As to these particular missiles, we have a family of Soviet missiles for which we have all accepted the specifications.

Bundy: I know that we have accepted them...

Carter: This is...

Bundy: ...and I know that we've had these things in charts for years, but I don't know how we know.

Carter: Well, we know from a number of sources, including our Ironbark sources, as well as from range firings, which we have been vetting for several years, as to the capabilities. But I would have to get the analysts in here to give you the play-by-play account.

Rusk: Pat, we don't know of any sixty-five-foot Soviet missile that has a range of, say, fifteen miles, do we?

Carter: Fifteen miles? No, we certainly don't.

Rusk: In other words, if they are missiles this size, they are missiles of considerable range, I think.

McNamara: I tried to prove today—I am, I'm satisfied—that these were not MRBMs. And I worked long on it. I got our experts out, and I could not find evidence that would support any conclusion other than that they are MRBMs. Now, whether they're eleven-hundred mile, six-hundred mile, nine-hundred mile is still a guess in my opinion. But that they are MRBMs seems the most probable assumption at the moment.

Speaker ?: I would apparently agree given the weight of it.

JFK: Is General Taylor coming over?

McNamara: He is Mr President.

JFK: Have you finished, General?

Carter: Yes, sir. That, I think that's at [*word unintelligible*]. . .

Rusk: [Because?] we've had some further discussion meetings on this but I might mention certain points that are, some of us are concerned about. The one is the chance that this might be the issue on which Castro would elect to break with Moscow if he knew that he were in deadly jeopardy. Now, this is one chance in a hundred, possibly. But, in any event we, we're very much interested in the possibility of a direct message to Castro as well as Khrushchev, might make some sense here before an actual strike is put on. Mr Martin will present you with outline, the kind of message to Castro that we had in mind.

Martin: This would be an oral note, message through a third party. First describing just what we know about what exists in the missile sites, so that he knows that we are informed about what's going on. Second, to point out that the issues this raises as far as the US security is concerned, it's a breach of two of the points that you have made public. First, the ground-to-ground missile, and, second, obviously, it's a Soviet-operated base in Cuba. Thirdly, this raises the greatest problems for Castro, as we see it. In the first place, by this action the Soviets have threatened him with attack from the United States, and therefore the overthrow of his regime; used his territory to make this, to put him in this jeopardy. And, secondly, the Soviets are talking to other people about the possibility of bargaining this support and these missiles against concessions in Berlin and elsewhere, and therefore are threatening to, to bargain him away. In these circumstances, we wonder whether he realizes the, the position that he's been put in and the way the Soviets are using him.

Then go on to say that we will have to inform our people of the threat that exists here, and we mean to take action about it in the next day or so. And we'll have to do this unless we receive word from him that he is prepared to take action to get the Soviets out of the site. He will have to show us that not only by statements, privately or publicly, but by action; that we intend to keep close surveillance by overflights of the site to make su-, to know what is being done. But we will have to know that he is doing something to remove this threat in order to withhold the action that we intend to, we will be compelled to take.

If Castro feels that an attempt by him to take the kind of action that we're suggesting to him would result in serious difficulties for him within Cuba, we at least want him to know that, and to convey to him and remind him of the statement that you, Mr President, made a year and a half ago in effect that there are two points that are non-negotiable. One is the Soviet tie and presence, and the second is aggression in Latin America. This is a, a hint, but no more than that, that we might have sympathy and help for him in case he ran into trouble trying to throw the old-line Communists and the Soviets out.

Rusk: Yes.

Martin: We'll give him 24 hours to respond.

Rusk: The disadvantage in that is, of course, the, the advance notice if he judges that we, we would not in this, in such approach here say exactly what we would do, but it might, of course, lead him to bring up mobile anti-aircraft weapons around these missiles themselves or take some other action that will make the strike that more difficult. But there is that, there is that.

There are two other problems that we are concerned about. If we strike these missiles, we would expect, I think maximum Communist reaction in Latin America. In the case of about six of those governments, unless the heads of government had some intimation, requiring some preparatory steps from the security point of view, one or another of those governments could could easily be overthrown—they, Venezuela for example or Guatemala, Bolivia, Chile, possibly even Mexico—and therefore the question will arise as to whether we should not somehow indicate to them in some way the seriousness of the situation so they can take precautionary steps, whether we tell them exactly what we have in mind or, or not.

The other is the NATO problem. We would estimate that the Soviets would almost certainly take some kind of action somewhere. For us to, to take an action of this sort without letting our closer allies know of a matter which could subject them to very great danger is a very far-reaching decision to make. And we could find ourselves isolated and the alliance crumbling, very much as it did for a period during the Suez affair, but at a moment of much greater danger over an issue of much greater danger than the Suez affair, for the alliance. I think that these are matters that we'll be working on very hard this evening, but I think I ought to mention them because it's necessarily a part of this problem.

JFK: Can we get a little idea about what the military thing is? Well, of course, one, would you suggest taking these out?

McNamara: Yes, Mr President. General Taylor has just been with the Chiefs, and the unified commanders went through this in detail. To take out only the missiles or to take out the missiles and the MiG aircraft and the associated nuclear storage facilities if we locate them could be done in 24-hours' warning. That is to say, 24 hours between the time of decision and the time of strike starting with a decision no later than, no earlier than this coming Friday and with the strike therefore on Saturday,★ or anytime thereafter with 24 hours between the decision and time of strike. General Taylor will wish to comment on this, but the Chiefs are strong in their recommendation against that kind of an attack, believing that it would leave too great a capability in Cuba undestroyed. The specific number of sorties required to, to accomplish this end has not been worked out in detail. The capability is for something in excess of 700 sorties per day. It seems highly unlikely that that number would be required to carry out that limited an objective, but at least that capability is available in the air force alone, and the navy sorties would rise on top of that number. The Chiefs have also considered other alternatives extending into the full invasion you may wish to discuss later. But that's the answer to your first question.

JFK: That would be taking out these three missile sites plus all the MiGs?

McNamara: Well, you can go from the three missile sites to the three missile sites plus the MiGs, to the three missile sites plus MiGs plus nuclear storage plus airfields and so on up through the offensive, potential offensive [*words unintelligible*]...

★ October 19 and 20.

JFK: Just the three missiles, however, would be?

McNamara: Could be done with 24-hours' notice and would require a relatively small number of sorties, less than a day's air attack, in other words.

JFK: Of course, all you'd really get there would be... What would you get there? You'd get the, probably you'd get the missiles themselves that are, have to be on the...

McNamara: You'd get the launchers ...

JFK: ... [*Words unintelligible*].

McNamara: ... the launchers and the missiles on the [*words unintelligible*] ...

JFK: The launchers are just what? They, they're not much are they?

McNamara: No, they're simply a mobile launchers device.

Taylor: This is a point target, Mr President. You're never sure of having, absolutely of getting everything down there. We intend to do a great deal of damage because we can [*words unintelligible*]. But, as the Secretary says here, there was unanimity among all the commanders involved in the Joint Chiefs that in our judgment, it would be a mistake to take this very narrow, selective target because it invited reprisal attacks and it may be detrimental. Now if the Soviets have been willing to give nuclear warheads to these missiles, there is every, just as good reason for them to give nuclear capability to these bases. We don't think we'd ever have a chance to take 'em again, so that we lose this, the first strike surprise capability. Our recommendation would be to get complete intelligence, get all the photography we need, the next two or three days, no, no hurry in our book. Then look at this target system. If it really threatens the United States, then take it right out with one hard crack.

JFK: That would be taking out the, some of those fighters, bombers and …

Taylor: Fighters, the bombers, IL–28s may turn up in this photography. It's not at all unlikely there're some there.

JFK: Think you could do that in one day?

Taylor: We think that the first strike, we'd get a great majority of this. We'll never get it all, Mr President. But we then have to come back day after day for several days—we said five days perhaps—to do the complete job. Meanwhile, we could then be making up our mind as to whether or not to go on and invade the island. I'm very much impressed with the need for a time something like five to seven days for this air purpose because of the parachute aspect of the in-, proposed invasion. You can't take parachute formations, close formations of troop carrier planes in in the face of any air opposition really. So the first job, before the, any land attack, including [parachutes or paratroops?], is really cleaning out the, the MiGs and the, the accompanying aircraft.

McNamara: Mr President, could I outline three courses …

JFK?: [Yes?].

McNamara: … of action we have considered and speak very briefly on each one? The first is what I would call the political course of action, in which we follow some of the possibilities that Secretary Rusk mentioned this morning by approaching Castro, by approaching Khrushchev, by discussing with our allies. An overt and open approach politically to the problem [attempting, or in order?] to solve it. This seemed to me likely to lead to no satisfactory result, and it almost stops subsequent military action. Because the danger of starting military action after they acquire a nuclear capability is so great I believe we would decide against it, particularly if that nuclear capability included aircraft as well as, as missiles, as it well might at that point.

A second course of action we haven't discussed but lies in between the military course we began discussing a moment ago and the political course of action is a course of action that would involve declaration of open surveillance; a statement that we would immediately impose a blockade against offensive weapons entering Cuba in the future; and an indication that with our open-surveillance reconnaissance, which we would plan to maintain indefinitely for the future, we would be prepared to immediately attack the Soviet Union in the event that Cuba made any offensive move against this country . . .

Bundy: Attack who?

McNamara: The Soviet Union. In the event that Cuba made any offensive move against this country. Now this lies short of military action against Cuba, direct military action against Cuba. It has some, some major defects.

But the third course of action is any one of these variants of military action directed against Cuba, starting with an air attack against the missiles. The Chiefs are strongly opposed to so limited an air attack. But even so limited an air attack is a very extensive air attack. It's not 20 sorties or 50 sorties or a hundred sorties, but probably several hundred sorties. We haven't worked out the details. It's very difficult to do so when we lack certain intelligence that we hope to have tomorrow or the next day. But it's a substantial air attack. And to move from that into the more extensive air attacks against the MiGs, against the airfields, against the potential nuclear storage sites, against the radar installations, against the SAM sites means, as, as Max suggested, possibly 700 to a thousand sorties per day for five days. This is the very, very rough plan that the Chiefs have outlined, and it is their judgment that that is the type of air attack that should be carried out. To move beyond that into an invasion following the air attack means the application of tens of thousands, between ninety and, over a hundred and fifty thousand men to the invasion forces.

It seems to me almost certain that any one of these forms of direct military action will lead to a Soviet military response of some type some place in the world. It may well be worth the price. Perhaps we should pay that. But I think we should recognize that possibility, and, moreover, we must recognize it in a variety of ways. We must recognize it by trying to deter it, which means we probably should alert SAC, probably put on an airborne alert, perhaps take other alert measures. These bring risks of their own, associated with them. It means we should recognize that by mobilization. Almost certainly, we should accompany the initial air strike with at least a partial mobilization. We should accompany an, an invasion following an air strike with a large-scale mobilization, a very large-scale mobilization, certainly exceeding the limits of the authority we have from Congress requiring a declaration therefore of a national emergency. We should be prepared, in the event of even a small air strike and certainly in the event of a larger air strike, for the possibility of a Cuban uprising, which would force our hand in some way. Either force us to accept an unsatisfactory uprising, with all of the adverse comment that result; or would, would force an invasion to support the uprising.

Rusk: Mr President, may I make a very brief comment on that? I think that any course of action involves heavy political involvement. It's going to affect all sorts of policies, positions, as well as the strategic situation. So I don't think there's any such thing as a nonpolitical course of action. I think also that we have to consider what political preparation, if any, is to occur before an air strike or in connection with any military action. And when I was talking this morning, I was talking about some steps which would put us in the best position to crack the ...

JFK: I think the difficulty ...

Rusk: ... the strength of Cuba.

JFK: ... it seems to me, is ... I completely agree that there isn't any doubt that if we announced that there were MRBM sites going up that that would change, we would secure a good deal of political support, after my statement; and the fact that we indicated our desire to restrain, this really would put the burden on the Soviet. On the other hand, the very fact of doing that makes the military ... We lose all the advantages of our strike. Because if we announce that it's there, then it's quite obvious to them that we're gonna probably do something about it. I would assume. Now, I don't know, that, it seems to me what we ought to be thinking about tonight is if we made an announcement that the intelligence has revealed that there are, and if we [did the note?] message to Khrushchev ... I don't think that Castro has to know we've been paying much attention to it any more than ... Over a period of time, it might have some effect, [have settled?] back down, change. I don't think he plays it that way. So [have?] a note to Khrushchev ... I don't ... It seems to me, my press statement was so clear about how we wouldn't do anything under these conditions and under the conditions that we would. He must know that we're going to find out, so it seems to me he just ...

Bundy: That's, of course, why he's been very, very explicit with us in communications to us about how dangerous this is, and ...

JFK: That's right, but he's . . .

Bundy: . . . the TASS statement and his other messages.

JFK: He's initiated the danger really, hasn't he? He's the one that's playing [his card, or God?], not us. So we could . . .

Rusk: And his statement to Kohler on the subject of his visit and so forth, completely hypocritical.

[Reel 1 ends.]

[Reel 2 begins mid-conversation.]

McNamara: . . . Cuba. Is a great possibility they can place them in operational condition quickly. Unless, as General Carter said, the system may have a, a normal reaction time, set-up time of six hours. Whether it has six hours or two weeks, we don't know how much time has started, nor do we know what air-launch capabilities they have for warheads. We don't know what air-launch capability they have for high explosives. It's almost certainly a substantial high-explosive capability in the sense that they could drop one or two or ten high-explosive bombs some place along the East Coast. And that's the minimum risk to this country we run as a result of advance warning, too.

Taylor: I'd like to stress this last point, Mr President. We are very vulnerable to conventional bombing attack, low-level bombing attacks in the Florida area. Our whole air defense has been oriented in other directions. We've never had low-level defenses prepared for this country. So it would be entirely possible for MiGs to come through with conventional weapons and do some amount, some damage.

JFK: Yeah. Not, talking overall, not a great deal of damage . . .

Taylor: No, but it certainly is fair to . . .

JFK: . . . if they get one strike.

Dillon: What if they carry a nuclear weapon?

JFK: Well, if they carry a nuclear weapon. . . . You assume they wouldn't do that.

Taylor: [*Words unintelligible*] I think we would expect some conventional weapon.

Rusk: I would not think that they would use a nuclear weapon unless they're prepared to [join?] a nuclear war, I don't think. I just don't see that possibility.

Speaker ?: I would agree.

Bundy?: I agree.

Rusk: That would mean that we could be just utterly wrong, but, we've never really believed that, that Khrushchev would take on a general nuclear war over Cuba.

Bundy: May I ask a question in that context?

JFK: We certainly have been wrong about what he's trying to do in Cuba. There isn't any doubt about that [*possibly a word unintelligible*] . . .

Bundy: [*Words unintelligible*] that we've been wrong.

JFK: . . . many of us thought that he was going to put MRBMs on Cuba.

Bundy: Yeah. Except John McCone.

Carter: Mr McCone.

JFK: Yeah.

Bundy: But, the question that I would like to ask is, quite aside from what we've said—and we're very hard-locked onto it, I know—What is the strategic impact on the position of the United States of MRBMs in Cuba? How gravely does this change the strategic balance?

McNamara: Mac, I asked the Chiefs that this afternoon, in effect. And they said, substantially. My own personal view is, not at all.

Bundy: Not so much.

McNamara: And, and I think this is an important element here. But it's all very ...

Carter: The reason our estimators didn't think that they'd put them in there because of ...

McNamara: That's what they said themselves ...

Bundy: That's what they said themselves ...

McNamara: ... in TASS statement.

Bundy: Yeah.

Carter: But then, going behind that ...

JFK: [But why? Did it indicate? Being?] valuable enough?

Bundy: Doesn't prove anything in the strategic balance [overall?].

Carter: Doesn't prove anything. That was what the estimators felt, and that the Soviets would not take the risk. Mr McCone's reasoning, however, was if this is so, then what possible reason have they got for going into Cuba in the manner in which they are with surface-to-air missiles and cruise-type missiles. He just couldn't understand while their, why the Soviets were so heavily bolstering Cuba's defensive posture. There must be something behind it, which led him then to the belief that they must be coming in with MRBMs.

Taylor: I think it was [cold-blooded?] ...

Carter: [*Words unintelligible*]

Taylor: ... point of view, Mr President. You're quite right in saying that these, these are just a few more missiles targeted on the United States. However, they can become a, a very, a rather important adjunct and reinforcement to the, to the strike capability of the Soviet Union. We have no idea how far they will go. But more than that, these are to our nation it means, it means a great deal more. You all are aware of that, in Cuba and not over in the Soviet Union.

Bundy: Well, I ask the question ...

Taylor: Yeah.

Bundy: ... with an awareness [laughter?] of the political ...

JFK: I will say, my understanding's that ...

Bundy: [*Words unintelligible*]

JFK: ... let's just say that they get, they get these in there and then you can't they get sufficient capacity so we can't, with warheads. Then you don't want to knock 'em out ['cause?], there's too much of a gamble. Then they just begin to build up those air bases there and then put more and more. I suppose they really ... Then they start getting ready to squeeze us in Berlin, doesn't that ... You may say it doesn't make any difference if you get blown up by an ICBM flying from the Soviet Union or one that was 90 miles away. Geography doesn't mean that much.

Taylor: We'd have to target them with our missiles and have the same kind of, of pistol-point:d-at-the-head situation as we have in the Soviet Union at the present time.

Bundy: No question, if this thing goes on, an attack on Cuba becomes general war. And that's really the question whether . . .

JFK: That's why it shows the Bay of Pigs was really right. [We've, or We'd?] got it right. That was better and better and worse and worse.

Taylor: I'm [a pessimist,?] Mr President. We have a war plan over there for you, calls for a, for a quarter of a million Americans—soldiers, marines and airmen—to take an island we launched eighteen hundred Cubans against a year and a half ago.

[Faint laughter]

Taylor: [We've changed?] our evaluations well.

RFK: Of course, the other problem is in South America a year from now. And the fact that you got these things in the hands of Cubans, here, and then you, say your, some problem arises in Venezuela you've got Castro saying, You move troops down into that part of Venezuela, we're going to fire these missiles.

Taylor: Well, I think you've [*words unintelligible*].

RFK: I think that's the difficulty . . .

Speaker ?: [*Words unintelligible*].

RFK: . . . rather than the [*words unintelligible*].

Speaker ?: [*Words unintelligible*].

RFK: I think it gives the [*word unintelligible*] image.

JFK: It makes them look like they're coequal with us and that . . .

Dillon: We're scared of the Cubans.

RFK: We let the . . . I mean like we'd hate to have it in the hands of the Chinese. [*Possibly words unintelligible*]

Dillon: [*Right?*] I agree with that sort of thing very strongly.

Martin: It's a psychological factor. It won't reach as far as Venezuela is concerned.

Dillon: Well, that's . . .

McNamara: It'll reach the US though. This is the point.

Speaker ?: That's the point.

Dillon: Yeah. That is the point.

Martin: Yeah. The psychological factor of our having taken it.

Dillon: Taken it, that's the best.

RFK: Well, and the fact that if you go there, we're gonna fire it.

JFK: What's that again, Ed? What are you saying?

Martin: Well, it's a psychological factor that we have sat back and let 'em do it to us, that is more important than the direct threat. It is a threat in the Caribbean . . .

JFK: [*Words unintelligible*] I said we weren't going to.

Martin: . . . [*Words unintelligible*].

Bundy?: That's something we could manage.

JFK: Last month I said we weren't going to.

[Laughter]

JFK: Last month I should have said we're . . .

Speaker ?: Well . . .

JFK: ... that we don't care. But when we said we're not going to and then they go ahead and do it, and then we do nothing, then ...

Speaker ?: That's right.

JFK: ... I would think that our risks increase. I agree. What difference does it make? They've got enough to blow us up now anyway. I think it's just a question of ... After all this is a political struggle as much as military. Well so where are we now? Where is the ... Don't think the message to Castro's got much in it. Let's try to get an answer to this question. How much ... It's quite obviously to our advantage to surface this thing to a degree before ... First to inform these governments in Latin America, as the Secretary suggests; secondly to the rest of NATO—[*one line of source text not declassified*]. How much does this diminish ... Not that we're going to do anything, but the existence of them, without any say about what we're gonna do. Let's say we, 24 hours ahead of our doing something about it, [*less than one line of source text not declassified*] we make a public statement that these have been found on the island. That would, that would be notification in a sense that of their existence, and everybody could draw whatever conclusion they wanted to.

Martin?: I would say this, Mr. President, that I would, that if you've made a public statement, you've got to move immediately, or they, you're going to have a ...

JFK: Oh, I ...

Martin?: ... a [*words unintelligible*] in this country.

JFK: ... oh, I understand that. We'll be talking about ... Say, say we're going to move on a Saturday and we would say on Friday that these MRBMs, that the existence of this presents the gravest threat to our security and that appropriate action must be taken.

RFK: Could you stick planes over them, until you made the announcement at six o'clock Saturday morning? And at the same time or simultaneously put planes over to make sure that they weren't taking any action or movement, and that you could move in if they started moving in the missiles in place or something, you would move in and knock, that would be the trigger that you would move your planes in and knock them out. Otherwise you'd wait until six o'clock or five o'clock that night. I don't, is that is that...

Taylor: I don't think anything like that... I can't visualize doing it, doing it successfully that way. I think that anything that shows our intent to strike is going to place the airplanes and, and the missiles into, these are por-, really mobile missiles. They can be...

RFK: [You mean they can just?] ...

Taylor: They can pull in under trees and forest and disappear almost at once, as I visualize.

McNamara: And they can also be readied, perhaps, between the time we, in effect, say we're going to come in and the time we do come in. This, this is a very, very great danger to this, this coast. I don't know exactly how to appraise it because ...

Speaker ?: I don't know.

McNamara: ... of the readiness period, but it is possible that these are field missiles, and then in that case they can be readied very promptly if they choose to do so.

Carter: These are field missiles, sir. They are mobile-support-type missiles.

Taylor: About a 40-minute countdown, something like that's been estimated.

Ball?: So you would say that the strike should precede any public discussion?

McNamara: I believe so, yes, if you're going to strike. I think before you make any announcements, you should decide whether you're going to strike. If you are going to strike, you shouldn't make an announcement.

Bundy: That's right.

Dillon: What is the advantage of the announcement earlier? Because it's, it's to build up sympathy or something for doing it; but you get the simultaneous announcement of what was there and why you struck, with pictures and all, I [believe?] would serve the same ...

Ball?: Well, the only announ-, the only advantage is, it's a kind of ultimatum, it's, there is an opportunity of a response that, which would preclude it. I mean it's, it's more, a more, for, for the appearance than as for the reality. 'Cause obviously you're not going to get that kind of response. But I would suppose that there is a course which is a little different, which is a private message from the President to [*less than one line of source text not declassified*] ...

Martin?: [*one line of source text not declassified*]

Ball?: And that this is, you're going to have to do this, you're compelled and you've gotta move quickly and you want them to know it. Maybe two hours before the strike, something like that ...

Dillon: Well, that's it, that's different.

Ball?: ... even the night before. But you ... But it has to be kept on that basis of total secrecy. And then the question of what you do with these Latin American governments is another matter. I think if you, if you notify them in advance ...

JFK: That's right. [Indicated?]

Ball?: . . . it may be all over.

JFK: Then you just have to, Congress would, take Congress along . . .

Bundy: I can't . . . I think that's just not, not right.

Speaker ?: [*Words unintelligible*]

JFK: I'm not completely, I don't think we ought to abandon just knocking out these missile bases as opposed to, that's much more defensible, explicable, politically or satisfactory-in-every-way action than the general strike which takes us . . .

Speaker ?: Move down . . .

JFK: . . . us into the city of Havana . . .

Speaker ?: . . . those two.

JFK: . . . and [it is plain to me?] takes us into much more . . .

Speaker ?: [*Words unintelligible*]

JFK: . . . hazardous, shot down. Now I know the Chiefs say, Well, that means their bombers can take off against us, but . . .

Bundy: Their bombers take off against us, then they have made a general war against Cuba of it, which is a, it then becomes much more their decision. We move this way . . . The political advantages are, are very strong, it seems to me, of the small strike. It corresponds to the, the punishment fits the crime in political terms, that we are doing only what we warned repeatedly and publicly we would have to do. We are not generalizing the attack. The things that we've already recognized and said that we have not found it necessary to attack and said we would not find it necessary to attack . . .

OCTOBER 17–18, 1962

Memorandum by Director of Central Intelligence McCone
Washington, October 17, 1962

Several alternatives indicated below were posed for consideration at the close of meeting covered by memorandum dated October 17th. All dealt with the specific
actions US Government should take against Cuba at this
time. The discussions centered around:

(a) Whether military action should be taken prior to a
     warning to, or discussions with, Khrushchev and
     Castro.

(b) Notification to or consultation with our allies, including NATO, OAS, and others.
(c) Referral to the United Nations.
(d) Effect on the "balance of nuclear power equation" of the MRBM installations in Cuba.

Three principal courses of action are open to us, and of course there are variations of each.

1. Do nothing and live with the situation. It was pointed out clearly that Western Europe, Greece, Turkey, and other countries had lived under the Soviet MRBMs for years; therefore, why should the United States be so concerned.

2. Resort to an all-out blockade which would probably require a declaration of war and to be effective would mean the interruption of all incoming shipping. This was discussed as a slow strangulation process, but it was stated that "intelligence reports" indicated that a blockade would bring Castro down in four months. (Note: I have seen no such estimate.)

3. Military action which was considered at several levels. The following alternatives are:

(a) Strafing identified MRBM installations.
(b) Strafing MRBM installations and airfields with MiGs.
(c) (a) and (b) plus all SAM sites and coastal missile sites.
(d) (a), (b), and (c) above plus all other significant military installations, none of which were identified.

Discussions of all of the above were inconclusive and it was asked that the group reassemble, and develop their views on the advantages and disadvantages and the effects of the following:

1. Warning to Khrushchev and Castro.

(a)   If the response is unsatisfactory, pursuing a course of military action.

(b)   If the response is unsatisfactory, referring to the OAS and the United Nations prior to taking military action.

2. Warning to Khrushchev and Castro and if the response is unsatisfactory convening Congress, seeking a declaration of war, and proceeding with an all-out blockade.

3. Strike militarily with no warning, the level of the military effort being dependent upon evolving circumstances. In all probability this type of action would escalate into invasion and occupation, although the meeting was not agreed on this point.

4. Blockade with no warning and no advance notice such as a declaration of war, with the President depending upon existing Congressional resolutions for authority.

JOHN A. MCCONE
Director

Memorandum of meeting attended in Secretary Ball's conference room by Secretary McNamara, Bundy, General Taylor, Robert Kennedy, Martin, and McCone
Washington, October 17, 1962, 8:30 a.m.

1. Meeting involved an inclusive exploration of alternatives open to us in connection with the Cuban matter.

Ball seemed to feel military action would throw the NATO allies in disarray and permit Britain and France to separate from us on Berlin policy. Stated Kohler discussions with Khrushchev did not fit in with Soviet action in Cuba. Suggested Cuban situation might be by inadvertence. Suggested we might give Khrushchev an "out" on the grounds that he does not know what is going on in

Cuba and discussed various types of action ranging from a limited military strike to minimize losses to the calling of a Summit conference.

2. During the discussion Taylor and Ball speculated as to whether this whole thing was not a "mock up" designed to draw out action by us, and that the warheads were not there. This view was not supported.

3. McNamara urged avoiding taking a position, considering all alternatives, with meetings this afternoon and this evening in preparation of final discussion with the President tomorrow.

4. Urged exploration of all facts and listed the following:

- About 50 or 60 MiG-17s and 19s now in Cuba and these apparently have no offensive capability.
- One MiG-21 has been seen and a number of suspicious crates also seen indicating some MiG-21 capability and we do not know whether the MiG-21 has an offensive capability.
- IL-28s have been delivered.
- Three MRBM sites under construction and can be ready in two weeks.
- Warhead locations unknown; also unknown whether MRBMs are nuclear or conventional. Also feels that if nuclear warheads supplied them, Soviet will also supply nuclear bombs for bombers with offensive capability.
- Shiploads of boxes of unknown purpose reported by Lundahl to DCI on October 14th.
- 28 Soviet ships en route to Cuba at the present time.
- Sited at Havana, mysterious excavations, revetments, covered buildings, railroad tracks through tunnels, etc., might be nuclear storage site.
- Other facts should be developed today.

5. General Taylor and Thompson discussed political nature of problem including possibility of forcing settlement in Berlin and elsewhere—Khrushchev wished showdown on Berlin and this gave a showdown issue. Believes Khrushchev would be surprised to find we know about MRBMs. Thompson emphasized Khrushchev wants Berlin settlement but on his terms. And will probably deny knowledge of Cuban situation but at any event would justify actions because of our missiles in Italy and Turkey. Also Khrushchev recognizes that action by us would be divisive among our allies.

6. McCone emphasized his views on political objectives as stated in paragraph 5 of the attached memorandum [page 149], and also repeated paragraph 2(c). Also made the point in paragraph 6.

7. McNamara discussed many operational questions concerning the use of Soviet nuclear warheads in Cuba; how communications could be arranged; what authority was in the field. Thompson believes Soviet nuclear warheads was under very tight control. McCone reviewed recent Chicadee reports, indicated considerable autonomy in hands of field commanders much more so than we have.

8. Bundy and McCone left for meeting with the President.

Memorandum of meeting, attended by Rusk, Ball (each part of the time), Martin, Johnson, McNamara, Gilpatric, Taylor, McCone, Bohlen, Thompson, Bundy, Sorensen, Dean Acheson (for a short time)
Washington, Wednesday, October 17, at 8:30 a.m. and again at 4:00 p.m.

Note: The 4:00 o'clock meeting adjourned at about 7:00, and reassembled at 10:00 p.m., in Secretary Ball's conference room, adjourning at 11:45 p.m.

Note: At 9:30 a.m. DCI went to see the President,★ then went to Gettysburg to see General Eisenhower. The purpose of the discussion was to develop a plan of action in connection with Cuba.

This memorandum will record views as they were expressed and developed throughout the meetings.

Ambassador Bohlen warned against any action against Cuba, particularly an air strike without warning, stating such would be divisive with all allies and subject us to criticism throughout the world. He advocated writing both Khrushchev and Castro; if their response was negative or unsatisfactory then we should plan action; advise our principal allies, seek a two-thirds vote from the OAS, and then act. The Attorney General and Bohlen exchanged views as to just what type of an answer we could expect from Khrushchev and what he might do if we threatened an attack. During this discussion Secretary Rusk seemed to favor asking Congress for a declaration of a state of war against Cuba and then proceed with OAS, NATO, etc., but always preserve flexibility as to the type of action. Bohlen consistently warned that world opinion would be against us if we carried out a military strike. Secretary Ball emphasized the importance of time, stating that if action was over quickly, the repercussions would not be too serious.

The Attorney General raised the question of the attitude of Turkey, Italy, Western European countries, all of which have been "under the gun" for years, and would take the position that now that the US has a few missiles in their backyard, they become hysterical. This point was

★ McCone's record of this meeting reads as follows: "President seemed inclined to act promptly if at all, without warning, targeting on MRBMs and possible airfields. Stated Congressional resolutions gave him all authority he needed and this was confirmed by Bundy, and therefore seemed inclined to act."

discussed back and forth by various people throughout both days of discussion.

Secretary McNamara made the point that missiles in Cuba had no great military consequence because of the stalemate mentioned in my October 18th memorandum. General Taylor supported this view in the early parts of the discussion, but in the later meetings expressed increasing concern over the importance of the missile threat from Cuba. Gilpatric supported McNamara's position. McCone doubted it, stating that McNamara's facts were not new as they had appeared in estimates months ago (which McNamara questioned). Nevertheless, he and McCone felt that a complex of MRBMs and IRBMs in Cuba would have very important military significance. McNamara took issue claiming that the military equation would not be changed by the appearance of these missiles.

Bohlen and Thompson questioned the real purpose of the Soviet's actions in Cuba and seemed to feel that their acts may be in preparation for a confrontation with President Kennedy at which time they would seek to settle the entire subject of overseas bases as well as the Berlin question. McCone indicated this might be one of several objectives and undoubtedly would be the subject of discussion at the time of confrontation; however, McCone doubted that this was the prime purpose of such an elaborate and expensive installation as the Soviets were going forward with in Cuba. Bohlen seemed to favor precipitating talks, and was supported by Thompson.

SecDef and Taylor both objected to political talks because it would give time for threatening missiles to become operational and also give the Soviets an opportunity to camouflage the missiles. McCone presented most recent photographs and indicated CIA opinion that the first missiles will be operational within one or two weeks.

Bohlen again raised the question of opening up discussions. McNamara agreed that this would be desirable but emphasized the importance of developing a sequence of events which would lead to military action.

There followed an extensive discussion of the advantages and disadvantages of a military blockade, total or partial.

It was at this point that McNamara and Taylor presented their schedule of alternative military strikes, and which was the subject of continual discussion in the ensuing meetings.

Dean Acheson then expressed his views as follows:

> We should proceed at once with the necessary military actions and should do no talking. The Soviets will react some place. We must expect this; take the consequences and manage the situations as they evolve. We should have no consultations with Khrushchev, Castro, or our allies, but should fully alert our allies in the most persuasive manner by high level people. This would include all NATO partners, and the OAS. The President should forget about the elections and should cancel all future campaign speeches.

As an alternate to military action, a plan was discussed involving a declaration of war and the creation of an all-out blockade. Thompson spoke strongly in favor of a blockade. General Taylor at this point indicated that he favored a blockade although in subsequent meetings he seemed inclined toward a military strike. McCone gave an intelligence estimate on the effects of a blockade, indicating its seriousness would depend upon how "hard" a blockade it turned out to be, and finally stated that the main objective of taking Cuba away from Castro had been lost and we have been overly consumed with the missile problem. McCone stated that we must all bear in mind that we have two objectives, one, disposing of the missile sites, and the other, getting rid of Castro's Communism in the Western Hemisphere.

∞◦◦◦∞

The meeting adjourned for dinner and in the evening Secretary Rusk came forward with the following plan.

The United States cannot accept operational MRBMs in Cuba. There is not much profit in preliminary exchanges with Khrushchev and Castro, because the President has said that the establishment of Soviet bases and offensive weapons in the Western Hemisphere would raise serious problems, and therefore on September 5th [4th] and 13th the President has in effect warned both Khrushchev and Castro.

Rusk continued that more talks with Khrushchev would result in extended parlays and therefore he recommended against such an approach. Rusk then proposed that we hold until the middle of next week and then follow the OD course No. 1 (52 sorties against MRBMs). Prior, we inform key allies probably on Tuesday (Macmillan, de Gaulle, Adenauer, possibly the Turks and a few Latin American Presidents). On Wednesday, we strike with missiles and simultaneously send a message to Khrushchev, NATO, OAS, etc. We should be alert for an attack on Turkey and be prepared for the consequences in Berlin, Quemoy, Matsu, Korea, etc. Rusk made the estimate that world opinion would go along, 42 allies would go along and some neutrals would be favorable. Latin Americans must be told that we are acting in the interests of the Western Hemisphere. Rusk advocated that the first step—we take out the missiles and thus remove the immediate problem of the establishment of an offensive capability, but that we be prepared for subsequent steps. He emphasized the United States cannot accept missiles in our security interests and in view of statements made by the President and others and our various policy declarations. Bohlen continued to persist for a diplomatic approach but Rusk and several others were not at this point persuaded. McNamara raised innumerable questions concerning military operations; the manner in which the strike could be properly covered with protective air and how it might be restricted; and also the advisability of case one, as contrasted with case one, two and/or three.

Both Ambassador Thompson and Secretary Martin in discussing the Rusk proposal favored a blockade, coupled with a declaration of war.

General Taylor at this point spoke in favor of a military strike taking out the MRBMs and the planes as well, and was supported by McCone, who took the opportunity to cover the points set forth in "talking paper for principals, October 17, 1962." Also during the course of these meetings, McCone reported to the group and later to the President the results of his discussions with General Eisenhower.

In addition, State tabled during the day's meetings the following:

(a) Possible course of action (undated) in 14 pages
(b) Possible world consequences in military action, undated, five pages
(c) Political actions (undated) four pages
(d) Political actions in support of major military action (undated) three pages

These were all referred to as State papers (draft) and some were revised the following day. Also State tabled the following papers:

(a) Limited one-time strike against MRBM sites, undated, six pages

(b) Plan of blockade (undated), four pages
(c) Paper labeled "Attack Three—Invasion" five pages with an attached scenario of four pages
(d) Possible Soviet reactions to the following alternatives, C.E. Bohlen, October 17th, two pages

Also, proposed letter to Khrushchev was tabled, paper dealing with probable Castro response to US appeal and a proposed letter to Fidel Castro, marked "To Mr F.C.," all included in State papers.

At the conclusion of the meetings, which served the purpose of airing the views of all parties responsible for giving advice to the President, the alternatives open to us were summarized by the Attorney General [see below].

JOHN A. MCCONE

1. On Tuesday, 23 October, inform Western European and some Latin American leaders of the situation. On Wednesday, attack the MRBMs, issue a public statement, and send a message to Premier Khrushchev. Then wait and see what happens. Secretary Rusk rejected this suggestion.

2. Same as 1, but notify Chairman Khrushchev beforehand and wait about three days to obtain his reply. Defense spokesmen argued against this solution.

3. Tell the Soviets that the United States was aware of the missiles and would prevent any more from arriving. Impose a blockade, declare war, and make preparations for invasion. Mr Rusk and Mr Ball seemed inclined to favor this course, but first wanted surveillance without air strikes.

4. After limited political preliminaries, attack targets in Categories III–IV and prepare for invasion.

5. Same as 4, but omit the political preliminaries.

Letter from the US Ambassador to the United Nations
(Stevenson) to President Kennedy
Washington, October 17, 1962

Dear Mr President

I have reviewed the planning thus far and have the following comments for you:

As I have said I think your personal emissaries should deliver your messages to C and K. There is no disagreement as to C. As to K an emissary could better supplement the gravity of the situation you have communicated to Gromyko. And talking with K would afford a chance of uncovering his motives and objectives far better than correspondence thru the "usual channels."

As to your announcement, assuming it becomes imperative to say something soon, I think it would be a mistake at this time to disclose that an attack was imminent and that merely reciting the facts, emphasizing the gravity of the situation and that further steps were in process, would be enough for the first announcement.

Because an attack would very likely result in Soviet reprisals somewhere—Turkey, Berlin, etc.—it is most important that we have as much of the world with us as possible. To start or risk starting a nuclear war is bound to be divisive at best and the judgments of history seldom coincide with the tempers of the moment.

If war comes, in the long run our case must rest on stopping while there was still time the Soviet drive to world domination, our obligations under the Inter-American System, etc. We must be prepared for the widespread reaction that if we have a missile base in Turkey and other places around the Soviet Union surely they have a right to one in Cuba. If we attack Cuba, an ally of the USSR, isn't an attack on NATO bases equally justified. One could go on and on. While the explanation of our action may be clear to us it won't be clear to many others. Moreover, if war is the consequence, the Latin American republics may well divide and some say that the US is not acting with their approval and consent. Likewise unless the issue is very clear there may be sharp differences with our Western Allies who have lived so long under the same threat of Soviet attack from bases in the satellite countries by the same IRBMs.

But all these considerations and obstacles to clear and universal understanding that we are neither rash, impetuous or indifferent to the fate of others are, I realize, only too familiar to you.

I know your dilemma is to strike before the Cuban sites are operational or to risk waiting until a proper groundwork of justification can be prepared. The national security must come first. But the means adopted have such incalculable consequences that I feel you should have made it clear that the existence of nuclear missile bases anywhere is negotiable* before we start anything.

Our position, then, is that we can't negotiate with a gun at our head, a gun that imperils the innocent, helpless Cuban people as much as it does the US, and that if they won't remove the missiles and restore the status quo ante we will have to do it ourselves—and then we will be ready to discuss bases in the context of a disarmament treaty or anything else with them. In short it is they, not the US, that have upset the balance and created this situation of such peril to the whole world.

I confess I have many misgivings about the proposed course of action, but to discuss them further would add little to what you already have in mind. So I will only repeat that it should be clear as a pikestaff that the US was, is and will be ready to negotiate the elimination of bases and

---

* The word "negotiable" is double underlined in the source text.

anything else; that it is they who have upset the precarious balance in the world in arrogant disregard of your warnings—by threats against Berlin and now from Cuba—and that we have no choice except to restore that balance, i.e., blackmail and intimidation never, negotiation and sanity always.

ADLAI S. STEVENSON

P.S. I'm returning to New York and can return, of course, at your convenience.

Memorandum for discussion
Washington, October 17, 1962

The Cuban situation

1. The establishment of medium-range strike capability in Cuba by the Soviets was predicted by me in at least a dozen reports since the Soviet build-up was noted in early August.

2. Purposes are to:

(a) Provide Cuba with an offensive or retaliatory power for use if attacked.
(b) Enhance Soviet strike capability against the United States.
(c) Establish a "hall mark" of accomplishment by other Latin American countries, most particularly Mexico, and other Central American countries within strike range of the United States.

3. The MRBM capability we have witnessed will expand and the defensive establishments to protect this capability likewise will be expanded. There appears to me to be no

other explanation for the extensive and elaborate air defense establishment.

4. In my opinion the missiles are Soviet, they will remain under Soviet operational control as do ours, they will be equipped with nuclear warheads under Soviet control (because conventional warheads would be absolutely ineffective), Cubans will supply most of the manpower needs with the Soviets permanently exercising operational command and control. Nevertheless, there will be a substantial number of Soviets on site at all times.

5. Soviet political objectives appears to me to be:

(a) The establishment of a "trading position" to force removal of US overseas bases and Berlin.
(b) To satisfy their ambitions in Latin America by this show of determination and courage against the American Imperialist.

6. Consequences of action by the United States will be the inevitable "spilling of blood" of Soviet military personnel. This will increase tension everywhere and undoubtedly bring retaliation against US foreign military installations, where substantial US casualties would result, i.e., Tule, Spanish bases, Moroccan bases, and possibly SAC bases in Britain or Okinawa. Jupiter installations in Southern Italy, Turkey, and our facilities [*less than one line of source text not declassified*] do not provide enough "American blood."

7. The situation cannot be tolerated. However, the United States should not act without warning and thus be forced to live with a "Pearl Harbor indictment" for the indefinite future. I would therefore:

(a) Notify Gromyko and Castro that we know all about this.
(b) Give them 24 hours to commence dismantling and

removal of MRBMs, coastal defense missiles, surface-to-air missiles, IL-28s and all other aircraft which have a dual defensive-offensive capability, including MiG-21s.

(c) Notify the American public and the world of the situation created by the Soviets.

(d) If Khrushchev and Castro fail to act at once, we should make a massive surprise strike at airfields, MRBM sites and SAM sites concurrently.

JOHN A. MCCONE

Memorandum of conversation
Washington, October 18, 1962, 5 p.m.

PARTICIPANTS: *US* The President, The Secretary, Ambassador Thompson, Mr Hillenbrand, Mr Akalovsky; *USSR* Foreign Minister Gromyko, Mr Semenov, Ambassador Dobrynin, Mr Sukhodrev

Cuba

After a discussion on Germany and Berlin, Mr Gromyko stated he wished to set forth the Soviet position on Cuba and to voice the views of the Soviet Government with regard to US actions relating to Cuba. Continuing to read from his prepared text, he asserted that the Soviet Government stood for peaceful coexistence and was against interference by one state in the internal affairs of another state, and this also applied to relations between big and small states. This, he said, was the basic core, the credo of Soviet foreign policy, and it was not just a statement.

The President was surely fully familiar with the attitude of the Soviet Government, and of Mr Khrushchev personally, toward recent developments and toward actions by the

United States Government in relation to Cuba. For quite
some time there had been an unabated anti-Cuban campaign in the United States, a campaign which was
apparently backed by the United States Government. Now
the United States Government wished to institute a blockade against trade with Cuba, and there had also been some
talk of organized piracy under the aegis of the United
States. All this could only lead to great misfortunes for
mankind. The United States Government seemed to
believe that the Cubans must settle their internal affairs not
at their own discretion, but at the discretion of the United
States. Yet Cuba belonged to Cubans and not to the United
States. If this was so, why then were statements being made
in the United States advocating invasion of Cuba? What did
the United States want to do with Cuba? What could Cuba
do to the United States? If one were to compare the human
and material resources of Cuba and the United States, one
would see immediately that the United States was a giant
and Cuba only a baby. Cuba could not constitute a threat to
any country in Latin America. It was strange to believe that
small Cuba could encroach upon any Latin American
country. Cuban leaders, including Castro personally, had
stated for all the world to know and in the most solemn
fashion that Cuba did not intend to impose its system and
was in favor of peaceful coexistence. However, those who
called for aggression against Cuba said that Cuban statements were insufficient, in spite of the fact that those
statements were substantiated by deeds. If one were to
approach problems this way, then it would be easy to justify
any aggression. All international problems must be resolved
by negotiation between the states concerned. After all, the
US and USSR were now negotiating and making statements which should be given credence. Was it not sufficient
for Cuba to state that it wished negotiations and a solution
of existing problems on a mutually acceptable basis? The

President was surely familiar with President Dorticos' speech at the General Assembly.

What the Cubans wanted was to make their home and country secure. They appealed to reason and conscience and called upon the United States not to resort to encroachments. Thus the question arose of why it was necessary to fan this campaign, to organize hostile actions, and to take actions directed against those countries which were extending their hand of friendship to Cuba? This was a violation of international law, and how could the Soviet Government just sit by and observe this situation idly?

Mr Gromyko said he knew that the President appreciated frankness. Mr Khrushchev's conversation with the President at Vienna had been frank and therefore, with the President's permission, he himself wished to be frank, too. The situation today could not be compared to that obtaining in the middle of the 19th century. Modern times were not the same as those when colonies had been divided among colonial powers. Modern times could not be compared to those when it took weeks or months for the voice of the attacked to be heard. Statements had been made that the US was a powerful and great nation; this was true, but what kind of a nation was the USSR? Mr Khrushchev had been favorably impressed with the President's statement at Vienna regarding the equality of forces of our two nations. Since this was so, i.e., since the USSR was also a great and strong nation, it could not stand by as a mere observer when aggression was planned and when a threat of war was looming. The US Government was surely aware of the Soviet Government's attitude toward the recent call-up of 150,000 Reservists in the United States. The Soviet Government believed that if both sides were for relaxation of international tensions and for solving the outstanding international problems, such demonstrations could be designed only for the purpose of increasing tensions and should therefore be avoided. If worse should come to worse and if war should occur, then surely 150,000 soldiers would be of no significance. As the President was surely aware, today was not 1812, when Napoleon had relied on the number of soldiers, sabres and rifles. Neither could today's situation be compared to 1941, when Hitler had relied on the number of tanks and guns. Today, life itself and military technology had created an entirely different situation, where it was better not to rely on arms.

As to Soviet assistance to Cuba, Mr Gromyko stated that he was instructed to make it clear, as the Soviet Government had already done, that such assistance, pursued solely for the purpose of contributing to the defense capabilities of Cuba and to the development of Cuba, toward the development of its agriculture and land amelioration, and training by Soviet specialists of Cuba nationals in handling defensive armaments were by no means offensive. If it were otherwise, the Soviet Government would have never become involved in rendering such assistance. This applied to any other country as well. Laos was a good and convincing illustration of this point. If the Soviet Government had pursued a different policy, the situation in that country today would be quite different. It was quite evident that the Soviet Union and its friends had broader opportunities of influencing the situation in that country than had the United States. However, the USSR had sought an understanding on that question, since it could not go back on the basic principle of its foreign policy, which was designed to alleviate tensions, to eliminate outstanding problems and to resolve them on a peaceful basis.

Such was the position of the Soviet Government with regard to Cuba. The Soviet Government and Mr Khrushchev personally appealed to the President and the United States Government not to allow such steps as would be incompatible with peace, with relaxation of tensions, and with the United Nations Charter under which both the US and the USSR had solemnly affixed their signatures. The Soviet Government addressed its appeal to the United States on this question because both our countries were major powers and should direct their efforts only to ensuring peace.

The President said he was glad that Mr Gromyko had referred to Laos because he believed that the Soviet policy on that problem was as Mr Gromyko had described it. So far the Soviet Union had apparently met its obligations just as the United States had met them. However, a most serious mistake had been made last summer with respect to Cuba. The US had not pressed the Cuban problem and had attempted to push it aside although of course a number of people in this country opposed the regime now prevailing in Cuba and there were many refugees coming to this country. However, there was no intention to invade Cuba. But then last July the USSR, without any communication from Mr Khrushchev to the President, had embarked upon the policy of supplying arms to Cuba. The President said he did not know the reasons for that shift in Soviet policy, because there was no threat of invasion and he would have been glad to give appropriate assurances to that effect had Mr Khrushchev communicated with him. Soviet arms supply had had a profound impact in the United States; Ambassador Dobrynin was surely aware of how the American people and the Congress felt on this matter. The Administration had tried to calm this reaction and he, the President, had made a statement that in view of the nature of Soviet assistance to Cuba at this time coolness was required. Yet, the President said, he wished to stress that Soviet actions were extremely serious and he could find no satisfactory explanation for them. The Soviet Union was surely aware of US feelings with regard to

Cuba, which was only 90 miles away from the United States. The President continued that the US planned no blockade of Cuba; it was only a question of ships taking arms to Cuba not being able to stop in the United States with their return cargo. Thus a very unfortunate situation had developed. The President said he did not know where it was taking us but it was the most dangerous situation since the end of the war. The US had taken the Soviet statement concerning the nature of armaments supplied to Cuba at its face value. He, the President, had attacked last Sunday in Indianapolis a Senator who was advocating invasion, and he had stated that the Cuban problem must be kept in perspective. The President reiterated that this was a dangerous situation, and said he did not know where the USSR planned to have it end.

Mr Gromyko said that there had already been an invasion, and it was well known how it ended. It was well known now, both from facts and statements, including the President's own, under what circumstances and by whom that invasion had been organized. Everyone knew that if the United States had merely lifted its little finger, Cuban émigrées and smaller Caribbean countries which had helped them would not have dared undertake any invasion.

The President interjected that he had discussed with Mr Khrushchev the April 1, 1961, invasion and had said that it was a mistake. He also pointed out he would have given assurances that there would be no further invasion, either by refugees or by US forces. But last July the Soviet Union took certain actions and the situation changed.

Mr Gromyko continued that Cubans and the Cuban Government had before them the vital question of whether they should remain unprepared to resist attack or to take steps to defend their country. He said he wished to reiterate that the Soviet Union had responded to appeals for assistance only because that assistance pursued the sole objective of giving bread to Cuba and preventing hunger in that country; also, as far as armaments were concerned, Soviet specialists were training Cubans in handling certain types of armaments which were only defensive—and he wished to stress the word defensive—in character, and thus such training could not constitute a threat to the United States. He reiterated that if it were otherwise the Soviet Union would never have agreed to render such assistance.

The President said that in order to be clear on this Cuban problem he wanted to state the following: The US had no intention of invading Cuba. Introduction last July of intensive armanents had complicated the situation and created grave danger. His own actions had been to prevent, unless US security was endangered, anything from being done that might provoke the danger of war. The President then read a portion of his September 4th statement on Cuba and stated that this had been US position and policy on this question. He noted that the Attorney General had discussed the Cuban situation with Ambassador Dobrynin so that the latter must be aware of what it was. The President again recalled his Indianapolis speech of last Sunday and said that we were basing our present attitude on facts as they had been described by Mr Gromyko; our presumption was that the armaments supplied by USSR were defensive.

Mr Gromyko stated the Soviet Union proceeded from the assumption that on the basis of Soviet Government's statements and his own today, the US Government and the President had a clear idea of the Soviet policy on this matter and of the Soviet evaluation of US action in relation to Cuba. He said he had nothing to add to what he had already said.

OCTOBER 19, 1962

Memorandum for the file
Washington, October 19, 1962

Early in the morning of October 18th, Secretary McNamara called Mr McCone at his residence expressing great concern over the reports from NPIC as a result of their examination of the two flights run on October 15th.

Lundahl was at the house with the enlargements which indicated that, in addition to the three mobile MRBM sites detected on flight October 14th, there appeared to be now two IRBM sites with fixed launchers zeroed in on the Eastern United States. McNamara felt that this development demanded more prompt and decisive action.

The group which had been meeting on Tuesday met in the Cabinet Room at 11:00 a.m. on Wednesday with the President. State tabled revisions in their papers on covering a limited one-time strike and blockade, most of which are dated 10/18–11:00 a.m.

At the opening of the meeting, McCone gave a brief résumé of current intelligence and Lundahl presented the most recent photography. President questioned Lundahl further if the uninitiated could be persuaded that the photographs presented offensive MRBM missiles. Lundahl stated probably not and that we must have low-level photography for public consumption.

Secretary Rusk then stated that developments in the last 24 hours had substantially changed his thinking. He first questioned whether, if it is necessary to move against Cuba, and then concluded that it was because Cuba can become a formidable military threat. He also referred to the President's recent public statements and indicated a feeling that if no action was taken, we would free the Soviets to act any place they wished and at their own will. Also, Rusk stated the failure on our part to act would make our situation unmanageable elsewhere in the world. He furthermore indicated that this would be an indication of weakness which would have serious effect on our Allies. Secretary pointed out to the President that action would involve risks. We could expect counter-action and the cost may be heavy. The President must expect action in Berlin, Korea and possibly against the United States itself. Rusk felt a quick strike would minimize the risk of counter-action. He raised the question of solidarity of the Alliance and seemed to dismiss this question, feeling that the Alliance would hold together. Rusk stated that if we enter upon positive action, we can not say for sure what the final

Soviet response will be and therefore what the final outcome will be. However he felt that the American people
will accept danger and suffering if they are convinced
doing so is necessary and that they have a clear conscience.
The Secretary reviewed the circumstances surrounding the
outbreak of World War I, World War II, and the Korean
war. These factors militated in favor of consulting with
Khrushchev and depending on the Rio pact. This, he indicated, might have the possibility of prevention of action
and settlement by political means. The other course open
was the declaration of war. Rusk expressed himself in favor
of leaning upon the Rio pact, but does not dismiss the
alternative of a unilateral declaration of war as the ultimate
action we must take. The alternate is a quick strike.

Ambassador Bohlen was not present but his views were
expressed in a message which was read in which he
strongly advocated diplomatic effort and stated that military action prior to this would be wrong. He urged against
action first and the decisive value of discussion. He also
stated that limited quick military action was an illusion and
that any military action would rapidly escalate into an
invasion. McNamara at this point presented the alternatives referred to the previous day [see p. 135] stating that
alternatives one and two were not conclusive and that we
would have to resort to alternative three and in fact this
would lead us ultimately into an invasion.

General Taylor generally reviewed the situation stating
that the Chiefs looked upon Cuba as a forward base of
serious proportions, that it cannot be taken out totally by
air; that the military operation would be sizeable, nevertheless necessary.

Ambassador Thompson urged that any action be preceded by a declaration of war; he strongly advocated that
we institute a blockade and not resort to military action
unless and until it is determined that Castro and

Khrushchev refuse to reverse their activities and actually remove the missiles which are now in place.

Secretary Dillon questioned what would be accomplished by talking to Khrushchev. He pointed out that we would probably become engaged in discussions from which we could not extract ourselves and therefore our freedom of action would be frustrated. Dillon was very positive that whatever action we take should be done without consultation with Khrushchev. Rusk seemed to disagree indicating there was a possibility that Khrushchev might be persuaded to reduce his efforts but he admitted also that he might step them up as a result of discussions.

President Kennedy was non-committal, however he seemed to continually raise questions of reactions of our allies, NATO, South America, public opinion and others. Raised the question whether we should not move the missiles out of Turkey. All readily agreed they were not much use but a political question was involved. Bundy thought this a good idea either under conditions of a strike or during a preliminary talk.

McNamara discussed in some detail the effects of a strike indicating that we could expect several hundred Soviet citizens to be killed; he pointed out that all of the SAM sites were manned exclusively by Soviets and a great many Soviet technicians were working on the MRBMs and at the airfields. He agreed that we could move out of Turkey and Italy; pointed out the political complications. At this point McNamara seemed to be reconsidering his prior position of advocating military action and laid special emphasis on the fact that the price of Soviet retaliation, whether in Berlin or elsewhere, would be very high and we would not be able to control it.

Secretary Ball throughout the conversation maintained the position that strike without warning was not acceptable and that we should not proceed without discussion with Khrushchev. President Kennedy then said that he thought at some point Khrushchev would say that if we made a move against Cuba, he would take Berlin. McNamara surmised perhaps that was the price we must pay and perhaps we'd lose Berlin anyway. There followed an exchange of view on the possibility of the Soviets taking Berlin and our prospect of retaining it.

President Kennedy rather summed up the dilemma stating that action of a type contemplated would be opposed by the alliance—on the other hand, lack of action will create disunity, lack of confidence and disintegration of our several alliances and friendly relations with countries who have confidence in us.

As a result of discussions of the "price" of a strike, there followed a long discussion of the possibilities of a blockade, the advantages of it, and manner in which it would be carried out, etc. There seemed to be differences of opinion as to whether the blockade should be total, or should only involve military equipment which would mean blockading Soviet ships. Also there were continued references to blockading ships carrying offensive weapons and there seemed to be a differentiation in the minds of some in the policy of blockading offensive weapons as contrasted to blockading all weapons.

There followed discussion as to policies the President should follow with respect to calling Congress into session, asking for a declaration of war, advising the country and authorizing action. Thompson continued to insist that we must communicate with Khrushchev. There was a discussion concerning the President's meeting with Gromyko and the position he should take should the Cuban question come up. The President was advised to draw Gromyko out and it was indicated he probably would receive a flat denial that there were any offensive weapons in Cuba.

Meeting adjourned with the President requesting that we organize into two groups. One to study the advantages of what might be called a slow course of action which would involve a blockade to be followed by such further actions as appeared necessary as the situation evolved. Second would be referred to as a fast dynamic action which would involve the strike of substantial proportions with or without notice.

JOHN A. MCCONE

Record of meeting
Washington, October 19, 1962, 11:00 a.m.

PARTICIPANTS: Secretary Rusk, Under Secretary Ball, Ambassador Thompson, Deputy Under Secretary Johnson, Assistant Secretary Martin, Leonard C. Meeker, Secretary Dillon, Secretary McNamara, Deputy Secretary Gilpatric, Assistant Secretary Nitze, General Taylor, Attorney General Kennedy, Deputy Attorney General Katzenbach, John A. McCone, Ray S. Cline, McGeorge Bundy, Theodore Sorensen, Dean Acheson

Secretary Rusk opened the meeting by asking Mr Johnson if he was ready to lay a program before the group. Mr Johnson said that he was not.

Then ensued a military photographic intelligence briefing on installations in Cuba, presented by a CIA representative (Arthur Lundahl). Following this, Mr McCone called on Mr Cline to give the most recent intelligence estimate conclusions of the United States Intelligence Board. Mr Cline did so on the basis of three papers which were distributed to the group. (As he started, Mr Cline spoke of China by inadvertence instead of Cuba; a few moments later this was called to his attention and corrected.)

Secretary Rusk then said he thought there should be an exposition of the legal framework surrounding possible military measures by the United States, turned to me, and seemed about to call on me, when the Attorney General signalled and said "Mr Katzenbach." Secretary Rusk then called on the latter. Mr Katzenbach said he believed the President had ample constitutional and statutory authority to take any needed military measures. He considered a declaration of war unnecessary. From the standpoint of international law, Mr Katzenbach thought United States action could be justified on the principle of self-defense.

I said that my analysis ran along much the same lines. I did not think a declaration of war would improve our position, but indeed would impair it. I said that a defensive quarantine of Cuba would involve a use of force, and this had to be considered in relation to the United Nations Charter. The Charter contained a general prohibition against the use of force except in certain limited kinds of situation. One of these was "armed attack," but the situation in Cuba did not constitute armed attack on any country. Another exception was collective action voted by the competent United Nations organ to deal with a situation under Chapter VII of the Charter. Obviously, no resolution could be obtained from the Security Council. And it seemed quite problematical whether we could obtain a recommendation from the General Assembly.

The Charter also contained Chapter VIII on regional arrangements. Article 52 provided that regional arrangements could deal with "such matters relating to the maintenance of international peace and security as are appropriate for regional action." Thus a case could be made under the Charter for the use of force if it were sanctioned by the American Republics acting under the Rio Treaty. The Organ of Consultation, pursuant to

Articles 6 and 8 of that Treaty, could recommend measures, including the use of armed force, to meet a situation endangering the peace of America. As to the prospects for securing the necessary two-thirds vote in the Organ of Consultation, Mr Martin would have something to say about that.

If the contention were advanced that a defensive quarantine voted under the Rio Treaty constituted "enforcement action" under Article 53 of the United Nations Charter, and therefore required the authorization of the Security Council, we would be able to make a reasonably good argument to the contrary. While our ability to persuade seven members of the Security Council to vote with us on this issue might be uncertain, we would in any event be able to prevent a vote going against our position.

Mr Martin then gave as his estimate that the United States could secure immediately a vote of 14 in the OAS. He thought the majority could be increased within 24 hours to 17 or perhaps even 18 or 19. He was hopeful in regard to Ecuador and Chile, and believed there was a good chance of getting Mexico. The Attorney General said the President would be placed in an impossible position if we went to the OAS and then failed to get the necessary votes, or if there were a delay. He asked if we could be perfectly sure of the outcome before seeking OAS concurrence. Mr Martin said he hated to guarantee anything, but he had a lot of confidence about this. You couldn't go to the American Republics in advance without loss of security, but he felt that a last-minute approach to heads of state, laying the situation on the line, would produce the votes. The Attorney General again expressed his great concern at the possibility of a slip.

There followed a discussion covering the meeting held the night before with the President. One participant looked back on the meeting as having arrived at a tentative conclusion to institute a blockade, and thought the President had been satisfied at the consensus by then arrived at among his advisers. General Taylor quickly indicated that he had not concurred and that the Joint Chiefs had reserved their position.

Mr Bundy then said that he had reflected a good deal upon the situation in the course of a sleepless night, and he doubted whether the strategy group was serving the President as well as it might, if it merely recommended a blockade. He had spoken with the President this morning, and he felt there was further work to be done. A blockade would not remove the missiles. Its effects were uncertain and in any event would be slow to be felt. Something more would be needed to get the missiles out of Cuba. This would be made more difficult by the prior publicity of a blockade and the consequent pressures from the United Nations for a negotiated settlement. An air strike would be quick and would take out the bases in a clean surgical operation. He favored decisive action with its advantages of surprises and confronting the world with a fait accompli.

Secretary Rusk asked Mr Acheson for his views. Mr Acheson said that Khrushchev had presented the United States with a direct challenge, we were involved in a test of wills, and the sooner we got to a showdown the better. He favored cleaning the missile bases out decisively with an air strike. There was something else to remember. This wasn't just another instance of Soviet missiles aimed at the United States. Here they were in the hands of a madman whose actions would be perfectly irresponsible; the usual restraints operating on the Soviets would not apply. We had better act, and act quickly. So far as questions of international law might be involved, Mr Acheson agreed with Mr Katzenbach's position that self-defense was an entirely sufficient justification. But if there were to be imported a qualification or requirement of approval by the OAS, as apparently suggested by Mr Meeker, he could not go along with that.

Secretary Dillon said he agreed there should be a quick air strike. Mr McCone was of the same opinion.

General Taylor said that a decision now to impose a blockade was a decision to abandon the possibility of an air strike. A strike would be feasible for only a few more days; after that the missiles would be operational. Thus it was now or never for an air strike. He favored a strike. If it were to take place Sunday morning, a decision would have to be made at once so that the necessary preparations could be ordered. For a Monday morning strike, a decision would have to be reached tomorrow. Forty-eight hours' notice was required.

Secretary McNamara said that he would give orders for the necessary military dispositions, so that if the decision were for a strike the Air Force would be ready. He did not, however, advocate an air strike, and favored the alternative of a blockade.

Under Secretary Ball said that he was a waverer between the two courses of action.

The Attorney General said with a grin that he too had had a talk with the President, indeed very recently this morning. There seemed to be three main possibilities as the Attorney General analyzed the situation: one was to do nothing, and that would be unthinkable; another was an air strike; the third was a blockade. He thought it would be very, very difficult indeed for the President if the decision were to be for an air strike, with all the memory of Pearl Harbor and with all the implications this would have for us in whatever world there would be afterward. For 175 years we had not been that kind of country. A sneak attack was not in our traditions. Thousands of Cubans would be killed without warning, and a lot of Russians too. He favored action, to make known unmistakably the seriousness of United States determination to get the missiles out of Cuba, but he thought the action should allow the Soviets some room for maneuver to pull back from their over-extended position in Cuba.

Mr Bundy, addressing himself to the Attorney General, said this was very well but a blockade would not eliminate the bases; an air strike would.

I asked at this point: who would be expected to be the government of Cuba after an air strike? Would it be anyone other than Castro? If not, would anything be solved, and would we not be in a worse situation than before? After a pause, Mr Martin replied that, of course, a good deal might be different after a strike, and Castro might be toppled in the aftermath. Others expressed the view that we might have to proceed with an invasion following a strike. Still another suggestion was that US armed forces seize the base areas alone in order to eliminate the missiles. Secretary McNamara thought this a very unattractive kind of undertaking from the military point of view.

Toward one o'clock Secretary Rusk said he thought this group could not make the decision as to what was to be done; that was for the President in consultation with his constitutional advisers. The Secretary thought the group's duty was to present to the President, for his consideration, fully staffed-out alternatives. Accordingly, two working groups should be formed, one to work up the blockade alternative and the other to work up the air strike. Mr Johnson was designated to head the former, and Mr Bundy the latter. Mr Johnson was to have with him Ambassador Thompson, Deputy Secretary Gilpatric, Mr Martin, Mr Nitze, and Mr Meeker. Mr Bundy was to have Secretary Dillon, Mr Acheson, and General Taylor. Mr McCone, when asked to serve with the air strike group, begged off on the ground that his position and duties on the US Intelligence Board made it undesirable for him to participate in the working group. Mr Katzenbach was detailed to the Johnson group, later visiting the Bundy group to observe and possibly serve as a devil's advocate.

Mr Sorensen commented that he thought he had absorbed enough to start on the draft of a speech for the President. There was some inconclusive discussion on the timing of such a speech, on the danger of leaks before then, and on the proper time for meeting with the President once more, in view of his current Western campaign trip.

Before the whole group dispersed, Ambassador Thompson said the Soviets attached importance to questions of legality and we should be able to present a strong legal case. The Attorney General, as he was about to leave the room, said he thought there was ample legal basis for a blockade. I said: yes, that is so provided the Organ of Consultation under the Rio Treaty adopted an appropriate resolution. The Attorney General said: "That's all political; it's not legal." On leaving the room, he said to Mr Katzenbach, half humorously: "Remember now, you're working for me."

The two groups met separately until four o'clock. They then reconvened and were joined once more by the cabinet officers who had been away in the earlier afternoon.

The Johnson group scenario, which was more nearly complete and was ready earlier, was discussed first. Numerous criticisms were advanced. Some were answered; others led to changes. There was again a discussion of timing, now in relation to a Presidential radio address. Mr Martin thought Sunday might be too early, as it would be virtually impossible to get to all the Latin American heads of state on Sunday. Ambassador Thompson made the point that 24 hours must be allowed to elapse between announcement of the blockade and enforcement, so as to give the Soviet Government time to get instructions to their ship captains.

Approximately two hours were spent on the Johnson scenario. About 6 o'clock the Bundy approach was taken up, its author saying, "It's been much more fun for us up to this point, since we've had a chance to poke holes in the blockade plan; now the roles will be reversed." Not much more than half an hour was spent on the Bundy scenario.

More than once during the afternoon Secretary McNamara voiced the opinion that the US would have to pay a price to get the Soviet missiles out of Cuba. He thought we would at least have to give up our missile bases in Italy and Turkey and would probably have to pay more besides. At different times the possibility of nuclear conflict breaking out was referred to. The point was made that, once the Cuban missile installations were complete and operational, a new strategic situation would exist, with the United States more directly and immediately under the gun than ever before. A striking Soviet military push into the Western Hemisphere would have succeeded and become effective. The clock could not be turned back, and things would never be the same again. During this discussion, the Attorney General said that in looking forward into the future it would be better for our children and grandchildren if we decided to face the Soviet threat, stand up to it, and eliminate it, now. The circumstances for doing so at some future time were bound to be more unfavorable, the risks would be greater, the chances of success less good.

Secretary Rusk, toward the end of the afternoon, stated his approach to the problem as follows: the US needed to move in a way such that a planned action would be followed by a pause in which the great powers could step back from the brink and have time to consider and work out a solution rather than be drawn inexorably from one action to another and escalate into general nuclear war. The implication of his statement was that he favored blockade rather than strike.

In the course of the afternoon discussion, the military representatives, especially Secretary McNamara, came to expressing the view that an air strike could be made some time after the blockade was instituted in the event the blockade did not produce results as to the missile bases in Cuba. The Attorney General took particular note of this shift, and toward the end of the day made clear that he firmly favored blockade as the first step; other steps subsequently were not precluded and could be considered; he thought it was now pretty clear what the decision should be.

At about six-thirty Governor Stevenson came into the room. After a few minutes, Secretary Rusk asked him if he had some views on the question of what to do. He replied: "Yes, most emphatic views." When queried as to them, he said that in view of the course the discussion was taking he didn't think it was necessary to express them then. When asked: "But you are in favor of blockade, aren't you?," he answered affirmatively. He went on to say he thought we must look beyond the particular immediate action of blockade; we need to develop a plan for a solution of the problem—elements for negotiation designed to settle the current crisis in a stable and satisfactory way and enable us to move forward on wider problems; he was working on some ideas for a settlement. One possibility would be the demilitarization of Cuba under effective international supervision, perhaps accompanied by neutralization of the island under international guaranties and with UN observers to monitor compliance.

Once again there was discussion of when another meeting with the President should be held. It was generally agreed that the President should continue on his trip until Sunday morning. He would be reachable by telephone prior to that time.

The meeting broke up about seven o'clock.

Special National Intelligence Estimate
Washington, October 19, 1962

SNIE 11-18-62: Soviet reactions to certain US courses of action on Cuba

The problem
To estimate probable Soviet reactions to certain US courses of action with respect to Cuba.

The estimate
1. A major Soviet objective in their military build-up in Cuba is to demonstrate that the world balance of forces has shifted so far in their favor that the US can no longer prevent the advance of Soviet offensive power even into its own Hemisphere. In this connection they assume, of course, that these deployments sooner or later will become publicly known.

2. It is possible that the USSR is installing these missiles primarily in order to use them in bargaining for US concessions elsewhere. We think this unlikely, however. The public withdrawal of Soviet missiles from Cuba would create serious problems in the USSR's relations with Castro; it would cast doubt on the firmness of the Soviet intention to protect the Castro regime and perhaps on their commitments elsewhere.

3. If the US accepts the strategic missile build-up in Cuba, the Soviets would continue the build-up of strategic

weapons in Cuba. We have no basis for estimating the force level which they would wish to reach, but it seems clear already that they intend to go beyond a token capability. They would probably expect their missile forces in Cuba to make some contribution to their total strategic capability vis-à-vis the US. We consider in Annex B [not included] the possible effects of a missile build-up in Cuba upon the overall relationship of strategic military power.

4. US acceptance of the strategic missile build-up would provide strong encouragement to Communists, pro-Communists, and the more anti-American sectors of opinion in Latin America and elsewhere. Conversely, anti-Communists and those who relate their own interests to those of the US would be strongly discouraged. It seems clear that, especially over the long run, there would be a loss of confidence in US power and determination and a serious decline of US influence generally.

Effect of warning
5. If the US confronts Khrushchev with its knowledge of the MRBM deployment and presses for a withdrawal, we do not believe the Soviets would halt the deployment. Instead, they would propose negotiations on the general question of foreign bases, claiming equal right to establish Soviet bases and assuring the US of tight control over the missiles. They would probably link Cuba with the Berlin situation and emphasize their patience and preference for negotiations, implying that Berlin was held hostage to US actions in Cuba.

6. There is some slight chance that a warning to Castro might make a difference, since the Soviets could regard this as a chance to stand aside, but it also would give time for offers to negotiate, continued build-up, and counterpressures, and we think the result in the end would be the same.

7. Any warning would of course degrade the element of surprise in a subsequent US attack.

Effect of blockade
8. While the effectiveness of Castro's military machine might be impaired by a total US blockade, Castro would be certain to tighten internal security and would take ruthless action against any attempts at revolt. There is no reason to believe that a blockade of itself would bring down the Castro regime. The Soviets would almost certainly exert strong direct pressures elsewhere to end the blockade. The attitudes of other states toward a blockade action are not considered in this paper. It is obvious that the Soviets would heavily exploit all adverse reactions.

Soviet reaction to use of military force
9. If the US takes direct military action against Cuba, the Soviets would be placed automatically under great pressure to respond in ways which, if they could not save Cuba, would inflict an offsetting injury to US interests. This would be true whether the action was limited to an effort to neutralize the strategic missiles, or these missiles plus airfields, surface-to-air missile sites, or cruise missile sites, or in fact an outright invasion designed to destroy the Castro regime.

10. In reaction to any of the various forms of US action, the Soviets would be alarmed and agitated, since they have to date estimated that the US would not take military action in the face of Soviet warnings of the danger of nuclear war. They would recognize that US military action posed a major challenge to the prestige of the USSR. We must of course recognize the possibility that the Soviets, under pressure to respond, would again miscalculate and respond in a way which, through a series of actions and reactions, could escalate to general war.

11. On the other hand, the Soviets have no public treaty with Cuba and have not acknowledged that Soviet bases are on the island. This situation provides them with a pretext for treating US military action against Cuba as an affair which does not directly involve them, and thereby avoiding the risks of a strong response. We do not believe that the USSR would attack the US, either from Soviet bases or with its missiles in Cuba, even if the latter were operational and not put out of action before they could be readied for firing.

12. Since the USSR would not dare to resort to general war and could not hope to prevail locally, the Soviets would almost certainly consider retaliatory actions outside Cuba. The timing and selection of such moves would depend heavily upon the immediate context of events and the USSR's appreciation of US attitudes. The most likely location for broad retaliation outside Cuba appears to be Berlin. They might react here with major harassments, interruptions of access to the city or even a blockade, with or without the signing of a separate peace treaty.

13. We believe that whatever course of retaliation the USSR elected, the Soviet leaders would not deliberately initiate general war or take military measures, which in their calculation, would run the gravest risks of general war.

OCTOBER 20, 1962

*Minutes of the 505th meeting of the National Security Council
Washington, October 20, 1962, 2:30–5:10 p.m.*

PARTICIPANTS: The President, Attorney General Robert F. Kennedy; *CIA* John A. McCone, Director, Mr Ray Cline, Mr Arthur Lundahl, Mr Chamberlain; *Defense* Robert S. McNamara, Secretary, Roswell Gilpatric, Deputy Secretary, Paul Nitze, Assistant Secretary (ISA); *JCS* General Maxwell D. Taylor, USA, Chairman; *OEP*

Edward A. McDermott, Director; *State* Dean Rusk, Secretary, George Ball, Under Secretary, U. Alexis Johnson, Deputy Under Secretary for Political Affairs, Adlai Stevenson, US Ambassador to the UN, Edwin Martin, Assistant Secretary, Inter-American Affairs, Llewellyn E. Thompson, Ambassador-at-Large; *Treasury* Douglas Dillon, Secretary; *White House* McGeorge Bundy, Special Assistant to the President for National Security Affairs, Theodore Sorensen, Special Counsel, Kenneth O'Donnell, Special Assistant to the President, Bromley Smith, Executive Secretary, National Security Council

Intelligence briefing

The first 20 minutes were spent in the presentation and discussion of photographic intelligence establishing the presence in Cuba of Soviet intermediate-range and medium-range missiles, mobile missile launchers, and missile sites.

Mr Ray Cline of the Central Intelligence Agency summarized the report of the Guided Missile and Astronautics Intelligence Committee, the Joint Atomic Energy Intelligence Committee, and the National Photographic Interpretation Center, dated October 19, 1962 (SC 09538-62). Mr Arthur Lundahl of CIA described the various missile sites and launching pads, displaying enlarged pictures identical to those in the Committee report.

In response to the President's question, Mr Cline stated that there were no U-2 photographic reconnaissance missions over Cuba from August 29th to October 14th. The gap in photographic coverage was in part due to bad weather and in part to a desire to avoid activating the SAM Air Defense installations which the Russians were hurriedly installing in Cuba during this period. Since October 14th, nine high altitude missions have been flown. Information from these missions is not fully processed, but will be available for presentation by Monday.

In summary, the Council was informed that 16 SS-4 missiles, with a range of 1,020 nautical miles were now operational in Cuba and could be fired approximately 18 hours after a decision to fire was taken. The bearing of these launchers was 315 degrees, i.e. toward the central area of the United States.

The President summarized the discussion of the intelligence material as follows. There is something to destroy in Cuba now and, if it is destroyed, a strategic missile capability would be difficult to restore.

Blockade track

Secretary McNamara explained to the President that there were differences among his advisers which had resulted in the drafting of alternative courses of action. He added that the military planners are at work on measures to carry out all recommended courses of action in order that, following a Presidential decision, fast action could be taken.

Secretary McNamara described his view as the "blockade route." This route is aimed at preventing any addition to the strategic missiles already deployed to Cuba and eventually to eliminate these missiles. He said to do this we should institute a blockade of Cuba and be prepared to take armed action in specified instances. (The President was handed a copy of Ted Sorensen's "blockade route" draft of a Presidential message, which he read.)

Secretary McNamara concluded by explaining that following the blockade, the United States would negotiate for the removal of the strategic missiles from Cuba. He said we would have to be prepared to accept the withdrawal of United States strategic missiles from Turkey and Italy and possibly agreement to limit our use of Guantánamo to a specified limited time. He added that we could obtain the removal of the missiles from Cuba only if we were prepared to offer something in return during negotiations. He opposed as too risky the suggestion that we should issue an ultimatum to the effect that we would order an air attack on Cuba if the missiles were not removed. He said he was prepared to tell Khrushchev we consider the missiles in Cuba as Soviet missiles and that if they were used against us, we would retaliate by launching missiles against the USSR.

Secretary McNamara pointed out that SNIE 11-19-62, dated October 20, 1962, estimates that the Russians will not use force to push their ships through our blockade. He cited Ambassador Bohlen's view that the USSR would not take military action, but would limit its reaction to political measures in the United Nations.

Secretary McNamara listed the disadvantages of the blockade route as follows:

(1) It would take a long time to achieve the objective of eliminating strategic missiles from Cuba.
(2) It would result in serious political trouble in the United States.
(3) The world position of the United States might appear to be weakening.

The advantages which Secretary McNamara cited are:

(1) It would cause us the least trouble with our allies.
(2) It avoids any surprise air attack on Cuba, which is contrary to our tradition.
(3) It is the only military course of action compatible with our position as a leader of the free world.
(4) It avoids a sudden military move which might provoke a response from the USSR which could result in escalating actions leading to general war.

The President pointed out that during a blockade, more missiles would become operational, and upon the completion of sites and launching pads, the threat would increase.

He asked General Taylor how many missiles we could destroy by air action on Monday.

General Taylor reported that the Joint Chiefs of Staff favor an air strike on Tuesday when United States forces could be in a state of readiness. He said he did not share Secretary McNamara's fear that if we used nuclear weapons in Cuba, nuclear weapons would be used against us.

Secretary Rusk asked General Taylor whether we dared to attack operational strategic missile sites in Cuba.

General Taylor responded that the risk of these missiles being used against us was less than if we permitted the missiles to remain there.

The President pointed out that on the basis of the intelligence estimate there would be some 50 strategic missiles operational in mid-December, if we went the blockade route and took no action to destroy the sites being developed.

General Taylor said that the principal argument he wished to make was that now was the time to act because this would be the last chance we would have to destroy these missiles. If we did not act now, the missiles would be camouflaged in such a way as to make it impossible for us to find them. Therefore, if they were not destroyed, we would have to live with them with all the consequent problems for the defense of the United States.

The President agreed that the missile threat became worse each day, adding that we might wish, looking back, that we had done earlier what we are now preparing to do.

Secretary Rusk said that a blockade would seriously affect the Cuban missile capability in that the Soviets would be unable to deploy to Cuba any missiles in addition to those now there.

Under Secretary Ball said that if an effective blockade was established, it was possible that our photographic intelligence would reveal that there were no nuclear warheads in Cuba; hence, none of the missiles now there could be made operational.

General Taylor indicated his doubt that it would be possible to prevent the Russians from deploying warheads to Cuba by means of a blockade because of the great difficulty of setting up an effective air blockade.

Secretary McNamara stated that if we knew that a plane was flying nuclear warheads to Cuba, we should immediately shoot it down. Parenthetically, he pointed out there are now 6,000 to 8,000 Soviet personnel in Cuba.

The President asked whether the institution of a blockade would appear to the free world as a strong response to the Soviet action. He is particularly concerned about whether the Latin American countries would think that the blockade was an appropriate response to the Soviet challenge.

The Attorney General returned to the point made by General Taylor, i.e. that now is the last chance we will have to destroy Castro and the Soviet missiles deployed in Cuba.

Mr Sorensen said he did not agree with the Attorney General or with General Taylor that this was our last chance. He said a missile build-up would end if, as everyone seemed to agree, the Russians would not use force to penetrate the United States blockade.

Air strike route

Mr Bundy handed to the President the "air strike alternative," which the President read. It was also referred to as the Bundy plan.

The Attorney General told the President that this plan was supported by Mr Bundy, General Taylor, the Joint Chiefs of Staff, and with minor variations, by Secretary Dillon and Director McCone.

General Taylor emphasized the opportunity available now to take out not only all the missiles, but all the Soviet medium bombers (IL-28) which were neatly lined up in the open on air bases in Cuba.

Mr McNamara cautioned that an air strike would not destroy all the missiles and launchers in Cuba, and, at best, we could knock out two-thirds of these missiles. Those missiles not destroyed could be fired from mobile launchers not destroyed. General Taylor said he was unable to explain why the IL-28 medium bombers had been left completely exposed on two airfields. The only way to explain this, he concluded, was on the ground that the Cubans and the Russians did not anticipate a United States air strike.

Secretary Rusk said he hesitated to ask the question but he wondered whether these planes were decoys. He also wondered whether the Russians were trying to entice us into a trap. Secretary McNamara stated his strong doubt that these planes were decoys. Director McCone added that the Russians would not have sent 100 shiploads of equipment to Cuba solely to play a "trick." General Taylor returned to the point he had made earlier, namely, that if we do not destroy the missiles and the bombers, we will have to change our entire military way of dealing with external threats.

The President raised the question of advance warning prior to military action—whether we should give a minimum of two hours notice of an air strike to permit Soviet personnel to leave the area to be attacked.

General Taylor said that the military would be prepared to live with a 24-hour advance notice or grace period if such advance notice was worthwhile politically. The President expressed his doubt that any notice beyond seven hours had any political value.

There was a brief discussion of the usefulness of sending a draft message to Castro, and a copy of such a message was circulated.

The President stated flatly that the Soviet planes in Cuba did not concern him particularly. He said we must be prepared to live with the Soviet threat as represented by Soviet bombers. However, the existence of strategic missiles in Cuba had an entirely different impact throughout Latin America. In his view the existence of 50 planes in Cuba did not affect the balance of power, but the missiles already in Cuba were an entirely different matter.

The Attorney General said that in his opinion a combination of the blockade route and the air strike route was very attractive to him. He felt we should first institute the blockade. In the event that the Soviets continued to build up the missile capability in Cuba, then we should inform the Russians that we would destroy the missiles, the launchers, and the missile sites. He said he favored a short wait during which time the Russians could react to the blockade. If the Russians did not halt the development of the missile capability, then we would proceed to make an air strike. The advantage of proceeding in this way, he added, was that we would get away from the Pearl Harbor surprise attack aspect of the air strike route.

Mr Bundy pointed out that there was a risk that we would act in such a way as to get Khrushchev to commit himself fully to the support of Castro.

Secretary Rusk doubted that a delay of 24 hours in initiating an air strike was of any value. He said he now favored proceeding on the blockade track.

Secretary Dillon mentioned 72 hours as the time between instituting the blockade and initiating an air strike in the event we receive no response to our initial action.

Director McCone stated his opposition to an air strike, but admitted that in his view a blockade was not enough. He argued that we should institute the blockade and tell the Russians that if the missiles were not dismantled within 72 hours, the United States would destroy the missiles by air attack. He called attention to the risk involved in a long drawn-out period during which the Cubans could, at will, launch the missiles against the United States. Secretary Dillon said that the existence of strategic missiles in Cuba was, in his opinion, not negotiable. He believed that any effort to negotiate the removal of the missiles would involve a price so high that the United States could not accept it. If the missiles are not removed or eliminated, he continued, the United States will lose all of its friends in Latin America, who will become convinced that our fear is such that we cannot act. He admitted that the limited use of force involved in a blockade would make the military task much harder and would involve the great danger of the launching of these missiles by the Cubans.

Deputy Secretary Gilpatric saw the choice as involving the use of limited force or of unlimited force. He was prepared to face the prospect of an air strike against Cuba later, but he opposed the initial use of all-out military force such as a surprise air attack. He defined a blockade as being the application of the limited use of force and doubted that such limited use could be combined with an air strike.

General Taylor argued that a blockade would not solve our problem or end the Cuban missile threat. He said that eventually we would have to use military force and, if we waited, the use of force would be much more costly.

Secretary McNamara noted that the air strike planned by the Joint Chiefs involved 800 sorties. Such a strike would result in several thousand Russians being killed, chaos in Cuba, and efforts to overthrow the Castro Government. In his view the probability was high that an air strike would lead inevitably to an invasion. He doubted that the Soviets would take an air strike on Cuba without resorting to a very major response. In such an event, the United States would lose control of the situation which could escalate to general war.

The President agreed that a United States air strike would lead to a major Soviet response, such as blockading Berlin. He agreed that at an appropriate time we would have to acknowledge that we were willing to take strategic missiles out of Turkey and Italy if this issue was raised by the Russians. He felt that implementation of a blockade would also result in Soviet reprisals, possibly the blockade of Berlin. If we instituted a blockade on Sunday, then by Monday or Tuesday we would know whether the missile development had ceased or whether it was continuing. Thus, we would be in a better position to know what move to make next.

Secretary Dillon called attention to the fact that even if the Russians agreed to dismantle the missiles now in Cuba, continuing inspection would be required to ensure that the missiles were not again made ready.

The President said that if it was decided to go the Bundy route, he would favor an air strike which would destroy only missiles. He repeated his view that we would have to live with the threat arising out of the stationing in Cuba of Soviet bombers.

Secretary Rusk referred to an air strike as chapter two. He did not think we should initiate such a strike because of the risk of escalating actions leading to general war. He doubted that we should act without consultation of our allies. He said a sudden air strike had no support in the law or morality, and, therefore, must be ruled out. Reading from notes, he urged that we start the blockade and only go on to an air attack when we knew the reaction of the Russians and of our allies.

At this point Director McCone acknowledged that we did not know positively that nuclear warheads for the missiles had actually arrived in Cuba. Although we had evidence of the construction of storage places for nuclear weapons, such weapons may not yet have been sent.

The President asked what we would say to those whose reaction to our instituting a blockade now would be to ask why we had not blockaded last July.

Both Mr Sorensen and Mr Ball made the point that we did not institute a blockade in July because we did not then know of the existence of the strategic missiles in Cuba.

Secretary Rusk suggested that our objective was an immediate freeze of the strategic missile capability in Cuba to be inspected by United Nations observation teams stationed at the missile sites. He referred to our bases in Turkey, Spain and Greece as being involved in any negotiation covering foreign bases. He said a United Nations group might be sent to Cuba to reassure those who might fear that the United States was planning an invasion.

Ambassador Stevenson stated his flat opposition to a surprise air strike, which he felt would ultimately lead to a United States invasion of Cuba. He supported the institution of the blockade and predicted that such action would reduce the chance of Soviet retaliation of a nature which would inevitably escalate. In his view our aim is to end the existing missile threat in Cuba without casualties and without escalation. He urged that we offer the Russians a settlement involving the withdrawal of our missiles from Turkey and our evacuation of Guantánamo base.

The President sharply rejected the thought of surrendering our base at Guantánamo in the present situation. He felt that such action would convey to the world that we had been frightened into abandoning our position. He was not opposed to discussing withdrawal of our missiles from Turkey and Greece, but he was firm in saying we should only make such a proposal in the future.

The Attorney General thought we should convey our firm intentions to the Russians clearly and suggested that we might tell the Russians that we were turning over nuclear weapons and missiles to the West Germans.

Ambassador Thompson stated his view that our first action should be the institution of a blockade. Following this, he thought we should launch an air strike to destroy the missiles and sites, after giving sufficient warning so that Russian nationals could leave the area to be attacked.

The President said he was ready to go ahead with the blockade and to take actions necessary to put us in a position to undertake an air strike on the missiles and missile sites by Monday or Tuesday.

General Taylor summarized the military actions already under way, including the quiet reinforcement of Guantánamo by infiltrating Marines and the positioning of ships to take out United States dependents from Guantánamo on extremely short notice.

The Attorney General said we could implement a blockade very quickly and prepare for an air strike to be launched later if we so decided.

The President said he was prepared to authorize the military to take those preparatory actions which they would have to take in anticipation of the military invasion of Cuba. He suggested that we inform the Turks and the Italians that they should not fire the strategic missiles they have even if attacked. The warheads for missiles in Turkey and Italy could be dismantled. He agreed that we should move to institute a blockade as quickly as we possibly can.

In response to a question about further photographic surveillance of Cuba, Secretary McNamara recommended, and the President agreed, that no low-level photographic reconnaissance should be undertaken now because we have decided to institute a blockade. Secretary Rusk recommended that a blockade not be instituted before Monday in order to provide time required to consult our allies.

Mr Bundy said the pressure from the press was becoming intense and suggested that one way of dealing with it was to announce shortly that we had obtained photographic evidence of the existence of strategic missiles in Cuba. This announcement would hold the press until the President made his television speech.

The President acknowledged that the domestic political heat following his television appearance would be terrific. He said he had opposed an invasion of Cuba but that now we were confronted with the possibility that by December there would be 50 strategic missiles deployed there. In explanation as to why we have not acted sooner to deal with the threat from Cuba, he pointed out that only now do we have the kind of evidence which we can make available to our allies in order to convince them of the necessity of acting. Only now do we have a way of avoiding a split with our allies.

It is possible that we may have to make an early strike with or without warning next week. He stressed again the difference between the conventional military build-up in Cuba and the psychological impact throughout the world of the Russian deployment of strategic missiles to Cuba. General Taylor repeated his recommendation that any air strike in Cuba included attacks on the MiGs and medium bombers.

The President repeated his view that our world position would be much better if we attack only the missiles. He directed that air strike plans should include only missiles and missile sites, and that preparations to be ready three days from now.

Under Secretary Ball expressed his view that a blockade should include all shipments of POL to Cuba. Secretary Rusk thought that POL should not now be included because such a decision would break down the distinction which we want to make between elimination of strategic missiles and the downfall of the Castro Government. Secretary Rusk repeated his view that our objective is to destroy the offensive capability of the missiles in Cuba, not, at this time, seeking to overthrow Castro!

The President acknowledged that the issue was whether POL should be included from the beginning or added at a later time. He preferred to delay possibly as long as a week.

Secretary Rusk called attention to the problem involved in referring to our action as a blockade. He preferred the use of the word "quarantine."

Parenthetically, the President asked Secretary Rusk to reconsider present policy of refusing to give nuclear weapons assistance to France. He expressed the view that in light of present circumstances a refusal to help the French was not worthwhile. He thought that in the days ahead we might be able to gain the needed support of France if we stopped refusing to help them with their nuclear weapons project.

There followed a discussion of several sentences in the "blockade route" draft of the President's speech. It was agreed that the President should define our objective in terms of halting "offensive missile preparations in Cuba." Reference to economic pressures on Cuba would not be made in this context.

The President made clear that in the United Nations we should emphasize the subterranean nature of the missile build-up in Cuba. Only if we were asked would we respond that we were prepared to talk about the withdrawal of missiles from Italy and Turkey. In such an eventuality, the President pointed out that we would have to make clear to the Italians and the Turks that withdrawing strategic missiles was not a retreat and that we would be prepared to replace these missiles by providing a more effective deterrent, such as the assignment of Polaris submarines. The President asked Mr Nitze to study the problems arising out of the withdrawal of missiles from Italy and Turkey, with particular reference to complications which would arise in NATO.

The President made clear that our emphasis should be on the missile threat from Cuba.

Ambassador Stevenson reiterated his belief that we must be more forthcoming about giving up our missile bases in Turkey and Italy. He stated again his belief that the present situation required that we offer to give up such bases in order to induce the Russians to remove the strategic missiles from Cuba.

Mr Nitze flatly opposed making any such offer, but said he would not object to discussing this question in the event that negotiations developed from our institution of a blockade.

The President concluded the meeting by stating that we should be ready to meet criticism of our deployment of missiles abroad but we should not initiate negotiations with a base withdrawal proposal.

Memorandum for the files
Washington, October 20, 1962

Following the White House meeting with the President on the afternoon of October 20th, I spoke privately to the Attorney General. The Attorney General was to meet alone with the President, presumably to discuss policy matters.

I told the AG I was very worried about some of the wording in the second draft of the speech of the President as prepared by Sorensen and I was most particularly worried about the approach of Ambassador Stevenson. I reasoned, as I had repeatedly in meetings over the last three or four days, that we must not lose sight of the very important objectives of removing the Castro Communist Government from Cuba and establishing a climate which would permit the Cuban people to establish a Government of their own choice. In my talk with the AG I pointed out that Stevenson's proposal would not only cause the removal of the Guantánamo Base, which was most undesirable, but it would also place a crown of jewels on the head of Castro and we nor anyone else could do much about it after such a position had been established publicly.

About 9 o'clock in the evening (time uncertain) the AG called me at my home and said he had discussed my views with the President who concurred and he felt I could rest assured that the situation that worried me would not develop further. I then mentioned to the AG that numbered paragraph 2 of the speech did not give the President latitude for military action which may be necessary without suffering the indictment of committing a "surprise attack" and that I had suggested some different wording to Sorensen.

The AG then asked I call the President to arrange for a briefing of General Eisenhower.

I immediately talked with the President by telephone and arranged to see Eisenhower on Sunday morning and possibly take him to the White House for a direct meeting with the President. Details to be worked out upon Eisenhower's arrival.

I then expressed my concern at the wording of paragraph 2 of the speech. The President concurred; said he had made up his mind to pursue the course which I had recommended and he agreed with the views I expressed in the afternoon meeting. He said that he would be careful to preserve the widest possible latitude for subsequent military action at any time after the commencement of the blockade.

I then mentioned the Castro problem to the President. He seemed alert to the situation.

JOHN A. MCCONE
Director

OCTOBER 21, 1962

Notes on meeting with President Kennedy
Washington, October 21, 1962

TOP SECRET

1. The meeting was held in the Oval Room of the White House and lasted from 11:30 am to approximately 12:30 pm. In attendance were the Attorney General, General Taylor, General Sweeney and the Secretary of Defense.

2. The Secretary of Defense stated that following the start of an air attack, the initial units of the landing force could invade Cuba within seven days. The movement of troops

in preparation for such an invasion will start at the time of the President's speech. No mobilization of Reserve forces is required for such an invasion until the start of the air strike. General LeMay had stated that the transport aircraft, from Reserve and Guard units, which would be required for participation in such an invasion, can be fully operational within 24 to 48 hours after the call to active duty.

3. The Secretary of Defense reported that, based on information which became available during the night, it now appears that there is equipment in Cuba for approximately 40 MRBM or IRBM launchers. (Mr McCone, who joined the group 15 or 20 minutes after the start of the discussion, confirmed this report.) The location of the sites for 36 of these launchers is known. Thirty-two of the 36 known sites appear to have sufficient equipment on them to be included in any air strike directed against Cuba's missile capability.

4. We believe that 40 launchers would normally be equipped with 80 missiles. John McCone reported yesterday that a Soviet ship believed to be the vessel in which the Soviets have been sending missiles to Cuba has made a sufficient number of trips to that island within recent weeks to offload approximately 48 missiles. Therefore, we assume there are approximately that number on the Island today, although we have only located approximately 30 of these.

5. General Sweeney outlined the following plan of air attack, the object of which would be the destruction of the known Cuban missile capability.

(a) The five surface-to-air missile installations in the vicinity of the known missile sites would each be attacked by approximately eight aircraft; the three MiG airfields defending the missile sites would be

covered by 12 US aircraft per field. In total, the
defense suppression operations, including the necessary replacement aircraft, would require
approximately 100 sorties.

(b) Each of the launchers at the eight or nine known
sites (a total of approximately 32 to 36 launchers)
would be attacked by six aircraft. For the purpose, a
total of approximately 250 sorties would be flown.

(c) The US aircraft covering the three MiG airfields
would attack the MiGs if they became airborne.
General Sweeney strongly recommended attacks on
each of the airfields to destroy the MiG aircraft.

6. General Sweeney stated that he was certain the air
strike would be "successful"; however, even under opti-
mum conditions, it was not likely that all of the known
missiles would be destroyed. (As noted in 4 above, the
known missiles are probably no more than 60% of
the total missiles on the island.) General Taylor stated:
"The best we can offer you is to destroy 90% of the
known missiles." General Taylor, General Sweeney and
the Secretary of Defense all strongly emphasized that in
their opinion the initial air strike must be followed by
strikes on subsequent days and that these in turn would
lead inevitably to an invasion.

7. CIA representatives, who joined the discussion at this
point, stated that it is probable the missiles which are operational (it is estimated there are now between eight and 12
operational missiles on the island) can hold indefinitely a
capability for firing with from 2½ to 4 hours' notice.
Included in the notice period is a countdown requiring 20
to 40 minutes. In relation to the countdown period, the
first wave of our attacking aircraft would give 10 minutes
of warning; the second wave, 40 minutes of warning; and
the third wave a proportionately greater warning.

8. As noted above, General Sweeney strongly recommended that any air strike include attacks on the MiG aircraft and, in addition, the IL-28s. To accomplish the destruction of these aircraft, the total number of sorties of such an air strike should be increased to 500. The President agreed that if an air strike is ordered, it should probably include in its objective the destruction of the MiG aircraft and the IL-28s.

9. The President directed that we be prepared to carry out the air strike Monday morning or any time thereafter during the remainder of the week. The President recognized that the Secretary of Defense was opposed to the air strike Monday morning, and that General Sweeney favored it. He asked the Attorney General and Mr McCone for their opinions.

(a) The Attorney General stated he was opposed to such a strike because:
    (1) "It would be a Pearl Harbor type of attack."
    (2) It would lead to unpredictable military responses by the Soviet Union which could be so serious as to lead to general nuclear war. He stated we should start with the initiation of the blockade and thereafter "play for the breaks."
(b) Mr McCone agreed with the Attorney General, but emphasized he believed we should be prepared for an air strike and thereafter an invasion.

R. S. McNamara

Minutes of the 506th meeting of the National Security Council Washington, October 21, 1962, 2:30–4:50 p.m.

PARTICIPANTS: The President, Attorney General Robert F. Kennedy; *CIA* John A. McCone, Director, Mr Ray Cline, Mr Whelan, Mr Arthur Lundahl; *Defense* Robert S.

McNamara, Secretary, Roswell Gilpatric, Deputy Secretary, Paul Nitze, Assistant Secretary (ISA); *JCS* General Maxwell D. Taylor; Admiral George W. Anderson, Jr, USN, Chief of Naval Operations; *OEP* Edward A. McDermott, Director; *State* Dean Rusk, Secretary, George Ball, Under Secretary, U. Alexis Johnson, Deputy Under Secretary for Political Affairs, Adlai Stevenson, US Ambassador to the UN, Edwin Martin, Assistant Secretary, Inter-American Affairs, Llewellyn E. Thompson, Ambassador-at-Large; *Treasury* Douglas Dillon, Secretary; *USIA* Donald Wilson, Acting Director; *White House* McGeorge Bundy, Special Assistant to the President for National Security Affairs, Theodore Sorensen, Special Counsel, Bromley Smith, Executive Secretary, National Security Council; *Others:* Mr Robert Lovett

Introduction
Intelligence officers summarized new information which had become available since yesterday's meeting. The Council members read the third draft of the President's speech. There was some discussion of the date when positive information as to the existence of strategic missiles in Cuba became available. The draft was revised to state that such information became available Tuesday morning, October 16th.

The draft speech summarized the number of missiles and the number of sites known to exist in Cuba. Secretary McNamara recommended, and the President agreed, that specific numbers of missiles and sites be deleted.

The question was raised as to whether the speech should emphasize Soviet responsibility for the missile deployment or Castro's irresponsibility in accepting them. Secretary Rusk argued that we must hold the USSR responsible because it is important to emphasize the extra-hemispheric aspect of the missile deployment in order to increase support for our contemplated actions.

The President referred to the sentence mentioning the deployment of missiles by the Soviet Union and called attention to our deployment of missiles to Italy. Secretary Rusk pointed out that our missiles were deployed to NATO countries only after those countries were threatened by deployed Soviet missiles. Hence, our deployment was part of the confrontation of Soviet power, and, therefore, unrelated to the Cuban deployment by the USSR.

The President pointed out that Soviet missiles were in place, aimed at European countries, before we deployed United States missiles to Europe.

Secretary Dillon recalled that we sent United States missiles to Europe because we had so many of them we did not know where to put them.

The President referred to the sentence in the draft speech which states that the USSR secretly transferred weapons to Cuba. He said we should emphasize the clandestine manner in which the USSR had acted in Cuba.

The Attorney General wanted to be certain that the text as drafted did not preclude us from giving nuclear weapons to Western Germany, West Berlin, and France in the event we decided to do so.

It was agreed that no message would be sent to President Dorticos of Cuba at the present time and the draft speech was so revised.

The question of whether our actions should be described as a blockade or a quarantine was debated. Although the legal meaning of the two words is identical, Secretary Rusk said he preferred "quarantine" for political reasons in that it avoids comparison with the Berlin blockade. The President agreed to use "quarantine" and pointed out that if we so desired we could later institute a total blockade.

Both Secretary Dillon and Director McCone urged that the speech state that we were seeking to prevent all military equipment from reaching Cuba. They argued that later we might act to prevent all equipment from reaching Cuba even though at present our objective was to block offensive missile equipment.

The President preferred the phrase "offensive missile equipment" on the grounds that within 48 hours we will know the Soviet reaction. At such time we will know whether, as is expected, the Soviets turn back their ships rather than submit to inspection. Secretary McNamara agreed we should proceed in two stages. Initially our objective is to block offensive weapons and later we can extend our blockade to all weapons, if we so decide.

The President parenthetically pointed out that we were not taking action under the Monroe Doctrine.

General Taylor returned to a sentence in the earlier part of the draft and asked whether we were firm on the phrase "whatever steps are necessary." The President agreed that these words should remain so that he would not be hindered from taking additional measures if we so decide at a later date.

(The President asked Under Secretary Ball to obtain assurances that Dakar would not be used by the Soviets for air shipments to Cuba.)

Secretary Rusk commented that our objective was to "put out the fire" in Cuba and get United Nations teams to inspect all missile activity in Cuba. The President felt that a better tactic was for us initially to frighten the United Nations representatives with the prospect of all kinds of actions and then, when a resolution calling for the withdrawal of missiles from Cuba, Turkey and Italy was proposed, we could consider supporting such a resolution.

Ambassador Stevenson said we should take the initiative by calling a UN Security Council meeting to demand an immediate missile standstill in Cuba. Secretary Rusk pointed out that following the President's speech we would either be in the posture of a complainant or of a defendant.

Mr Sorensen said our posture should be to accuse the Soviets of being the aggressors and seek to persuade others to agree with us. He foresaw that some nations in the United Nations would immediately try to label us as the aggressors because of the actions which we had taken.

Secretary Rusk raised the question of whether we should move first in the United Nations or first in the OAS. He said our United Nations action should be aimed at removing the missile threat while our objective on the OAS would be to persuade other Latin American countries to act with us under the Rio Treaty.

In response to the President's question, Assistant Secretary Martin said that if there were a United Nations action before the OAS acted, the usefulness of the OAS would be seriously affected. Secretary Rusk felt we should act first in the OAS, then in the United Nations where our action program could be more flexible.

The President agreed that a reference in the draft speech to a Caribbean security force should be dropped.

The President said we should pin the responsibility for the developments in Cuba directly on Khrushchev. In response to the President's question, Ambassador Thompson agreed—naming Khrushchev would make it harder for him to reverse his actions in Cuba, but such reference to him would be more effective in producing favorable actions.

The President asked that the phrases describing the horrors of war should be deleted.

Ambassador Thompson urged, and the President agreed, that we should use the part of the TASS statement on Cuba which flatly states that the Russians have all the weapons they need and require no more for their defense. Therefore, the only reason for Soviet deployment of weapons to Cuba is the aim of dominating the Western Hemisphere.

The President agreed that the invitation to a summit meeting should be deleted.

Ambassador Stevenson repeated that he favored an early conference with the Russians on terms acceptable to us, to be held in an atmosphere free of threat. The President responded that he did not want to appear to be seeking a summit meeting as a result of Khrushchev's actions. Ambassador Thompson agreed. The President added that we should not look toward holding a meeting until it is clear to us what Khrushchev really thinks he will obtain worldwide as a result of his actions in Cuba.

Secretary Rusk said our first objective was to get a fully inspected missile standstill in Cuba before we sit down to talk with the Russians. Mr McCone was concerned that if we let it be known that we are prepared to talk to the Russians now, it would appear to outsiders that our only response to Khrushchev's challenge was to negotiate.

The Attorney General said that in his view we should anticipate a Soviet reaction involving a movement in Berlin. Secretary Dillon felt that the Soviet reaction in Berlin would be governed by the actions we would take in response to the Russian missile deployment in Cuba.

Following a discussion of ways in which we could reach the Cuban people through television despite Cuban jamming efforts, the President told Mr Wilson that we should go ahead with the television project involving the relay of signals via instruments aboard a ship at sea for use anywhere.

The Attorney General felt that the paragraphs in the President's draft speech addressed to the Cuban people were not personal enough. The President asked that these paragraphs be rewritten.

Following discussion of the pressure by the press for information, the President decided that no information on the missile deployment would be given out today.

In response to a Presidential question, General Taylor said an invasion of Cuba could be carried out seven days after the decision to invade had been taken. Secretary McNamara said the President had asked a question which was difficult to answer precisely. Present plans called for invasion to follow seven days after an initial air strike. The timing could be reduced, depending upon whether certain decisions were taken now. Some actions which were irreversible would have to be taken now in order to reduce the time when forces could be landed. He promised the President a breakdown of the decisions which he would have to take immediately in order to reduce the seven-day period.

The President said that in three or four days we might have to decide to act in order that we would not have to wait so long prior to the landing of our forces. As he understood the situation, a decision taken today would mean that an air strike could not be undertaken before seven days, and then seven days later the first forces could be ashore.

General Taylor explained that air action would be necessary to bring the situation under control prior to the dropping of paratroopers. He added that 90,000 men could be landed within an 11-day period.

Secretary McNamara said that planning was being done under two assumptions. The first called for an air strike, and seven days later, landings would begin. Twenty-five thousand men would be put ashore the first day, and on the eighteenth day, 90,000 would be ashore. The second plan provided for the landing of 90,000 men in a 23-day period. The President told General Taylor that he wanted to do those things which would reduce the length of time between a decision to invade and the landing of the first troops.

The President said he believed that as soon as he had finished his speech, the Russians would: (a) hasten the construction and the development of their missile capability in Cuba, (b) announce that if we attack Cuba, Soviet rockets will fly, and (c) possibly make a move to squeeze us out of Berlin.

Secretary Dillon said that in his view a blockade would either inevitably lead to an invasion of Cuba or would result in negotiations, which he believes the Soviets would want very much. To agree to negotiations now would be a disaster for us. We would break up our alliances and convey to the world that we were impotent in the face of a Soviet challenge. Unless the Russians stop their missile build-up at once, we will have to invade Cuba in the next week, no matter what they say, if we are to save our world position. We cannot convey firm intentions to the Russians otherwise and we must not look to the world as if we were backing down.

Secretary McNamara expressed his doubt that an air strike would be necessary within the next week.

Admiral Anderson described, in response to the President's question, the way the blockade would be instituted. He added that the Navy did not need to call up Reserves now to meet the immediate situation. He said that 40 Navy ships were already in position. The Navy knew the positions of 27 to 30 ships en route to Cuba. Eighteen ships were in Cuban ports, and 15 were on their way home.

Admiral Anderson described the method to be used in the first interception of a Soviet ship. It was hoped that a cruiser rather than a destroyer would make this interception. It would follow accepted international rules. He favored a 24-hour grace period, beginning with the President's speech, during which the Russians could communicate with their ships, giving them instructions as to what to do in the event they were stopped by United States ships.

Secretary McNamara said he would recommend to the President later today which kinds of reserve forces should be called up. He felt that air reserves would be necessary if it were decided to make an air strike, but probably would not be needed if our action was limited to a blockade.

Admiral Anderson said we had a capability to protect United States ships in the Caribbean. If the KOMAR ships took any hostile action, they could be destroyed, thereby creating a new situation. If a MiG plane takes hostile action, he would like to be in a position to shoot it down, thereby creating again a new situation. He estimated that the Soviets could not get naval surface ships to the area in less than 10 days and Soviet submarines could not get to the area in less than 10 to 14 days.

In response to a question, Admiral Anderson said that if the Navy received information that a Soviet submarine was en route to Havana, he would ask higher authority for permission to attack it.

Secretary McNamara said he favored rules of engagement which would permit responses to hostile actions, including attacks to destroy the source of the hostile action.

The President answered a question as to whether we were to stop all ships, including allied ships by saying that he favored stopping all ships in the expectation that allied ships would soon become discouraged and drop out of the Cuban trade.

Diplomatic measures
Under Secretary Ball summarized a scenario providing for consultation with our allies. He said Dean Acheson would brief de Gaulle and the NATO Council, Ambassador Dowling would brief Adenauer, and Ambassador Bruce would brief Macmillan. Present at such briefings would be

technical experts from CIA who could answer questions concerning the photographic intelligence which reveals the missile sites.

The President said we must assume that Khrushchev knows that we know of his missile deployments, and, therefore, he will be ready with a planned response. He asked that the draft speech emphasize his belief that the greatest danger to the United States in the present situation is doing nothing but acknowledging that in days to come we would be seriously threatened.

Ambassador Stevenson read from a list of problems which he foresaw in the United Nations. Secretary Rusk said we must decide on tactics for the Security Council meeting. He repeated his view that the aim of all our actions is to get a standstill of the missile development in Cuba to be inspected by United Nations observers and then be prepared to negotiate other issues.

The President asked Assistant Secretary of Defense Nitze to study the problem of withdrawing United States missiles from Turkey and Italy. Mr Nitze said such a withdrawal was complicated because we must avoid giving the Europeans the impression that we are prepared to take nuclear weapons of all kinds out of Europe.

Secretary McNamara stated his firm view that the United States could not lift its blockade as long as the Soviet weapons remained in Cuba.

The President asked why we could not start with a demand for the removal or the withdrawal of the missiles and if at a later time we wanted to negotiate for a less favorable settlement, we could then decide to do so. The Attorney General said we should take the offensive in our presentation to the United Nations. Our attitude should not be defensive, especially in view of the fact that Soviet leaders had lied to us about the deployment of strategic missiles to Cuba.

The President interjected a directive that we reverse our policy on nuclear assistance to France in the light of the present situation.

Ambassador Stevenson repeated his view that the United States would be forced into a summit meeting and preferred to propose such a meeting.

The President disagreed, saying that we could not accept a neutral Cuba and the withdrawal from Guantánamo without indicating to Khrushchev that we were in a state of panic. An offer to accept Castro and give up Guantánamo must not be made because it would appear to be completely defensive. He said we should be clear that we would accept nothing less than the ending of the missile capability now in Cuba, no reinforcement of that capability, and no further construction of missile sites.

Secretary McNamara stated his view that in order to achieve such a result we would have to invade Cuba.

The President said what he was talking about was the dismantlement of missiles now in Cuba.

Ambassador Stevenson thought that we should institute a blockade, and when the Russians rejected our demand for a missile standstill in Cuba, we should defer any air strike until after we had talked to Khrushchev.

There followed a discussion as to whether we wanted to rely primarily on the United Nations or primarily on the OAS. Assistant Secretary of State Martin indicated that if we did not use the OAS in preference to the United Nations, we would jeopardize the entire hemispheric alliance. Under Secretary Ball agreed that we should put primary emphasis on the OAS and he preferred that any inspectors going to Cuba should be OAS inspectors rather than United Nations inspectors.

The President indicated a need for further discussion of this matter and suggested that Secretary Rusk speak to him later about it.

As the meeting concluded, the President asked that the word "miscalculate" be taken out of the draft letter prepared for him to send to Khrushchev. He recalled that in Vienna Khrushchev had revealed a misunderstanding of this word when translated into Russian. He also requested that reference to a meeting with Khrushchev be deleted from the draft letter.

OCTOBER 22, 1962

*Telegram from the Department of State to the Embassy in the
United Kingdom*
Washington, October 22, 1962, 12:17 a.m.

Elite eyes only for the Ambassador. Following is text of letter to Prime Minister Macmillan to be delivered at 10:00
a.m. Monday London time:

> My dear friend: We are now in possession of
> incontrovertible military evidence obtained through
> photographic reconnaissances, that the Soviets have already

installed offensive nuclear missiles in Cuba, and that some of these may already be operational. This constitutes a threat to the peace which imperils the security not only of this hemisphere but of the entire free world. You will recall that last month I stated publicly that the Government of the United States would consider the presence of ground-to-ground missiles in Cuba as an offensive threat. In response to my remarks, the Soviets stated that such armaments and military equipment as had been shipped by them to Cuba were exclusively of a defensive nature, and this was repeated to me only last Thursday by Gromyko under instructions.

The foregoing has created a highly critical situation which must be met promptly and fearlessly. This evening at 19:00 hours Washington time I shall be making a public statement of which Ambassador Bruce will be giving you a draft together with this message. This text is not necessarily final in every detail, but the essentials of the problem, and the means by which I intend to meet it, have already been decided as set forth in the present text. Ambassador Bruce will also be prepared fully to explain to you the evidence on which we have based our conclusions.

I am also writing to Chairman Khrushchev to bring home to him how perilous is his present course of action, but expressing the hope that we can agree to resume the path of peaceful negotiation.

I am quite clear in my mind that these missiles have got to be withdrawn, and you will see that I intend to state this publicly in my speech as well as telling Chairman Khrushchev this in my letter to him.

The object of the quarantine, which will be put into effect immediately, is to prevent the Soviet Union from introducing additional missiles into Cuba and to lead to the elimination of the missiles that are already in place.

I shall also be sending a personal message to Prime Minister Diefenbaker, General de Gaulle, Chairman

Adenauer, and Prime Minister Fanfani and have sent Dean
Acheson to Paris [to] assist Ambassador Finletter in
briefing the North Atlantic Council shortly before I make
my public statement. However, I wanted you to be the first
to be informed of this grave development, in order that we
should have the opportunity, should you wish it, to discuss
the situation between ourselves by means of our private
channel of communication.

This is a solemn moment for our two countries, indeed
for the fate of the entire world. It is essential that the
already great dangers before us should not be increased
through miscalculation or underestimation by the Soviets
of what we intend to do, and are prepared to endure, in
the face of the course on which they have so recklessly
embarked.

I need not point out to you the possible relation of this
secret and dangerous move on the part of Khrushchev to
Berlin. We must together be prepared for a time of testing.
It is a source of great personal satisfaction to me that you
and I can keep in close touch with each other by rapid
and secure means at a time like this, and I intend to keep
you fully informed of my thinking as the situation evolves.

In the meanwhile I am also requesting an urgent
meeting of the United Nations Security Council. I have
asked Ambassador Stevenson to present on behalf of the
United States a resolution calling for the withdrawal of
missile bases and other offensive weapons in Cuba under
the supervision of United Nations observers. This would
make it possible for the United States to lift its quarantine.
I hope that you will instruct your representative in New
York to work actively with us and speak forthrightly in
support of the above program in the United Nations.

RUSK

Minutes of the 507th meeting of the National Security Council
Washington, October 22, 1962, 3:00 p.m.

The President opened the meeting by asking Secretary Rusk to read the attached message from Prime Minister Macmillan which had just been received.*

Secretary Rusk observed that for a first reaction to information of our proposed blockade it was not bad. He added that it was comforting to learn that the British Prime Minister had not thought of anything we hadn't thought of.

The President commented that the Prime Minister's message contained the best argument for taking no action. What we now need are strong arguments to explain why we have to act as we are acting.

Secretary Rusk stated that the best legal basis for our blockade action was the Rio Treaty. The use of force would be justified on the ground of support for the principles of the United Nations Charter, not on the basis of Article 51, which might give the Russians a basis for attacking Turkey.

The Attorney General said that in his opinion our blockade action would be illegal if it were not supported by the OAS. In his view the greatest importance is attached to our obtaining the necessary 14 favorable votes in the OAS. Secretary Rusk commented that if we do not win the support of the OAS, we are not necessarily acting illegally. He referred to the new situation created by modern weapons and he thought that rules of international law should not be taken as applying literally to a completely new situation. He said we need not abandon hope so early.

---

*Not included. It expressed sympathy and support for the US position but worried about how the USSR might respond.

Mr Salinger reported that Gromyko had departed from New York without making other than a usual departure statement containing nothing about Cuba.

Secretary Rusk said the Department had decided to hold off calling a Security Council meeting despite the possibility that the Russians might ask for one first. The basis of this decision was that we would have to name Cuba in the documents requesting the Security Council meeting and this we did not wish to do.

Director McCone summarized the latest intelligence information and read from the attached document. He added that we have a report of a fleet of Soviet submarines which are in a position to reach Cuba in about a week. He also mentioned that the London *Evening Standard* had printed a great deal of information about the existence of Soviet strategic missiles in Cuba. In response to a suggestion by Mr Bundy, the President outlined the manner in which he expected Council members to deal with the domestic aspects of the current situation. He said everyone should sing one song in order to make clear that there was now no difference among his advisers as to the proper course to follow. He pointed out the importance of fully supporting the course of action chosen which, in his view, represented a reasonable consensus. Any course is extremely troublesome and, as in the case of the Berlin wall, we are once again confronted with a difficult choice. If we undertake a tricky and unsatisfactory course, we do not even have the satisfaction of knowing what would have happened if we had acted differently. He mentioned that former Presidents, Eisenhower, Truman and Hoover, had supported his decision during telephone conversations with each of them earlier in the day.

The President then summarized the arguments as to why we must act. We must reply to those whose reaction to the blockade would be to ask what had changed in view of the fact that we had been living in the past years under a threat of a missile nuclear attack by the USSR.

(a) In September we had said we would react if certain actions were taken in Cuba. We have to carry out commitments which we had made publicly at that time.

(b) The secret deployment by the Russians of strategic missiles to Cuba was such a complete change in their previous policy of not deploying such missiles outside the USSR that if we took no action in this case, we would convey to the Russians an impression that we would never act, no matter what they did anywhere.

(c) Gromyko had left the impression that the Soviets were going to act in Berlin in the next few months. Therefore, if they acted now in response to our blockade action, we would only have brought on their Berlin squeeze earlier than expected.

(d) The effect in Latin America would be very harmful to our interests if, by our failure to act, we gave the Latinos the impression that the Soviets were increasing their world position while ours was decreasing.

Two questions were raised which the President hoped would be discussed and settled the following day:

(a) What is our response if one of our U-2 planes is shot down by a SAM missile?

(b) If the missile development in Cuba continues, what is our next course of action?

The President concluded by acknowledging the difficulties which he was asking the military to accept because of the necessity of our taking action which warned Cuba of the possibility of an invasion.

Secretary Rusk commented that if anyone thought our response was weak, they were wrong because he believed that a "flaming crisis" was immediately ahead of us.

The President read from a list of questions and suggested answers which might be made public. The first question was why we had not acted earlier. The response is that we needed more evidence of the existence of Soviet strategic missiles in Cuba. This additional evidence was required in order to gain the necessary 14 votes in the OAS. In addition, if we had acted earlier, we might have jeopardized our position in Berlin because our European Allies would have concluded that our preoccupation with Cuba was such as to reveal our lack of interest in Berlin, thus tempting the Russians to act in Berlin. Earlier action would undoubtedly have forced us to declare war on Cuba and this action, without the evidence we now have, would have thrown Latin American support to Castro.

There followed a discussion of why evidence of Soviet missiles was lacking. Information about the strategic missile sites was reported by the refugees but these reports could not be substantiated from aerial photography. Aerial photographs taken on August 29 revealed no missile sites. It was not until October 14 that photographic evidence of the sites and missiles was available. The cloud cover prevented photography for a period of time and the possibility of an attack on an overflying American plane led to a restriction on the number of U-2 flights. Mr McCone felt that the information given to Senator Keating about the missile sites had come from refugee sources, which he had accepted without further substantiation. The Attorney General pointed out that even if there had been U-2 flights, construction at the missile sites was not far enough along to have been detected by photography much earlier than October 14. It was pointed out that all Soviet experts agreed that Khrushchev would not send strategic missiles to Cuba. Therefore, there was a tendency to downgrade the refugee reports.

Commenting on what should be said publicly about our actions in Cuba, Secretary Rusk cautioned that we should say nothing now which might tie our hands later in the event we wanted to take additional actions.

The President referred again to the question of distinguishing between Soviet missiles in Cuba and United States missiles in Turkey and Italy. Secretary Rusk read extracts from the NATO communiqué of 1959. The President thought that it was most important that everyone be fully briefed as to why these situations with respect to the deployment of missiles do not match. He again called attention to the secret deployment of the weapons and the TASS statement saying that the Russians had no need to position strategic missiles in foreign countries. Soviet missiles in Cuba have a quite different psychological effect than Soviet missiles positioned in the USSR in that the Soviet action in Cuba may in fact be a probing action to find out what we would be prepared to do in Berlin.

Secretary Rusk added that the threat to the United States from Soviet missiles in Cuba was of worldwide importance because this threat was to a country which in effect provided the sole defense of some 40 Free World States.

The President suggested that we should make clear the difference between our Cuban blockade and the Berlin blockade by emphasizing that we were not preventing shipments of food and medicine to Cuba, but only preventing the delivery of offensive military equipment.

General Taylor asked how we should reply to the question: Are we preparing to invade? The President responded by saying that we should ask the press not to push this line of questioning and to accept our statement that we are taking all precautionary moves in anticipation of any contingency. Secretary McNamara agreed that we should say that the Defense Department had been ordered to be prepared for any contingency and that we were not now ready to say anything more than was in the President's speech.

In response to a Presidential question, Secretary McNamara said that an information group was working on the problem of voluntary press censorship based on experience during the Korean War.

[*one paragraph (four lines of source text) not declassified*]

Secretary McNamara reported that the Defense Department was working on how we would prevent the introduction into Cuba of nuclear weapons by airplanes. He said some planes could fly non-stop from the Soviet Union if refueled en route. Present arrangements provided that we would be informed of any plane flying to Cuba and we would then decide what action to take against it.

It was agreed that no Reserves would be called today, but that a review would be made tonight as to the necessity of such action.

Acting Secretary Fowler raised several questions involving domestic controls, including gold transfers, foreign exchange controls, and control of the stock market. He said, in response to the President's question, that another look would be taken the following day before any recommendation would be made as to closing the stock market.

Secretary Rusk said that if we were asked whether our blockade was an act of war, we should say that it was not. The President asked whether friendly ships would be halted and Admiral Anderson replied in the affirmative, saying that we would challenge all ships. The President agreed that we should stop all Soviet Bloc and non-Bloc ships when the order to institute the blockade was given.

Portion of the NSC meeting minutes, Monday, October 22, 1962

The President discussed the reasons why he had decided against an air strike now. First, there was no certainty that an air strike would destroy all missiles now in Cuba. We would be able to get a large percentage of these missiles, but could not get them all.

In addition we would not know if any of these missiles were operationally ready with their nuclear warheads and we were not certain that our intelligence had discovered all the missiles in Cuba. Therefore, in attacking the ones we had located, we could not be certain that others unknown to us would not be launched against the United States. The President said an air strike would involve an action comparable to the Japanese attack on Pearl Harbor. Finally, an air strike would increase the danger of a worldwide nuclear war.

The President said he had given up the thought of making an air strike only yesterday morning. In summary, he said an air strike had all the disadvantages of Pearl Harbor. It would not insure the destruction of every strategic missile in Cuba, and would end up eventually in our having to invade.

Mr Bundy added that we should not discuss the fact that we were not able to destroy all the missiles by means of an air strike because at some later time we might wish to make such an attack.

National Security Action Memorandum 196
Washington, October 22, 1962

To: Vice President, Secretary of State, Secretary of Defense, Secretary of the Treasury, Attorney General, Chairman, Joint Chiefs of Staff, Director of Central Intelligence

Establishment of an Executive Committee of the National Security Council

I hereby establish, for the purpose of effective conduct of the operations of the Executive Branch in the current crisis, an Executive Committee of the National Security Council. This committee will meet, until further notice, daily at 10:00 a.m. in the Cabinet Room. I shall act as Chairman of this committee, and its additional regular members will be as follows: the Vice President, the Secretary of State, the Secretary of Defense, the Secretary of the Treasury, the Attorney General, the Director of Central Intelligence, the Under Secretary of State, the Deputy Secretary of Defense, the Chairman of the Joint Chiefs of Staff, the Ambassador-at-Large, the Special Counsel, and the Special Assistant to the President for National Security Affairs.

The first meeting of this committee will be held at the regular hour on Tuesday, October 23rd, at which point further arrangements with respect to its management and operation will be decided.

JOHN KENNEDY

Memorandum for the file
Washington, October 24, 1962

Leadership meeting on October 22nd at 5:00 p.m.

ATTENDED BY: The Leadership [Democrat and Republican members of Congress and Senate], except for Senator Hayden; The President, Rusk, McNamara, McCone and Ambassador Thompson

McCone read a summary of the situation. This had been discussed with the President, Attorney General and Bundy and had been modified to conform to their views.

There were a few questions of a substantive nature, Hickenlooper asked when missiles would be in operational status. McCone replied with the existing figures as reported in the morning report. Hickenlooper then asked if the Cuban situation is tied in to the China/India confrontation. McCone replied that we have no information one way or the other. Thompson then indicated it was more probable that Cuba may force a showdown on Berlin.

Secretary Rusk then reviewed his current appraisal of the Soviet Union indicating there had been some radical moves within the USSR which were indicating a tougher line. It appeared the hard-liners are coming in to ascendancy and the soft co-existent line seems to be disappearing. Peking seems somewhat more satisfied with Moscow now. Rusk stated that he did not wish to underestimate the gravity of the situation; the Soviets were taking a very serious risk, but this in his opinion represents the philosophy of the "hard-liners". Russell questioned the Secretary as to whether things will get better in the future, whether we will have a more propitious time to act than now, the thrust of his questioning being, "Why wait?" Rusk answered that he saw no opportunity for improvement.

The President then reviewed the chronology of the situation, starting on Tuesday, October 16th, when the first information was received from the photographic flight of October 14th. He stated that he immediately ordered extensive overflights; that McCone briefed President Eisenhower; that we must recognize that these missiles might be operational and therefore military action on our part might cause the firing of many of them with serious consequences to the United States; furthermore the actions taken, and further actions which might be required, might cause the Soviets to react in various areas, most particularly Berlin, which they could easily grab and if they do, our European Allies would lay the blame in our lap. The President concluded whatever we do involves a risk; however we must make careful calculations and take a chance. To do nothing would be a great mistake. The blockade of Cuba on the importation of offensive weapons was to be undertaken, all ships would be stopped and those containing offensive weapons would not be permitted to proceed. We have no idea how the Bloc will react but the indications are, from unconfirmed sources, they will attempt to run the blockade. Initially the blockade would not extend to petroleum. This might be a further step. We are taking all military preparations for either an air strike or an invasion. It was the President's considered judgment that if we have to resort to active military actions, then this would involve an invasion. Rusk then stated that our proposed action gave the other side a chance to pause. They may pull back or they may rapidly intensify the entire situation existing between the Soviet Union and the United States.

Senator Russell then demanded stronger steps, stated he did not think we needed time to pause. The President had warned them in September and no further warning was necessary. We must not take a gamble and must not temporize; Khrushchev has once again rattled his missiles; he can become firmer and firmer, and we must react. If we delay, if we give notification, if we telegraph our punches, the result will be a more difficult military action and more American lives will be sacrificed. The thrust of Senator Russell's remarks were to demand military action. He did not specifically say by surprise attack; however he did not advocate warning.

McNamara then described the blockade, indicating that this might lead to some form of military action; that there would be many alternative courses open to us. The President then reviewed in some detail the time required to assemble an invasion force which would involve 90,000 men in the actual landings and a total of about 250,000 men. He stated this could not be done in 24 or 36 hours but would take a number of days and that many preliminary steps had been taken.

Halleck recalled a recent briefing by Secretary McNamara in which he stated it would take three months to prepare adequately to invade Cuba. McNamara then reaffirmed the 250,000-man figure, with 90,000 of them actually involved in the landing force. He stated that he could be ready in seven days and that the landing would be preceded by a substantial air strike. Russell again questioned the delay. He also seriously criticized any policy which involved extensive airborne alerts of SAC in the interests of our state of readiness, pointing out that the consequences would be the serious attrition of our SAC forces, most particularly the B-47s, which are now quite old. McNamara stated that we could carry on an airborne alert indefinitely because preliminary plans had been made, repair parts, etc., secured and were in position.

Vinson then asked if the Joint Chiefs of Staff actually approved the plans for the invasion. McNamara answered, "Yes." The plans had been developed over a 10-month period and had been submitted to the President by the JCS on a number of occasions. Note: This question did not refer to whether the JCS did or did not approve the proposed actions of blockade against Cuba.

The President then reviewed matters again, read an intelligence note from a United Nations source which indicated Soviet intention to grab Berlin. Russell promptly replied that Berlin will always be a hostage. He then criticized the decision, stated we should go now and not wait.

Halleck questioned whether we were absolutely sure these weapons were offensive. The President answered affirmatively. McNamara then made a most unusual statement. He said: "One might question whether the missiles are or are not

offensive. However there is no question about the IL–28s."
Note: This was the first time anyone has raised doubt as to
whether the MRBMs and the IRBMs are offensive missiles.

Questions were then raised concerning the attitude of
our Allies. The President advised steps taken to inform our
major Allies. He then read the message received from the
Prime Minister which in effect agreed to support us in the
United Nations and then raised many warnings including
the dangers to Berlin, Turkey, Pakistan, Iran, etc., etc.

Senator Saltonstall brought up the question of the legality of the blockade. A great many Senators expressed
concern over the proposed action with the OAS, indicating that they felt the OAS would delay rather than act.
Saltonstall then asked whether a blockade would be legal
if the OAS did not support it. The President answered that
it probably would not; however we would proceed anyway.

Fulbright then stated that in his opinion the blockade was
the worst of the alternatives open to us, and it was a definite
affront to Russia and that the moment that we had to damage or sink a Soviet ship, because of their failure to recognize
or respect the blockade, we would be at war with Russia and
the war would be caused because of our own initiative. The
President disagreed with this thinking. Fulbright then
repeated his position and stated in his opinion it would be far
better to launch an attack and to take out the bases from
Cuba. McNamara stated that this would involve the spilling
of Russian blood since there were so many thousand
Russians manning these bases. Fulbright responded that this
made no difference because they were there in Cuba to help
on Cuban bases. These were not Soviet bases. There was no
mutual defense pact between the USSR and Cuba. Cuba was
not a member of the Warsaw Pact. Therefore he felt the
Soviets would not react if some Russians got killed in Cuba.
The Russians in the final analysis placed little value on
human life. The time has come for an invasion under the

President's statement of February 13th. Fulbright repeated that an act [attack] on Russian ships is an act of war against Russia and on the other hand, an attack or an invasion of Cuba was an act against Cuba, not Russia. Fulbright also expressed reservations concerning the possible OAS action.

The President took issue with Fulbright, stating that he felt that an attack on these bases, which we knew were manned by Soviet personnel, would involve large numbers of Soviet casualties and this would be more provocative than a confrontation with a Soviet ship.

Vinson urged that if we strike, we strike with maximum force and wind the matter up quickly as this would involve the minimum of American losses and insure the maximum support by the Cuban people at large who, he reasoned, would very quickly go over to the side of the winner. The meeting was concluded at 6:35 to permit the President to prepare for his 7 o'clock talk to the nation.

It was decided to hold a meeting on Wednesday, October 24th. During this meeting Senator Hickenlooper expressed himself as opposed to the action and in favor of direct military action. He stated that in his opinion ships which were accosted on the high sea and turned back would be a more humiliating blow to the Soviets and a more serious involvement to their pride than the losing of as many as 5,000 Soviet military personnel illegally and secretly stationed in Cuba.

JOHN A. McCONE

*President John F. Kennedy's speech announcing the
quarantine against Cuba
Washington, October 22, 1962*

Good evening my fellow citizens:
This Government, as promised, has maintained the closest surveillance of the Soviet military build-up on the island

of Cuba. Within the past week, unmistakable evidence has established the fact that a series of offensive missile sites is now in preparation on that imprisoned island. The purpose of these bases can be none other than to provide a nuclear strike capability against the Western Hemisphere.

Upon receiving the first preliminary hard information of this nature last Tuesday morning at 9:00 a.m., I directed that our surveillance be stepped up. And having now confirmed and completed our evaluation of the evidence and our decision on a course of action, this Government feels obliged to report this new crisis to you in fullest detail.

The characteristics of these new missile sites indicate two distinct types of installations. Several of them include medium-range ballistic missiles, capable of carrying a nuclear warhead for a distance of more than 1,000 nautical miles. Each of these missiles, in short, is capable of striking Washington, DC, the Panama Canal, Cape Canaveral, Mexico City, or any other city in the southeastern part of the United States, in Central America, or in the Caribbean area. Additional sites not yet completed appear to be designed for intermediate range ballistic missiles—capable of traveling more than twice as far—and thus capable of striking most of the major cities in the Western Hemisphere, ranging as far north as Hudson Bay, Canada, and as far south as Lima, Peru. In addition, jet bombers, capable of carrying nuclear weapons, are now being uncrated and assembled in Cuba, while the necessary air bases are being prepared.

This urgent transformation of Cuba into an important strategic base—by the presence of these large, long-range, and clearly offensive weapons of sudden mass destruction—constitutes an explicit threat to the peace and security of all the Americas, in flagrant and deliberate defiance of the Rio Pact of 1947, the traditions of this Nation and hemisphere, the joint resolution of the 87th Congress, the Charter of the

United Nations, and my own public warnings to the Soviets on September 4 and 13. This action also contradicts the repeated assurances of Soviet spokesmen, both publicly and privately delivered, that the arms build-up in Cuba would retain its original defensive character, and that the Soviet Union had no need or desire to station strategic missiles on the territory of any other nation.

The size of this undertaking makes clear that it has been planned for some months. Yet only last month, after I had made clear the distinction between any introduction of ground-to-ground missiles and the existence of defensive antiaircraft missiles, the Soviet Government publicly stated on September 11 that, and I quote, "the armaments and military equipment sent to Cuba are designed exclusively for defensive purposes," that, and I quote the Soviet Government, "there is no need for the Soviet Government to shift its weapons . . . for a retaliatory blow to any other country, for instance Cuba," and that, and I quote their government, "the Soviet Union has so powerful rockets to carry these nuclear warheads that there is no need to search for sites for them beyond the boundaries of the Soviet Union." That statement was false.

Only last Thursday, as evidence of this rapid offensive build-up was already in my hand, Soviet Foreign Minister Gromyko told me in my office that he was instructed to make it clear once again, as he said his government had already done, that Soviet assistance to Cuba, and I quote, "pursued solely the purpose of contributing to the defense capabilities of Cuba," that, and I quote him, "training by Soviet specialists of Cuban nationals in handling defensive armaments was by no means offensive, and if it were otherwise," Mr Gromyko went on, "the Soviet Government would never become involved in rendering such assistance." That statement also was false.

Neither the United States of America nor the world community of nations can tolerate deliberate deception and offensive threats on the part of any nation, large or small. We no longer live in a world where only the actual firing of weapons represents a sufficient challenge to a nation's security to constitute maximum peril. Nuclear weapons are so destructive and ballistic missiles are so swift, that any substantially increased possibility of their use or any sudden change in their deployment may well be regarded as a definite threat to peace.

For many years, both the Soviet Union and the United States, recognizing this fact, have deployed strategic nuclear weapons with great care, never upsetting the precarious status quo which insured that these weapons would not be used in the absence of some vital challenge. Our own strategic missiles have never been transferred to the territory of any other nation under a cloak of secrecy and deception; and our history—unlike that of the Soviets since the end of World War II—demonstrates that we have no desire to dominate or conquer any other nation or impose our system upon its people. Nevertheless, American citizens have become adjusted to living daily on the bull's-eye of Soviet missiles located inside the USSR or in submarines.

In that sense, missiles in Cuba add to an already clear and present danger—although it should be noted the nations of Latin America have never previously been subjected to a potential nuclear threat.

But this secret, swift, and extraordinary build-up of Communist missiles—in an area well known to have a special and historical relationship to the United States and the nations of the Western Hemisphere, in violation of Soviet assurances, and in defiance of American and hemispheric policy—this sudden, clandestine decision to station strategic weapons for the first time outside of Soviet soil—is a deliberately provocative and unjustified change in the status quo which cannot be accepted by this country, if our courage and our commitments are ever to be trusted again by either friend or foe.

The 1930s taught us a clear lesson: aggressive conduct, if allowed to go unchecked, ultimately leads to war. This nation is opposed to war. We are also true to our word. Our unswerving objective, therefore, must be to prevent the use of these missiles against this or any other country, and to secure their withdrawal or elimination from the Western Hemisphere.

Our policy has been one of patience and restraint, as befits a peaceful and powerful nation, which leads a world-wide alliance. We have been determined not to be diverted from our central concerns by mere irritants and fanatics. But now further action is required—and it is under way; and these actions may only be the beginning. We will not prematurely or unnecessarily risk the costs of worldwide nuclear war in which even the fruits of victory would be ashes in our mouth—but neither will we shrink from that risk at any time it must be faced.

Acting, therefore, in the defense of our own security and of the entire Western Hemisphere, and under the authority entrusted to me by the Constitution as endorsed by the Resolution of the Congress, I have directed that the following *initial* steps be taken immediately:

First: To halt this offensive build-up, a strict quarantine on all offensive military equipment under shipment to Cuba is being initiated. All ships of any kind bound for Cuba from whatever nation or port will, if found to contain cargoes of offensive weapons, be turned back. This quarantine will be extended, if needed, to other types of cargo and carriers. We are not at this time, however, denying the necessities of life as the Soviets attempted to do in their Berlin blockade of 1948.

Second: I have directed the continued and increased close surveillance of Cuba and its military build-up. The foreign ministers of the OAS, in their communiqué of October 6, rejected secrecy on such matters in this hemisphere. Should these offensive military preparations continue, thus increasing the threat to the hemisphere, further action will be justified. I have directed the Armed Forces to prepare for any eventualities; and I trust that in the interest of both the Cuban people and the Soviet technicians at the sites, the hazards to all concerned of continuing this threat will be recognized.

Third: It shall be the policy of this Nation to regard any nuclear missile launched from Cuba against any nation in the Western Hemisphere as an attack by the Soviet Union on the United States, requiring a full retaliatory response upon the Soviet Union.

Fourth: As a necessary military precaution, I have reinforced our base at Guantánamo, evacuated today the dependents of our personnel there, and ordered additional military units to be on a standby alert basis.

Fifth: We are calling tonight for an immediate meeting of the Organ of Consultation under the Organization of American States, to consider this threat to hemispheric security and to invoke articles 6 and 8 of the Rio Treaty in support of all necessary action. The United Nations Charter allows for regional security arrangements—and the nations of this hemisphere decided long ago against the military presence of outside powers. Our other allies around the world have also been alerted.

Sixth: Under the Charter of the United Nations, we are asking tonight that an emergency meeting of the Security Council be convoked without delay to take action against this latest Soviet threat to world peace. Our resolution will call for the prompt dismantling and withdrawal of all offensive weapons in Cuba, under the supervision of UN observers, before the quarantine can be lifted.

Seventh and finally: I call upon Chairman Khrushchev to halt and eliminate this clandestine, reckless, and provocative threat to world peace and to stable relations between our two nations. I call upon him further to abandon this course of world domination, and to join in an historic effort to end the perilous arms race and to transform the history of man. He has an opportunity now to move the world back from the abyss of destruction—by returning to his government's own words that it had no need to station missiles outside its own territory, and withdrawing these weapons from Cuba—by refraining from any action which will widen or deepen the present crisis—and then by participating in a search for peaceful and permanent solutions.

This Nation is prepared to present its case against the Soviet threat to peace, and our own proposals for a peaceful world, at any time and in any forum—in the OAS, in the United Nations, or in any other meeting that could be useful—without limiting our freedom of action. We have in the past made strenuous efforts to limit the spread of nuclear weapons. We have proposed the elimination of all arms and military bases in a fair and effective disarmament treaty. We are prepared to discuss new proposals for the removal of tensions on both sides—including the possibilities of a genuinely independent Cuba, free to determine its own destiny. We have no wish to war with the Soviet Union—for we are a peaceful people who desire to live in peace with all other peoples.

But it is difficult to settle or even discuss these problems in an atmosphere of intimidation. That is why this latest Soviet threat—or any other threat which is made either independently or in response to our actions this week—must and will be met with determination. Any hostile move anywhere in the world against the safety and freedom of peoples to whom we are committed—including in particular the brave people of West Berlin—will be met by whatever action is needed.

Finally, I want to say a few words to the captive people of Cuba, to whom this speech is being directly carried by special radio facilities. I speak to you as a friend, as one who knows of your deep attachment to your fatherland, as one who shares your aspirations for liberty and justice for all. And I have watched and the American people have watched with deep sorrow how your nationalist revolution was betrayed—and how your fatherland fell under foreign domination. Now your leaders are no longer Cuban leaders inspired by Cuban ideals. They are puppets and agents of an international conspiracy which has turned Cuba against your friends and neighbors in the Americas—and turned it into the first Latin American country to become a target for nuclear war—the first Latin American country to have these weapons on its soil.

These new weapons are not in your interest. They contribute nothing to your peace and well-being. They can only undermine it. But this country has no wish to cause you to suffer or to impose any system upon you. We know that your lives and land are being used as pawns by those who deny your freedom. Many times in the past, the Cuban people have risen to throw out tyrants who destroyed their liberty. And I have no doubt that most Cubans today look forward to the time when they will be truly free—free from foreign domination, free to choose their own leaders, free to select their own system, free to own their own land, free to speak and write and worship without fear or degradation. And then shall Cuba be welcomed back to the society of free nations and to the associations of this hemisphere.

My fellow citizens: let no one doubt that this is a difficult and dangerous effort on which we have set out. No one can foresee precisely what course it will take or what costs or casualties will be incurred. Many months of sacrifice and self-discipline lie ahead—months in which both our patience and our will will be tested—months in which many threats and denunciations will keep us aware of our dangers. But the greatest danger of all would be to do nothing.

The path we have chosen for the present is full of hazards, as all paths are—but it is the one most consistent with our character and courage as a nation and our commitments around the world. The cost of freedom is always high—but Americans have always paid it. And one path we shall never choose, and that is the path of surrender or submission.

Our goal is not the victory of might, but the vindication of right—not peace at the expense of freedom, but both peace *and* freedom, here in this hemisphere, and, we hope, around the world. God willing, that goal will be achieved.

Thank you and good night.

Letter from President Kennedy to Chairman Khrushchev
Washington, October 22, 1962

Dear Mr Chairman: A copy of the statement I am making tonight concerning developments in Cuba and the reaction of my Government thereto has been handed to your Ambassador in Washington. In view of the gravity of the developments to which I refer, I want you to know immediately and accurately the position of my Government in this matter.

In our discussions and exchanges on Berlin and other international questions, the one thing that has most concerned me has been the possibility that your Government would not correctly understand the will and determination of the United States in any given situation, since I have not assumed that you or any other sane man would, in this nuclear age, deliberately plunge the world into war which it is crystal clear no country could win and which could only result in catastrophic consequences to the whole world, including the aggressor.

At our meeting in Vienna and subsequently, I expressed our readiness and desire to find, through peaceful negotiation, a solution to any and all problems that divide us. At the same time, I made clear that in view of the objectives of the ideology to which you adhere, the United States could not tolerate any action on your part which in a major way disturbed the existing over-all balance of power in the world. I stated that an attempt to force abandonment of our responsibilities and commitments in Berlin would constitute such an action and that the United States would resist with all the power at its command.

It was in order to avoid any incorrect assessment on the part of your Government with respect to Cuba that I publicly stated that if certain developments in Cuba took place, the United States would do whatever must be done to protect its own security and that of its allies.

Moreover, the Congress adopted a resolution expressing its support of this declared policy. Despite this, the rapid development of long-range missile bases and other offensive weapons systems in Cuba has proceeded. I must tell you that the United States is determined that this threat to the security of this hemisphere be removed. At the same time, I wish to point out that the action we are taking is the minimum necessary to remove the threat to the security of the nations of this hemisphere. The fact of this minimum response should not be taken as a basis, however, for any misjudgment on your part.

I hope that your Government will refrain from any action which would widen or deepen this already grave crisis and that we can agree to resume the path of peaceful negotiation.

Sincerely,
JFK

Memorandum of telephone conversation between President Kennedy and Prime Minister Macmillan
October 22, 1962

The clandestine way that the Soviets have made their build-up in Cuba would have unhinged us in all of Latin America. To allow it to continue would have thrown into question all our statements about Berlin.

PM spoke.
We have the potential to occupy Cuba but we didn't start that way.

There would be a gap of some days before invasion could be mounted. Preparations for invasion would have public notice. This way provides action without immediate escalation to war.

Action is limited now. Greater force would give him the same excuse in Berlin.

It may be necessary to expand blockade to include fuel, lubricants and so forth.

PM spoke (about possible Russian actions).
He may require us to seize their ships by force.

There is no telling what he will do—probably it will be something in Berlin.

PM spoke.
We have had no plan to invade Cuba. We must get their missiles out. What exchange possible is not known. But getting the missiles out is the object of our policy.

We are aware that this action is not complete application of force—does not immediately solve the problem.

The alternatives were air strike or invasion. These may be necessary but going completely into Cuba now invites him into Berlin.

PM spoke.

If we had the force on hand to take Cuba tonight that would be okay, but it would take a week to build up.

PM spoke.

We are attempting to begin the escalation in a way to prevent WW III. Maybe this will result anyway, but we cannot accept his actions.

PM spoke (about talking to K on phone).

No, but I sent a letter to him one hour ago. Khrushchev is playing a double game. He said he wasn't going to do anything until after the election. He said weapons in Cuba were not offensive.

It is obvious that he was attempting to face us in November with a bad situation.

PM answered.

Mr Bundy suggested the following point which the President made.

The build-up in Cuba, if completed, would double the number of missiles the Soviets could bring to bear on the US. They would also overcome our warning system which does not face south. Furthermore, the short distance involving short times of flight would tempt them to make a first strike.

PM spoke.

Some action was necessary. It could result in WW III; we could lose Berlin.

PM spoke.

Invasion may yet be required. It requires seven days for mobilization of the necessary forces. In any event we won't invade until I speak again with you.

PM spoke.
It faces Khrushchev with action taken which has unpleasant options for him also.

*Telegram from the Embassy in France to the
Department of State
Paris, October 22, 1962, 9:00 p.m.*

1901. Eyes only for the Secretary. Deptel 2300. I accompanied Mr Acheson this afternoon when he called on President de Gaulle at five pm local time. Mr Acheson began conversation by presenting President de Gaulle with copy of President's letter contained Deptel 2304. He also handed President de Gaulle part one of President's speech since other sections not yet received by Embassy. However, they will be delivered to President de Gaulle's Chef de Cabinet as soon as received.

President de Gaulle read both communications carefully and then remarked that he would welcome further elucidation by Mr Acheson.

Mr Acheson outlined background of present situation in Cuba, reason for President's proposed action, going into considerable detail, emphasizing that maximum build-up had occurred within past week, and saying that he had Mr Sherman Kent with him who was prepared to brief President de Gaulle in more detail.

President de Gaulle listened with obvious interest and then remarked that US for first time felt itself threatened since missiles in Cuba were aimed at US and they had no other reason to be in Cuba save threaten US. He continued that President Kennedy wishes to react, and to react now, and certainly France can have no objection to that since it is legal for a country to defend itself when it finds itself in danger.

He then referred to blockade and said that of course there would be no objection on part of France to US initiating such blockade, but he himself had doubts as to its effectiveness. He wondered whether it would be sufficiently effective to cause Cubans [Soviets] to remove missiles and their bases. He admitted it would at least stop additional missiles going to Cuba.

President de Gaulle then referred to our proposal to consult with other American nations, asked whether that would be effective, and remarked he himself did not know.

With respect to proposed action in Security Council, President de Gaulle remarked that he realized that this was in line with our policy. Personally he did not think it would be practical. There might be much talk, but he doubted whether Security Council would be effective.

In conclusion, President de Gaulle said that he felt blockade was one positive step, and he repeated that France made no objection thereto. President de Gaulle said he believed that if blockade were initiated USSR would react perhaps in neighborhood of Cuba, but more likely in area where they could act more effectively. President de Gaulle felt they would choose Berlin since they would want to make West suffer, and this was where they could do so most effectively. If they choose Berlin, President de Gaulle said, three powers would have to take necessary steps; number of countersteps have been prepared and they would have to be taken.

President de Gaulle continued that perhaps Soviets wished, and perhaps US also wished to some extent, to intensify international situation somewhat to bring about talks. Perhaps that is Mr Khrushchev's view. President de Gaulle said he did not think we would have war but if Soviets forced US in such places as Berlin, France would be with US, "France will act in accord with you."

President de Gaulle expressed appreciation for having been informed by President. He said that he realized this had been done after decision had been made, but nevertheless appreciated being informed. He said he would reply to President's letter as soon as possible, but meanwhile if Mr Acheson saw President please explain de Gaulle's appreciation and tell him he would be replying to his message.

President de Gaulle said that in this serious time it was important that governments keep in close contact. This would be done in Washington through Ambassador Alphand and through Ambassador Bohlen when he arrives here shortly. President de Gaulle ruminated that while one never knew what real intentions of Soviets were, he did not think present situation would lead to war. He thought it might be great maneuver to engage US in talks on Berlin and on Cuba. Berlin was the sensitive point and it was there that Soviets no doubt would press. Perhaps also Khrushchev had in mind impressing other Latin American states by showing them that USSR could establish themselves anywhere in Western Hemisphere and could not be moved out. He repeated he hoped blockade would be effective, but did not think it would be.

At this point Mr Kent was called into room to brief President de Gaulle. President de Gaulle was obviously very interested in briefing and showed keen interest, asking pertinent questions, which revealed his military background. In addition to specific technical questions, he inquired as to Cuba's self-sufficiency with respect to food, petroleum, etc.

His obvious concern with this Cuban development was expressed in his statement: "US has been defending Europe in order that Europe may not become base against US. Now there is base in America directed against US. This is not a good thing."

President de Gaulle inquired what countries were being informed in similar manner. Mr Acheson replied UK, France, Germany.

President de Gaulle was friendly, relaxed and deeply interested. He appreciated significance of situation rapidly, and obviously found here a subject which interested him considerably. His Chef de Cabinet was extremely cooperative in maintaining secrecy of interview, and we drove to Elysée in Elsyée motorcars and were taken in back door to avoid any leakage to press of Mr Acheson's visit.

LYON

OCTOBER 23, 1962

*Minutes of meeting of the Executive Committee of the
National Security Council
Washington, October 23, 1962, 10:00 a.m.*

1. Intelligence
The meeting began with a briefing by Mr McCone in
which, in addition to written material, he emphasized the
strength of evidence substantiating the non-participation
of Cubans in Soviet missile installations in Cuba.

2. Unity on the home front
There was general discussion of the problem of adequate
briefing of Members of the Congress and of the press on

the way in which the crisis had developed and on the reasons for the decisions which had been taken. A number of assignments were given to individual members of the Committee for further work on this problem.

3. Blockade effects estimates
The President asked the Director of Central Intelligence for an analysis of effects of the blockade on Cuba, not to include food and medicine, and for a comparable analysis of the effects of a comparable blockade on Berlin.

4. Items presented by the Department of Defense
(a) The President approved plans for the issue of the Proclamation of Interdiction of ship delivery of offensive weapons to Cuba. The Proclamation was to be issued at 6:00 p.m. and the Interdiction to become effective at dawn October 24.

(b) The President approved and later signed an Executive Order authorizing the extension of tours of duty of certain members of the Armed Forces.

(c) The President approved the following contingency plan for action in the event of an incident affecting U-2 overflights. The President will be informed through SAC/DOD channels, and it is expected that if there is clear indication that the incident is the result of hostile action, the recommendation will be for immediate retaliation upon the most likely surface-to-air site involved in this action. The President delegated authority for decision on this point to the Secretary of Defense under the following conditions:

(1) that the President himself should be unavailable
(2) that evidence of hostile Cuban action should be very clear.

(d) It was expected, but not definitely decided, that if hostile actions should continue after such a single incident and single retaliation, it would become necessary to take action to eliminate the effectiveness of surface-to-air missiles in Cuba.

(e) The Secretary reported that he was not ready to make a recommendation on air intercept of Soviet flights to Cuba, that he was maintaining aircraft on alert for prompt reaction against known missile sites, that preparations for invasion were proceeding at full speed, that the quarantine would initially exclude POL, though this decision should be reexamined continuously.

(f) The Attorney General was delegated to check the problem of the legal possibility of permitting foreign flag ships to participate in US coastwise trade, in order to prevent shipping requirements for an invasion from disrupting US commerce.

(g) The Secretary of Defense recommended, and the President approved, about six low-level reconnaissance flights for the purpose of obtaining still more persuasive photography of Soviet missile sites.

(h) The President, on hearing these reports, asked whether US air forces in Southeastern United States were properly deployed against possible hostile reaction, and after discussion he directed that photographs be taken of US airfields to show their current condition.

5. State Department business

(a) Secretary Ball reported the urgent need for persuasive evidence in New York as described by Ambassador Stevenson and Mr McCloy, and the President directed Secretary Ball and Mr McCone to work together to meet this requirement as well as possible.

(b) There was a brief discussion of possible reactions in Berlin, and the President indicated that he would wish to consider whether additional Soviet inspection of convoys would be acceptable. After the meeting, the President designated Assistant Secretary Nitze to be Chairman of a Subcommittee of the Executive Committee, for Berlin Contingencies.

(c) The President decided that it would be advisable not to make his forthcoming trip to Brazil, and the assignment of diplomatic disengagement was given to the Department of State.

There was discussion of the problem of effective communications and it was agreed that for the present, Dr Wiesner will be asked informally to lead an inter-departmental review of this matter and to report on the problem on Wednesday, October 24.

McGEORGE BUNDY

Telegram from the Embassy in the Soviet Union to the Department of State
Moscow, October 23, 1962, 5:00 p.m.

Policy. Embtel 1041. Embassy translation follows of Khrushchev's letter of October 23 to President. Kuznetsov informed me letter would not be published "for time being."

Begin text.
Mr President. I have just received your letter, and have also acquainted myself with text of your speech of October 22 regarding Cuba.

I should say frankly that measures outlined in your statement represent serious threat to peace and security of peoples. United States has openly taken path of gross violation of Charter of United Nations, path of violation of international norms of freedom of navigation on high seas, path of aggressive actions both against Cuba and against Soviet Union.

Statement of Government of United States of America cannot be evaluated in any other way than as naked interference in domestic affairs of Cuban Republic, Soviet Union, and other states. Charter of United Nations and international norms do not give right to any state whatsoever to establish in international waters control of vessels bound for shores of Cuban Republic.

It is self-understood that we also cannot recognize right of United States to establish control over armaments essential to Republic of Cuba for strengthening of its defensive capacity.

We confirm that armaments now on Cuba, regardless of classification to which they belong, are destined exclusively for defensive purposes, in order to secure Cuban Republic from attack of aggressor.

I hope that Government of United States will show prudence and renounce actions pursued by you, which would lead to catastrophic consequences for peace throughout world.

Viewpoint of Soviet Government with regard to your statement of October 22 is set forth in statement of Soviet Government, which is being conveyed to you through your Ambassador in Moscow.

N. Khrushchev

End text.

Original of letter being airpouched today.

Kohler

Record of action of the second meeting of the Executive Committee of the National Security Council Washington, October 23, 1962, 6:00 p.m.

1. There was a preliminary report of low level reconnaissance.

2. The Proclamation of Interdiction was reviewed, slightly revised, and approved in the version later signed by the President.

3. A further message to Khrushchev was agreed in the form later dispatched by the Department of State.

4. The President requested the Secretary of Defense to give a further review to the process of naval action and engagement under the quarantine.

5. The Secretary of Defense was requested to consider and recommend appropriate arrangements for the continuation of General Norstad as Supreme NATO Commander during the crisis.

6. Assistant Secretary Pittman reported briefly on civil defense capability and was requested to produce recommendations for a special plan covering the southeastern area of the United States during the period of a possible invasion of Cuba. The President expected to review these plans at a separate meeting on October 24th.

7. Assistant Secretary Nitze was confirmed as Chairman of a subcommittee on Berlin preparations of the Executive Committee. The President invited Mr Nitze to sit regularly with the Executive Committee in this capacity.

8. Counselor W.W. Rostow was confirmed as Chairman of a second subcommittee on advance planning.

MG. B.

Memorandum for the files
Washington, October 23, 1962

Executive Committee Meeting on October 23, 1962, 6:00 p.m.
All members present plus Counsel for Defense Department
1. Committee reviewed the blockade proclamation and approved it. It was signed by the President at 6:00 p.m.

2. The President instructed McNamara to review all details of instructions to the Fleet Commanders regarding procedures to be followed in the blockade. There was an extended discussion of actions to be taken under various assumed Soviet resistance activities such as (a) failing to stop, (b) refusing right to board, (c) ships turning around, heading in another direction, etc.

3. Discussion of the effect on US industry by chartering and preempting the use of 20 or 30 American ships. Gilpatric reported that this would have little or no effect on the American economy. McCone questioned these findings; however Gilpatric said that this had been thoroughly studied and McCone's concerns as expressed at the morning meeting were unfounded. The Attorney General stated that it was within the law to use foreign bottoms, however decision was made to preempt US bottoms and not worry about the consequences because they would not be serious.

4. The President urged that Norstad be retained at SHAPE during the period of crisis, perhaps until February 1, 63. He indicated Lemnitzer might be used as CINCEUR with Norstad remaining as SACEUR. Bundy stated that this is complicated as the two posts are so co-mingled that they really must be held by one man. Taylor raised question that if this was done it would hurt Lemnitzer's prestige. The President said that he felt that Norstad was so experienced and so capable and his judgment so sound, as evidenced by today's cable, copy of which I have not seen, that he would take the risk of NATO country criticisms, he did not think that Lemnitzer would be hurt, and he wished Norstad to remain. Defense to take under advisement and report within 24 hours.

5. In the prolonged discussion of report on civil defense problems, the President seemed particularly concerned over the situation if we should launch attacks which

might result in four or five missiles being delivered on the United States. DOD spokesmen stated that the area covered by the 1,100-mile missiles involved 92 million people. They felt that fall-out space was available though not equipped for about 40 million. The President asked what emergency steps could be taken. Replied that many arrangements could be made without too much publicity, such as repositioning food, actually obtaining space, putting up shelter signs, etc. I got the conclusion that not very much could or would be done; that whatever was done would involve a great deal of publicity and public alarm.

Prior to the departure of Secretary McNamara at approximately 7 o'clock, McCone (who had not been called upon for an intelligence appraisal) stated to the President that he felt certain intelligence should be reported to the meeting prior to the departure of Secretary McNamara as some items observed by the Intelligence Community might prove of great significance.

[*one paragraph (17½ lines of source text) not declassified*]

JOHN A. MCCONE

BY THE PRESIDENT OF THE UNITED STATES OF AMERICA
A PROCLAMATION

WHEREAS the peace of the world and the security of the United States and of all American states are endangered by reason of the establishment by the Sino–Soviet powers of an offensive military capability in Cuba, including bases for ballistic missiles with a potential range covering most of North and South America;

WHEREAS by a joint resolution passed by the Congress of the United States and approved on October 3, 1962, it was declared that the United States is determined to prevent by whatever means may be necessary, including the use of arms, the Marxist–Leninist regime in Cuba from expanding, by force or the threat of force, its aggressive or subversive activities to any part of this hemisphere, and to prevent in Cuba the creation or use of an externally supported military capability endangering the security of the United States; and

WHEREAS the Organ of Consultation of the American Republics meeting in Washington on October 23, 1962, recommended that the member states, in accordance with Articles 6 and 8 of the Inter-American Treaty of Reciprocal Assistance, take all measures, individually and collectively, including the use of armed force, which they may deem necessary to insure that the Government of Cuba cannot continue to receive from the Sino–Soviet powers military material and related supplies which may threaten the peace and security of the continent and to prevent the missiles in Cuba with offensive capability from ever becoming an active threat to the peace and security of the continents:

Now, THEREFORE, I, John F. Kennedy, President of the United States of America, acting under and by virtue of the authority conferred upon me by the Constitution and statutes of the United States, in accordance with the aforementioned resolutions of the United States Congress and of the Organ of Consultation of the American Republics, and to defend the security of the United States, do hereby proclaim that the forces under my command are ordered, beginning at 2:00 p.m. Greenwich time October 24, 1962, to interdict, subject to the instructions herein contained, the delivery of offensive weapons and associated material to Cuba.

For the purposes of this proclamation, the following are declared to be prohibited material:

Surface-to-surface missiles; bomber aircraft; bombs; air-to-surface rockets and guided missiles; warheads for any of the above weapons; mechanical or electronic equipment to support or operate the above items; and any other classes of material hereafter designated by the Secretary of Defense for the purpose of effectuating this proclamation.

To enforce this order, the Secretary of Defense shall take appropriate measures to prevent the delivery of prohibited material to Cuba, employing the land, sea, and air forces of the United States in cooperation with any forces that may be made available by other American states.

The Secretary of Defense may make such regulations and issue such directives as he deems necessary to ensure the effectiveness of this order, including the designation, within a reasonable distance of Cuba, of prohibited or restricted zones and of prescribed routes.

Any vessel or craft which may be proceeding toward Cuba may be intercepted and may be directed to identify itself, its cargo, equipment, and stores and its ports of call, to stop, to lie to, to submit to visit and search, or to proceed as directed. Any vessel or craft which fails or refuses to respond to or comply with directions shall be subjected to being taken into custody. Any vessel or craft which is believed en route to Cuba and may be carrying prohibited material or may itself constitute such material shall, wherever possible, be directed to proceed to another destination of its own choice and shall be taken into custody if it fails or refuses to obey such directions. All vessels or craft taken into custody shall be sent into a port of the United States for appropriate disposition.

In carrying out this order, force shall not be used except in case of failure or refusal to comply with directions, or with regulations or directives of the Secretary of Defense issued hereunder, after reasonable efforts have been made to communicate them to the vessel or craft, or in case of self-defense. In any case, force shall be used only to the extent necessary.

IN WITNESS WHEREOF, I have hereunto set my hand and caused the seal of the United States of America to be affixed.

Done in the city of Washington this 23rd day of October in the year of Our Lord, 1962, and of the independence of the United States of America the 187th.

JOHN F. KENNEDY
By the President:
DEAN RUSK, *Secretary of State*

Telegram from the Department of State to the Embassy in the Soviet Union
Washington, October 23, 1962, 6:51 p.m.

You should deliver following letter addressed by the President to Chairman Khrushchev immediately. This replaces message contained in Deptel 982.

Dear Mr Chairman:

I have received your letter of October twenty-third. I think you will recognize that the steps which started the current chain of events was the action of your Government in secretly furnishing offensive weapons to Cuba. We will be discussing this matter in the Security Council. In the meantime, I am concerned that we both show prudence and do nothing to allow events to make the situation more difficult to control than it already is.

I hope that you will issue immediately the necessary instructions to your ships to observe the terms of the quarantine, the basis of which was established by the vote of the Organization of American States this afternoon, and which will go into effect at 14:00 hours Greenwich time October twenty-four.

Sincerely, JFK

RUSK

Memorandum from the Acting Chairman of the Board of
National Estimates (Smith) to Director of
Central Intelligence McCone
Washington, October 23, 1962

Soviet challenge to the quarantine

1. Our best guess is that:

(a) A challenge at sea to the quarantine is unlikely, at least for a day or two.

(b) Thereafter a challenge is likely if the Soviets believe that their political efforts are not succeeding and a heightening of the crisis is required.

(c) In staging any challenge, they would probably employ a vessel with nonmilitary cargo, refuse boarding, and exploit the subsequent attack by the US.

(d) Retaliatory actions would follow if the incident itself failed to produce quick political results. It would be aimed either at a US ship elsewhere or at access to Berlin; we think the latter somewhat more likely.

2. Today's TASS statement suggests that the Soviets wish to retain full freedom of action while they consider their initial moves. There is some intelligence, dating from before the President's speech, indicating that the Soviets had decided to run any US blockade which might be established. Nevertheless, we think it likely that, at least for a day or two, they will avoid a challenge at sea while they observe the results of their political efforts to get the quarantine lifted.

3. If the USSR feels that these efforts are succeeding, the Soviets will probably continue to avoid challenges, lest an incident interrupt this favorable trend. On the other hand, if Soviet political tactics are bearing little fruit, they may

judge that an incident would be useful as a means of heightening the crisis further and bringing extra international pressure on the US.

4. If and when they decide to permit an incident of this sort, the Soviets would not allow the US to board a vessel, since this would mean acceptance in principle of quarantine. Instead, their tactics would probably be to choose a ship carrying a nonmilitary cargo and to allow it to be attacked.

5. It is possible that the Soviets, in deciding to test the quarantine, would accompany their probe ship with a submarine which would counterattack the US vessel after the Soviet ship was struck. Or the counterattack might be made by an aircraft from Cuba. We think this unlikely, however, because the Soviets would almost certainly estimate that the US would respond by tightening the blockade and launching a full-scale effort to seek out and destroy a Soviet submarine in the area of quarantine operations.

6. After an incident, the Soviets would probably allow a pause while they exploited this incident and observed its effects. Unless the US showed signs of quickly yielding, however, we believe that they would then follow with some form of retaliation.

7. We do not believe that this would take the form of major military action. Instead, the Soviets would choose between an attack on a US ship elsewhere or a move on the access routes to Berlin, designed to remind the US of the vulnerability of its position there. In most circumstances, they probably would regard a Berlin move as both more effective and easier to control. Still, they would probably exercise care to avoid giving the impression that they were moving toward a general showdown with the US.

8. The USSR might use a submarine, however, to deliver through the quarantine some particularly critical item and to demonstrate, with a subsequent announcement, its ability to frustrate US efforts.

For the Board of National Estimates:
ABBOT SMITH

OCTOBER 24, 1962

Record of action of the third meeting of the Executive Committee of the National Security Council Washington, October 24, 1962, 10:00 a.m.

1. Intelligence
The Director of Central Intelligence summarized the intelligence briefing. The President directed that the Secretary of the Treasury and the Director of Central Intelligence take immediate action to obtain more "black boxes."

2. Defense operations

(a) The Secretary of Defense presented photographs of dispersal of existing US planes in the southeast US, and the Chairman of the Joint Chiefs of Staff reported that modifications of readiness were being considered to permit improvement of the situation.

(b) The Secretary of Defense reported the plans for naval interception, noted the presence of a submarine near the more interesting ships, and warned that radio silence might be imposed. There was discussion of the problem of dealing with such submarines, and it was understood that in the event of intervention by a submarine in the process of interception the submarine might have to be destroyed.

3. In the middle of the meeting there were reports that certain Soviet ships had appeared to have stopped or turned back, and the President directed that there be no interception of any target for at least another hour while clarifying information was sought.

4. Dr Wiesner presented an initial briefing on the communications situation and the President directed that most urgent action be taken by State, Defense and CIA to improve communications worldwide, but particularly in the Caribbean area. After the meeting, the President, in discussion with the Secretary of State and the Secretary of Defense, directed that special responsibilities should be assigned to designated individuals and a plan for this purpose will be presented for approval by State, Defense and White House officers at the next meeting of the Committee.

5. The President directed that State and USIA should give immediate attention to increasing understanding in Europe of the fact that any Berlin crisis would be fundamentally the result of Soviet ambition and pressure, and that inaction by

the United States in the face of the challenge in Cuba would have been more and not less dangerous for Berlin.

6. The President directed that a senior representative of USIA should regularly be present at meetings of the Executive Committee.

McGEORGE BUNDY

Memorandum from Attorney General Kennedy to President Kennedy about his meeting with Soviet Ambassador Dobrynin
Washington, October 24, 1962

TOP SECRET. A copy was sent to Rusk.

I met with Ambassador Dobrynin last evening on the third floor of the Russian Embassy and as you suggested made the following points:*

I told him first that I was there on my own and not on the instructions of the President. I said that I wanted to give him some background on the decision of the United States Government and wanted him to know that the duplicity of the Russians had been a major contributing factor. When I had met with him some six weeks before, I said, he had told me that the Russians had not placed any long-range missiles in Cuba and had no intention to do so in the future. He interrupted at that point and confirmed this statement and said he specifically told me they would not put missiles in Cuba which would be able to reach the continental United States.

I said based on that statement which I had related to the President plus independent intelligence information at that time, the President had gone to the American people and assured them that the weapons being furnished by the Communists to Cuba were defensive and that it was not

---

* The meeting took place on October 23, 9:30 p.m.

necessary for the United States to blockade or take any military action. I pointed out that this assurance of Dobrynin to me had been confirmed by the TASS statement and then finally, in substance, by Gromyko when he visited the President on Thursday (October 18). I said that based on these assurances the President had taken a different and far less belligerent position than people like Senators Keating and Capehart, and he had assured the American people that there was nothing to be concerned about.

I pointed out, in addition, that the President felt he had a very helpful personal relationship with Mr Khrushchev. Obviously, they did not agree on many issues, but he did feel that there was a mutual trust and confidence between them on which he could rely. As an example of this statement I related the time that Mr Khrushchev requested the President to withdraw the troops from Thailand and that step was taken within 24 hours.

I said that with the background of this relationship, plus the specific assurances that had been given to us, and then the statement of Dobrynin from Khrushchev to Ted Sorensen and to me that no incident would occur before the American elections were completed, we felt the action by Khrushchev and the Russians at this time was hypocritical, misleading and false. I said this should be clearly understood by them as it was by us.

Dobrynin's only answer was that he had told me no missiles were in Cuba but that Khrushchev had also given similar assurances through TASS and as far as he (Dobrynin) knew, there were still no missiles in Cuba.

Dobrynin in the course of the conversation made several other points. The one he stressed was why the President did not tell Gromyko the facts on Thursday. He said this was something they could not understand and that if we had the information at the time why didn't we tell Gromyko.

I answered this by making two points:

Number one, there wasn't anything the President could tell Gromyko that Gromyko didn't know already and after all, why didn't Gromyko tell the President this instead of, in fact, denying it. I said in addition the President was so shocked at Gromyko's presentation and his failure to recite these facts that he felt that any effort to have an intelligent and honest conversation would not be profitable.

Dobrynin went on to say that from his conversations with Gromyko he doesn't believe Gromyko thought there were any missiles in Cuba. He said he was going to contact his government to find out about this matter.

I expressed surprise that after all that had appeared in the papers, and the President's speech, that he had not had a communication on that question already.

Dobrynin seemed extremely concerned. When I left I asked him if ships were going to go through to Cuba. He replied that was their instructions last month and he assumed they had the same instructions at the present time. He also made the point that although we might have pictures, all we really knew about were the sites and not missiles and that there was a lot of difference between sites and the actual missile itself. I said I did not have to argue the point—there were missiles in Cuba—we knew that they were there and that I hoped he would inform himself also.

I left around 10:15 p.m. and went to the White House and gave a verbal report to the President.

Telegram from the Department of State to the Embassy in Turkey raising the possibility of missile removal
Washington, October 24, 1962, 11:24 a.m.

SECRET; PRIORITY; EYES ONLY. Drafted by Ball, cleared with Tyler and NEA, approved by Rusk. Also sent to Paris for USRO

445. For Ambassadors Hare and Finletter from Secretary. Soviet reaction Cuban quarantine likely involve efforts compare missiles in Cuba with Jupiters in Turkey. While such comparison refutable, possible that negotiated solution for removal Cuban offensive threat may involve dismantling and removal Jupiters. Recognize this would create serious politico-military problems for US–Turkish relations and with regard to Turkey's place in NATO Alliance. Therefore need to prepare carefully for such contingency in order not to harm our relations with this important ally.

Urgently request Ambassador Hare's assessment political consequences such removal under various assumptions, including outright removal, removal accompanied by stationing of Polaris submarine in area, or removal with some other significant military offset, such as seaborn multilateral nuclear force within NATO.

Ambassador Finletter also requested comment standpoint NATO aspect problem. Do not discuss with any foreigners.

Memorandum from the Chairman of the Planning Subcommittee of the Executive Committee of the National Security Council (Rostow) to President Kennedy
Washington, October 24, 1962

Representatives of State and Defense, the Attorney General, and Mr Lovett, met to consider the course of action to be followed with respect to the Soviet vessels which have altered course (Group A), and those vessels still proceeding toward Cuba (Group B). With respect to Group A, it is recommended:

That the Department of Defense intercept, trail, and photograph, but not interfere with, such vessels. The object is to record the fact of their turnaround and, to the extent possible, the character of their cargo.

With respect to Group B, it is recommended that:

(1) They be stopped and searched in accordance with the Proclamation;
(2) That the order to search be determined by the order of their operational availability to our forces;
(3) Should a vessel refuse to comply with orders to stop, we should proceed to execute the terms of the Proclamation with special attention to the minimum use of force, given the likelihood that their cargoes will prove innocent.

It is recommended that a Department of Defense spokesman announce that:

(1) Some of the Bloc vessels proceeding toward Cuba appear to have altered course;
(2) No intercepts have yet been necessary;
(3) Other vessels are proceeding toward Cuba and will be intercepted in accordance with the Proclamation.

On a background basis, it will be explained that those vessels which altered course were those we had reason to believe contained offensive weapons; but that inspection of other vessels is required, now and in the future, until offensive weapons and installations are removed from Cuba, because such vessels could contain essential components for offensive weapons.

W. W. R.

Memorandum of telephone conversation between the Under Secretary of State (Ball) and the President's Special Assistant for National Security Affairs (Bundy)
Washington, October 24, 1962, 3:25 p.m.

Bundy: Have you got the word in on what is happening at sea?
Ball: No.
Bundy: The six most interesting ships have turned back. Two others are coming on. We are starting over here a thinking session as to what might be done which will be going on all afternoon. If you want to come, it would be helpful to have you. Walt is here. If there is anyone you want to send, send him. I have told the Secretary and you are the only two I have told. Will you alert anyone else you wish to alert?
Ball: I will. The other ships are going forward?
Bundy: Two tankers are coming on, but six interesting ships have turned back; six may not be a precise figure. Khrushchev told Lord Russell he thought it would be useful to have a top level meeting.
Ball: I'll be over.

Letter from Chairman Khrushchev to President Kennedy
Moscow, October 24, 1962

A copy of this letter, transmitted in telegram 1070 from Moscow, October 24, arrived in the Department of State at 9:24 p.m.

Dear Mr President: I have received your letter of October 23, have studied it, and am answering you.

Just imagine, Mr President, that we had presented you with the conditions of an ultimatum which you have presented us by your action. How would you have reacted to this? I think that you would have been indignant at such a step on our part. And this would have been understandable to us.

In presenting us with these conditions, you, Mr President, have flung a challenge at us. Who asked you to do this? By what right did you do this? Our ties with the Republic of Cuba, like our relations with other states, regardless of what kind of states they may be, concern only the two countries between which these relations exist. And if we now speak of the quarantine to which your letter refers, a quarantine may be established, according to accepted international practice, only by agreement of states between themselves, and not by some third party. Quarantines exist, for example, on agricultural goods and products. But in this case the question is in no way one of quarantine, but rather of far more serious things, and you yourself understand this.

You, Mr President, are not declaring a quarantine, but rather are setting forth an ultimatum and threatening that if we do not give in to your demands you will use force. Consider what you are saying! And you want to persuade me to agree to this! What would it mean to agree to these demands? It would mean guiding oneself in one's relations with other countries not by reason, but by submitting to arbitrariness. You are no longer appealing to reason, but wish to intimidate us.

No, Mr President, I cannot agree to this, and I think that in your own heart you recognize that I am correct. I am convinced that in my place you would act the same way.

Reference to the decision of the Organization of American States cannot in any way substantiate the demands now advanced by the United States. This Organization has absolutely no authority or basis for adopting decisions such as the one you speak of in your letter. Therefore, we do not recognize these decisions. International law exists and universally recognized norms of conduct exist. We firmly adhere to the principles of international law and observe strictly the norms which regulate navigation on the high seas, in international waters. We observe these norms and enjoy the rights recognized by all states.

You wish to compel us to renounce the rights that every sovereign state enjoys, you are trying to legislate in questions of international law, and you are violating the universally accepted norms of that law. And you are doing all this not only out of hatred for the Cuban people and its government, but also because of considerations of the election campaign in the United States. What morality, what law can justify such an approach by the American Government to international affairs? No such morality or law can be found, because the actions of the United States with regard to Cuba constitute outright banditry or, if you like, the folly of degenerate imperialism. Unfortunately, such folly can bring grave suffering to the peoples of all countries, and to no lesser degree to the American people themselves, since the United States has completely lost its former isolation with the advent of modern types of armament.

Therefore, Mr President, if you coolly weigh the situation which has developed, not giving way to passions, you will understand that the Soviet Union cannot fail to reject the arbitrary demands of the United States. When you confront us with such conditions, try to put yourself in our place and consider how the United States would react to these conditions. I do not doubt that if someone attempted to dictate similar conditions to you—the United States— you would reject such an attempt. And we also say—no.

The Soviet Government considers that the violation of the freedom to use international waters and international air space is an act of aggression which pushes mankind toward the abyss of a world nuclear-missile war. Therefore, the Soviet Government cannot instruct the captains of Soviet vessels bound for Cuba to observe the orders of American naval forces blockading that Island. Our instructions to Soviet mariners are to observe strictly the universally accepted norms of navigation in international waters and not to retreat one step from them. And if the American side violates these rules, it must realize what responsibility will rest upon it in that case. Naturally we will not simply be bystanders with regard to piratical acts by American ships on the high seas. We will then be forced on our part to take the measures we consider necessary and adequate in order to protect our rights. We have everything necessary to do so.

Respectfully,

N. KHRUSHCHEV

Memorandum of telephone conversation between the Under Secretary of State (Ball) and the President's Special Assistant for National Security Affairs (Bundy)
Washington, October 24, 1962, 8:25 p.m.

Bundy: I am getting a little groggy, so many people have different views, but the current situation is this. Bob thinks that it may well be important to intercept a tanker and to turn him back. His own understanding was that that was his orders. I understand that there are complications. He is going to go down to Flag Plot and look hard and find out what he knows and what anyone knows about where these things will be. He agrees that we must not do this at night time. Therefore, the question is really what orders Admiral Innison (?) [Dennison] has for dawn, that they require Presidential action and a meeting of the

Committee tonight. You had better argue with your Secretary.

Ball: Yes. Right.

Bundy: I understand that he is an anti-tanker interceptor. I think we have to leave the question of further discussion in suspense until McNamara has reviewed it and come in and said. If he comes in and says let's let it go until the meeting tomorrow morning, which we might as well have at 10 as at 8, because we miss dawn in either case. If he comes in and says that, does the Department wish to say no, no, we want orders for interception at dawn?

Ball: I don't think that we feel that strongly about that. My position is that since we are not singling out any special ships, then we ought to just take anything that comes on a completely nondiscriminatory basis, and not indulge any presumptions about what any particular kind of vessel might—

Bundy: I think that you will find that to do that requires a very distinct adjustment in the basic orders to the Navy. They are not operating on the basis of enforcing a blockade in that sense. They are enforcing a blockade with instructions from McNamara as to which ship to enforce it upon.

Ball: Adm. Ricker [Rickover?] felt that that was the easiest operational kind of—

Bundy: All I'm saying is that means different orders from what they now have.

Ball: My own view, you may pick out certain ships as we were preparing to do, those ships are not now in the equation; therefore, the thing to do is to take anything that comes and I would feel happier if the first ship that came along was a Belgian or Moroccan ship, so that we could establish the principle of what we are doing.

Bundy: Right.

Ball: If it happens to be a Soviet tanker . . .

Bundy: Right.

Ball: I will probably hear later tonight from Bob after he has been out there and had a look.

Bundy: I would think that when Bob has had a look at Flag Plot, he will call me and I will call you.

Ball: Very good.

Memorandum of telephone conversation between President Kennedy and the Under Secretary of State (Ball) Washington, October 24, 1962, 10:30 p.m.

Ball: The letter from Khrushchev is garbled, and I am trying to fill it in. As far as shipping goes, it is pretty repetitious. The significant part is the last paragraph. It says: [*Ball reads last paragraph*]. It simply says that the OAS has no authority in these matters; that one has to abide by international law; we are committing an act of piracy; if you were in his place you would take the same view. The significant part is the part I read to you. I don't think we have any option but to go ahead and test this thing out, in the morning, but at least this is the notice he has given to us.

President: Do you want to call up Bob McNamara because we have got the tanker we talked about stopping.

Ball: I'll talk to Bob about it and I will also get hold of Dean and maybe we had better get back to you.

President: I will be around.

Ball: The second thing is this. U Thant has just gotten through speaking, and I am waiting for a call from Stevenson. Stevenson is kicking like a steer about reply tonight, but I think we have to reply tonight.

President: He doesn't want to reply tonight?

Ball: He is concerned primarily about the conditions which we put in that proposed reply because he feels that those are in effect conditions to talking rather than the kind of conditions that might emerge out of talk. My own feeling is that we have got to be quite specific about them, otherwise we will get ourselves in a hopeless harass, and I don't think we can afford to do it at this point.

President: How does he want us to change it?

Ball: I think he would like to suggest some concessions we are prepared to make. I am waiting for a call from him. If it is agreeable to you, I am going to take a very firm line that we have to get this thing back to U Thant tonight even though it isn't published because I think we ought to be very prompt in getting some reply back before the Soviet Union comes in with an acceptance of the U Thant proposal. I may not be able to hold the line with him and he may insist on talking with you. I think we have got to go ahead.

President: They are obviously not going to stop. He is stopping the ones he doesn't want us to have. I suppose we will have to stop these. The press will give the impression that we are easing the situation.

Ball: That is inevitable. I have told them that there was no decision not to stop tankers, but only the fact that the initial version does not include POL. They are confused on this. I think we have worked it out so that story will be all right.

President: I think the impression tonight seems to be that the Russians are giving way, which is not quite accurate. They want to believe that it is giving way. I think that, after you talk to McNamara and the Sec., they ought to have either State and Defense put out the indication that Russian ships are approaching.

Ball: I'll do that. Maybe I can persuade Adlai, if not he may insist on talking to you. In the meantime, I will get hold of Bob and Dean, and we may have to get back to you.

Memorandum of telephone conversation between Secretary of State Rusk and the Under Secretary of State (Ball)
Washington, October 24, 1962, 11:25 p.m.

Ball: The President called me again and we've been talking about what we might do about getting some kind of a message to K [Khrushchev]. The Pres. had the idea that maybe we ought to do with U Thant tonight instead of trying to get a message back to K because there isn't much we can say that we didn't say in that message he sent last night. Try to get U Thant to make a direct appeal to Mr K to hold off his ships on the ground that there is going to be a confrontation in the morning which could escalate until there is a chance for a discussion on the modalities of negotiation. The Pres. is very reluctant to face this thing particularly with a tanker involved tomorrow until we make one last try to see if the UN can get itself in between.

Secretary: I must say that I don't think a tanker is the best case.

Ball: It isn't the best case. I talked to McNamara and what he said they had in mind with regard to the tanker was simply to hail it and ask it what it is carrying, where it was going, and if it answered satisfactory to let it go, not to board it. In fact the Commander has no instructions to do more than that. If it goes on through, then we have lost the principle of the quarantine, having done that. On the other hand, we could let this one go but then there will probably be a whole day without stopping a ship, and I am afraid this would be misinterpreted in Moscow, particularly in the light of this letter. The President's idea, this was a kind of an idea we were developing together, was possibly if we could get Thant tonight to make the appeal on the ground that there was going to be a likelihood of a confrontation and ask K to instruct his fellows to talk with ours and see if a negotiation could be gotten under way. In the mean-time, to hold his ships away from Cuba that something might be done.

Secretary: I don't think there is a chance in the world that K would get instructions to this tanker by 2 a.m.

Ball: In the meantime, we could hold off til, actually we could even change the thing for half a day as far as that goes. We could outrun the tanker.

Secretary: I should think that we ought to wait til daylight anyhow.

Ball: Well, we are going to wait til daylight as I understood it.

Secretary: I think you might talk to Adlai about this and see if U Thant on his own responsibility will ask Mr K not to send his ships pending modalities.

Ball: Let me see what we can do.

Secretary: All right, fine. What about the answer?

Ball: If we did that, I suppose we wouldn't answer.

Secretary: Hold off until in the morning?

Ball: Yes. There really isn't anything much that we can say that hasn't been said. If we can now get Thant to do some-thing rather than doing it ourselves.

Secretary: Right.

Ball: Let me see what I can work out when I talk to Stevenson.

Memorandum of telephone conversation between the Under Secretary of State (Ball) and the Ambassador to the United Nations (Stevenson)
October 24, 1962, 11:45 p.m.

Ball: We've got another idea that I would like to try out on you. Do you think there is any chance that U Thant would be willing to send Mr K a [letter?]. Let me bring you up to date. We've had a message from K in which he says in effect that he can't give instructions to his ships to abide by the blockade and that if we violate these rules, that will be our fault and they will be forced to take measures that they deem necessary and adequate to protect their rights, and they have what's necessary to do that. Implications being knowing that there may be a submarine or two in the waters, that could be an attempt to torpedo one of our ships. Would U Thant under all the circumstances knowing the possibility of a confrontation tomorrow be prepared to send a message to K along the lines that he is very concerned about possibility of a confrontation in connection with this quarantine, and that he asked K to hold his ships away from Cuban waters on the condition that we will not molest them while there is a discussion of the modalities of a possible negotiation.

Stevenson: Yes, I think he might do something like this.

Ball: If we could get something out like that tonight, I think we would hold off, because all we've got is a tanker coming through. We've just given instructions not to touch the thing tonight. We can buy a day or two here and see how it goes.

Stevenson: I think it would be a lot more helpful for me in trying to get U Thant to do this if I could have a copy of the message that we have from K.

Ball: I can give you. It's a garbled message, and it hasn't been cleaned up yet.

Stevenson: Well, if you could put it on the wire to me, so that I would have it first thing in the morning a substantial text of it.

Ball: I think it would have to be done tonight if we're going to do it because we've got a time dislocation and things are moving so swiftly. Is there a chance of getting hold of Thant tonight?

Stevenson: He's awful hard to get when he goes home. I am afraid it will be almost impossible to do anything with him tonight.

Ball: If you could even talk to him tonight.

Stevenson: I could talk to him on the phone and tell him what the burden of this thing is and that I'm going to be around in the morning with a suggestion that he send a message to K saying that he, I don't know whether he should say that he has this word.

Ball: I don't think he needs to say that he has any word.

Stevenson: See, what he's already said is please hold off on everything.

Ball: What he can say is that he is disturbed about the possibility of a confrontation at sea under the quarantine before further action could be taken toward trying to get this into political channels and he would therefore like an agreement from K that he will hold his ships off on the condition, away from Cuban waters, we won't molest them while the discussion of modalities goes forward.

Stevenson: He says that all concerned should refrain from any actions which may aggravate the situation and bring with it the risk of war. He will say, well I've already said that.

Ball: Yes, but this is giving specific content to it in terms of what the real danger, an immediate confrontation, may be.

Stevenson: I think if he had some feeling that we were likely to present this thing in general subject or conditions, which he knows about, I think maybe he would send such a message.

Ball: This position, I don't want to misrepresent the President on it, but this position that I have from him is that we could hold off for a while while there is some discussions on the modalities of the thing if they will hold their ships away while we do that.

Stevenson: As I understand it, are there any ships nearby?

Ball: There is a ship which was going to be challenged at 2 o'clock tomorrow morning, which is just about 2½ hours from now. We have got that held off.

Stevenson: That was a tanker?

Ball: Yes, and we can continue to hold that one off until we can see if something like this would work.

Stevenson: Would we stop it anyway?

Ball: Yes, we were going to stop it.

Stevenson: Although it was not carrying—

Ball: That is on the theory that we stop everything and challenge it and find out what's on board.

Stevenson: Let me call him. I think he may have trouble getting this message off tonight.

Ball: You know, there is a little flexibility in this because we are challenging these ships 500 miles out; we could outrun most of them and we could challenge them 200 miles out if necessary.

Stevenson: What's next . . .

Ball: I'm not very clear just what comes how soon. But we could adjust that. We don't want to let ships go through because this discredits our firmness of attention. What I think, if we could get an agreement from the Russians to hold their ships off while we talk about this, the modalities.

Stevenson: For a couple of days?

Ball: Yes, I think it would be that long probably before we get something settled. We won't take any action as long as their ships are held off, that way we avoid a confrontation until we can see if we can get the modalities with negotiation.

Stevenson: He has diverted the armed ships?

Ball: Yes.

Stevenson: Let me call him and see what I get.

Ball was in Washington; Stevenson was in New York.

OCTOBER 25, 1962

Memorandum of telephone conversation between the Under Secretary of State (Ball) and the President's Special Assistant for National Security Affairs (Bundy)
Washington, October 25, 1962, 12:30 a.m.

Bundy: We have now written, and everybody but you have signed off on it, and I hope you won't object, a message to the Chairman telling him it's your fault and not ours on the basic ground that they misled us—the thing that we think we ought to get back into his chest—. The word of the Soviet Government is what caused the trouble. David

Cline [Klein] is arranging to send it out. Do you want to hear it?

Ball: I would like to hear it. I'll tell you about my conversation with Stevenson.

Bundy: How did it go?

Ball: With Stevenson?

Bundy: Yes, mine is in the typewriter.

Ball: The situation with Stevenson is that he finally got Thant out of bed and Thant has agreed to send a message to K which he probably can't do tonight because of the communications but will do it first thing in the morning.

Bundy: Why don't we offer him some communications?

Ball: I think it is probably a matter of his composing it.

Bundy: Nothing is going to happen tonight.

Ball: He says that first thing in the morning he will send the message to K saying that he, pending some consideration of his proposal, he would hope that K will keep his ships away and prevent a confrontation because he thinks there is a chance the Americans are prepared to discuss the modalities of a negotiation.

Bundy: Does that pin us to anything?

Ball: I raised this with Stevenson and in the first place this is not a public thing, this is a private—

Bundy: It will be public soon enough.

Ball: He doesn't.

Bundy: U Thant is on and we are not on on this?

Ball: That's it.

Bundy: Stevenson may go down the drain.

Ball: He just gives his impression. I think it's worth a play.

Bundy: It's worth a try.

Ball: I asked Stevenson to try to get the thing from him in the morning and shoot it down to us as soon as he can. I think I would have put it up in tougher terms, but that's the way it went.

Bundy: Yes, I think the main thing is that Adlai should know what he has sent in the morning.

Ball: I asked him to get it from Thant first thing and let us know, and he said he would and I hope Thant doesn't give too much of an impression of our willingness, but in any event it's just Thant giving an impression.

Bundy: *Bundy reads reply to K.*

Ball: There is only one very minor point, but I think it might be a major one. That is we use these offensive weapons; actually, my understanding in the conversation with Gromyko, that Gromyko was explicit that they had no weapons that could reach the US.

Bundy: He didn't say it that way.

Ball: I got this from the Secretary.

Bundy: He didn't say it. At least it did not appear in any transcript we had.

Ball: This may have been given by Dobrynin.

Bundy: It is true that Dobrynin has said things. I think this language is more precise in the case than we can document to the Chairman.

Ball: Well, of course his answer will be that they are not offensive.

Bundy: Well, he never said that actually.

Ball: Well, except that this was the implication of what was said by—

Bundy: Then change it to "such as long-range nuclear missiles."

Ball: Yes, I think we can do that. It takes it out of that dialectical argument as to what's offensive and what isn't.

Bundy: "Such weapons as long-range nuclear missiles."

Ball: Yes.

Bundy: That doesn't let us off the bombers. "Such weapons as (we don't want quite long-range) nuclear missiles?"

Ball: I think that would be all right.

Bundy: "Of considerable range?" I don't know George; I have cleared it with everybody else; I think we had better leave it as it is. The point is clear enough.

Ball: Yes. We will deliver that tonight then.

Bundy: It'll be along. Klein is handling that.

Ball: The only thing that concerns me about the Stevenson thing is that he has probably given the impression to U Thant that we will go further than we will go. That's what worries me.

Bundy: I don't know how to advise you on that other than to say that we probably will not go further than we will go.

Ball: If it indicates a weakness in relation to K that will create another element of miscalculation.

Bundy: If he will hold off his ships, then the Americans are interested in the modalities?

Ball: Yes.

Bundy: Has Stevenson showed him our answer?

Ball: No. That is reserved for tomorrow morning.

Bundy: It would seem to me that you should say to Adlai that nothing in, from the point of view of us in Washington, any message to K should be inconsistent with that message.

Ball: I think I will get hold of Adlai first thing in the morning and let him go over and talk to Thant.

Bundy: If Adlai knows early in the morning that he must not sign the US to anything that would make that letter impossible without checking back with us.

Ball: I think that's the way to leave it.

Bundy: Right.

*Telegram from the Department of State to the Embassy
in the Soviet Union
Washington, October 25, 1962, 1:59 a.m.*

Signed original following message from President to Khrushchev delivered to Soviet Embassy 1:45 a.m. Washington time October 25. Please deliver to highest-ranking Soviet official immediately available.

October 25, 1962

Dear Mr Chairman:

I have received your letter of October 24, and I regret very much that you still do not appear to understand what it is that has moved us in this matter.

The sequence of events is clear. In August there were reports of important shipments of military equipment and technicians from the Soviet Union to Cuba. In early September I indicated very plainly that the United States would regard any shipment of offensive weapons as presenting the gravest issues. After that time, this Government received the most explicit assurance from your Government and its representatives, both publicly and privately, that no offensive weapons were being sent to Cuba. If you will review the statement issued by TASS in September, you will see how clearly this assurance was given.

In reliance on these solemn assurances I urged restraint upon those in this country who were urging action in this matter at that time. And then I learned beyond doubt what you have not denied—namely, that all these public assurances were false and that your military people had set out recently to establish a set of missile bases in Cuba. I ask you to recognize clearly, Mr Chairman, that it was not I who issued the first challenge in this case, and that in the light of this record these activities in Cuba required the responses I have announced.

I repeat my regret that these events should cause a
deterioration in our relations. I hope that your
Government will take the necessary action to permit a
restoration of the earlier situation.
Sincerely yours,
John F. Kennedy

Please report time delivery.

RUSK

*Telegram from the Department of State to the Mission
to the United Nations
Washington, October 25, 1962, 2:00 a.m.*

Deliver to Ambassador Stevenson personally 8:30 a.m.

On further checking with White House believe it
important that you follow up first thing Thursday morning on suggestion you made to Secretary General late
Wednesday night to make sure his message to Khrushchev
reflects following general line:

(1) Concern that Soviet vessels may be under
    instructions to challenge quarantine and thus bring
    on a confrontation at sea between Soviet ships and
    Western Hemisphere ships which could lead to
    escalation of violence.
(2) Concern that such confrontation would destroy
    possibility of talks such as Secretary General has
    suggested as prelude to political settlement.
(3) Hope that Khrushchev will hold his ships out of
    interception area for limited time in order to permit
    discussions of modalities of agreement.
(4) Confidence, on basis that Soviet ships are not
    proceeding to Cuba, that United States will avoid
    direct confrontation with them during same period
    in order to minimize chances of untoward incidence.

FYI: While we are quite ready to begin conversations on modalities as suggested by SYG we should not give SYG impression nor encourage him to give Khrushchev impression that we can agree on any interim arrangement for uninspected moratorium or "voluntary suspension" without explicit provision for adequate UN observation to ensure against weapons being imported, work on sites continued, or offensive weapons being operational. In other words White House feels it undesirable to give any impression to SYG that would be inconsistent with draft answer to SYG's proposal that was cleared by President and sent you Wednesday night.

RUSK

Memorandum for the files
Washington, October 25, 1962

Executive Committee meeting, all members present
McCone reported on intelligence, reviewing summary of 25 October, including penciled memorandums as indicated, plus Cline memorandum of 25 October on talks with Sir Kenneth Strong, and the Watch Report of same date.

I called special attention to the *Belovodsk* and reported on page II-5 and the searching of the Cuban airplane by Canadians as reported on page IV-2. Also the shipping schedule.

McNamara reported that at 7 o'clock a destroyer intercepted the tanker *Bucharest* which responded destination was Havana, cargo was petroleum and the *Bucharest* was permitted to proceed under surveillance. He stated that no United States Navy ships had orders to board. He recommended orders be issued to immediately board Bloc ships and then the *Bucharest* be boarded. Decision was reached that Navy be instructed to board the next Soviet ship contacted which would be the *Graznyy*, a tanker, but which was carrying a deck load which might be missile field tanks. Later in the meeting decision was reached not to board the *Bucharest*. Contact was to be made with the *Graznyy* as early as possible and that was estimated to be about 8 o'clock in the evening, Friday, October 26th.

McNamara recommended several recurring low-level surveillance strikes of multiple aircraft in an operation that would resemble an air strike. [*6½ lines of source text not declassified*] It was the Secretary's opinion that since all of these were indicators of some indecision on the part of the Soviets, that we should pursue low-level surveillance in the interests of gathering intelligence, simulating air attack, demonstrating our intention to watch construction, familiarizing ourselves with camouflage, and to determine whether the Soviets are building additional sites. This recommendation was approved and eight sorties were ordered immediately to cover the nine missile sites, the IL-28 site, the MiG-21 airfield, and the nuclear storage sites and the KOMAR missile ship sites. It was decided this reconnaissance should not be announced but, if questioned, we should refer to the President's statement.

McCone then noted the number of ships in the Eastern Atlantic and in the Baltic and Mediterranean which had turned back. Dillon asked about ships in the Pacific. The President asked whether Soviet ships bound elsewhere than Cuba had changed course. McCone said he would report on this in the afternoon.

There was a further discussion of the policy of stopping or hailing non-Bloc ships. It was decided that all ships must be hailed.

Rusk raised the question of discussions with the United Nations. Draft of US reply to the U Thant letter was approved with modifications. It was agreed at the meeting that we must insist upon the removal of missiles from Cuba in addition to demands that construction be stopped and that UN inspectors be permitted at once.

Bundy reviewed Khrushchev letter to the President of the 24th of October and the Kennedy reply. McNamara raised the question of accelerating or raising the escalation of the actions we have so far taken, expressing concern over the plateau, indicating determination to meet our ultimate objective of taking out the missile sites.

Rusk then asked certain actions on the part of CIA as follows: (1) An answer to questions of the effect on Cuba because ships were turned about as indicated in recent reports; (2) What had happened to Soviet ships which were bound elsewhere than Cuba; (3) The general Cuban reaction to our actions to date: (a) Do they know about Soviet missiles? (b) Have they heard the President's speech? (c) What is the morale in Cuba?

McCone promised answers.

JOHN A. McCONE
Director

Record of action of the fourth meeting of the Executive Committee of the National Security Council
Washington, October 25, 1962

1. Mr McCone presented the intelligence briefing.

2. The President requested Mr McCone to prepare a careful analysis of the present situation inside Cuba, and he asked for further consideration by USIA of the possibility of dropping propaganda leaflets.

3. The Secretary of Defense reported the current military situation, and on the President's direction instructions were issued for selective investigation and boarding of non-Bloc ships, excluding tankers.

4. The Secretary reported that all armed forces in Cuba have been instructed to fire only in response to attack. Many installations are so camouflaged as to be in a low state of readiness. The Secretary recommended a program of low-level reconnaissance for the purpose of improving intelligence, camouflaging the possibility of a later low-level attack, and emphasizing our concern with offensive installations already in Cuba. The President approved an immediate daylight mission of eight low-level reconnaissance aircraft to cover missile sites, airfields holding IL-28s and MiGs, KOMAR naval vessels, coastal installations, nuclear storage sites, and selected SAM sites.

5. The President directed that the tanker *Bucharest* not be intercepted for the present. Her status as a tanker with no contraband cargo made it desirable to allow her to proceed. He directed further that the Defense Department be prepared to make an intercept of an appropriate Bloc ship on Friday in daylight.

6. The President approved a version of an answer to U Thant, but in later discussion a revised version was worked out between New York and Washington and approved by the President at 1:15 p.m.

7. There was preliminary discussion of alternative courses of action in the immediate future, and the President asked the other members of the Committee to make appropriate arrangements for preparing alternative courses of action for discussion with him at a later meeting.

8. The President approved the recommendation of the Secretary of Defense that missile fuel be added to the list of contraband goods under the Proclamation of Interdiction.

McGEORGE BUNDY

Telegram from the Mission to the United Nations to the Department of State
New York, October 25, 1962, 8:40 p.m.

For Harriman—State; Forrestal—White House. From Schlesinger. Following is text of memo I sent to Stevenson October 24:

Memorandum to Ambassador Stevenson.

I had a talk this evening with Averell Harriman. He made the following points:

1. Khrushchev, he said, is sending us desperate signals to get us to help take him off the hook. He is sending messages exactly as he did to Eisenhower directly after the U-2 affair. Eisenhower ignored these messages to his cost. We must not repeat Eisenhower's mistake.

2. The signals are (1) the instructions to the Soviet ships to change their course; (2) the message to Bertrand Russell; (3) his obviously premeditated appearance last night at an American concert in Moscow and his subsequent visit with the American singer.

3. In view of these signals from Khrushchev, the worst mistake we can possibly make is to get tougher and to escalate. Khrushchev is pleading with us to help him find a way out.

4. The best way out is the resolution recommended by Cleveland as Tab C in his memorandum (the defanging resolution). However, Harriman disagrees with Cleveland's

view that we should try to negotiate this resolution. He thinks we should try to get Ireland to introduce the resolution tomorrow. We cannot afford to lose any time. Incidents—stopping of ships, etc.—will begin the process of escalation, engage Soviet prestige, and reduce the chances of a peaceful resolution. If we act shrewdly and speedily, we can bail Khrushchev out and discredit the tough guys around him—the ones who sold him the Cuban adventure on the theory that Americans were too liberal to fight.

ARTHUR SCHLESINGER, JR

Statement by Soviet Ambassador Zorin
United Nations Security Council Meeting, October 25, 1962

When Mr Stevenson today attempted to accuse the Soviet Union as the prime cause for these aggressive actions on the part of the United States, I should like to draw attention of the Council to a completely surprising fact.

In the statement of President Kennedy of the 22nd of October, Mr Kennedy said that during the last week unmistakable evidence has established the fact that a series of offensive missile sites is now in preparation on that island.

On the 16th of October the President of the United States had in his hands incontrovertible information. What happened after that? On the 18th of October the President of the United States was receiving the representative of the Soviet Union, the Minister of Foreign Affairs, Mr Gromyko, two days after he had already in his hands incontrovertible evidence.

One may well ask why did the President of the United States in receiving the minister of another power which the Government of the United States is now accusing of dispatching offensive arms to Cuba against the United States, why then did he not say a word to the Minister of

Foreign Affairs of the Soviet Union with respect to these incontrovertible facts?

Why? Because no such facts exist. The Government of the United States has no such fact in its hands except these [sic] falsified information of the United States Intelligence Agency, which are being displayed for review in halls and which are sent to the press.

Falsity is what the United States has in its hands, false evidence.

The Government of the United States has deliberately intensified the crisis, has deliberately prepared this provocation and had tried to cover up this provocation by means of a discussion in the Security Council.

You cannot conduct world policies and politics on such an opportunistic matter. Such steps can lead you to catastrophic consequences for the whole world, and the Soviet Government has issued a warning to the United States and to the world on that score.

The Soviet Union considers that the Government of the United States of America must display reserve and stay the execution of its piratical threats, which are fraught with the most serious consequence.

The question of war and peace is so vital that we should consider useful a top level meeting in order to discuss all the problems which have arisen to do everything to remove the danger of unleashing a thermonuclear war.

Statement by Ambassador Stevenson to UN Security Council
October 25, 1962

I want to say to you, Mr Zorin, that I do not have your talent for obfuscation, for distortion, for confusing language, and for doubletalk. And I must confess to you that I am glad that I do not!

But if I understood what you said, you said that my position had changed, that today I was defensive because we did not have the evidence to prove our assertions, that your Government had installed long-range missiles in Cuba.

Well, let me say something to you, Mr Ambassador—we do have the evidence. We have it, and it is clear and it is incontrovertible. And let me say something else—those weapons must be taken out of Cuba.

Next, let me say to you that, if I understood you, with a trespass on credibility that excels your best, you said that our position had changed since I spoke here the other day because of the pressures of world opinion and the majority of the United Nations. Well, let me say to you, sir, you are wrong again. We have had no pressure from anyone whatsoever. We came in here today to indicate our willingness to discuss Mr U Thant's proposals, and that is the only change that has taken place.

But let me also say to you, sir, that there has been a change. You—the Soviet Union has sent these weapons to Cuba. You—the Soviet Union has upset the balance of power in the world. You—the Soviet Union has created this new danger, not the United States.

And you ask with a fine show of indignation why the President did not tell Mr Gromyko on last Thursday about our evidence, at the very time that Mr Gromyko was blandly denying to the President that the USSR was placing such weapons on sites in the new world.

Well, I will tell you why—because we were assembling the evidence, and perhaps it would be instructive to the world to see how a Soviet official—how far he would go in perfidy. Perhaps we wanted to know if this country faced another example of nuclear deceit like that one a year ago, when in stealth, the Soviet Union broke the nuclear test moratorium.

And while we are asking questions, let me ask you why your Government—your Foreign Minister—deliberately, cynically deceived us about the nuclear build-up in Cuba.

And, finally, the other day, Mr Zorin, I remind you that you did not deny the existence of these weapons. Instead, we heard that they had suddenly become defensive weapons. But today again if I heard you correctly, you now say that they do not exist, or that we haven't proved they exist, with another fine flood of rhetorical scorn.

All right, sir, let me ask you one simple question: Do you, Ambassador Zorin, deny that the USSR has placed and is placing medium- and intermediate-range missiles and sites in Cuba? Yes or no—don't wait for the translation—yes or no?

(The Soviet representative refused to answer.)

You can answer yes or no. You have denied they exist. I want to know if I understood you correctly. I am prepared to wait for my answer until hell freezes over, if that's your decision. And I am also prepared to present the evidence in this room.

(The President called on the representative of Chile to speak, but Ambassador Stevenson continued as follows.)

I have not finished my statement. I asked you a question. I have had no reply to the question, and I will now proceed, if I may, to finish my statement.

I doubt if anyone in this room, except possibly the representative of the Soviet Union, has any doubt about the facts. But in view of his statements and the statements of the Soviet Government up until last Thursday, when Mr Gromyko denied the existence or any intention of installing such weapons in Cuba, I am going to make a portion of the evidence available right now. If you will indulge me for a moment, we will set up an easel here in the back of the room where I hope it will be visible to everyone.

The first of these exhibits shows an area north of the village of Candelaria, near San Cristóbal, southwest of Habana. A map, together with a small photograph, shows precisely where the area is in Cuba.

The first photograph shows the area in late August 1962; it was then, if you can see from where you are sitting, only a peaceful countryside.

The second photograph shows the same area one day last week. A few tents and vehicles had come into the area, new spur roads had appeared, and the main road had been improved.

The third photograph, taken only 24 hours later, shows facilities for a medium-range missile battalion installed. There are tents for 400 or 500 men. At the end of the new spur road there are seven 1,000-mile missile trailers. There are four launcher-erector mechanisms for placing these missiles in erect firing position. This missile is a mobile weapon, which can be moved rapidly from one place to another. It is identical with the 1,000-mile missiles which have been displayed in Moscow parades. All of this, I remind you, took place in 24 hours.

The second exhibit, which you can all examine at your leisure, shows three successive photographic enlargements of another missile base of the same type in the area of San Cristóbal. These enlarged photographs clearly show six of these missiles on trailers and three erectors.

And that is only one example of the first type of ballistic missile installation in Cuba.

A second type of installation is designed for a missile of intermediate range—a range of about 2,200 miles. Each site of this type has four launching pads.

The exhibit on this type of missile shows a launching area being constructed near Guanajay, southwest of the city of Habana. As in the first exhibit, a map and small photograph show this area as it appeared in late August 1962, when no military activities were apparent.

A second large photograph shows the same area about six weeks later. Here you will see a very heavy construction effort to push the launching area to rapid completion. The pictures show two large concrete bunkers or control centers in process of construction, one between each pair of launching pads. They show heavy concrete retaining walls being erected to shelter vehicles and equipment from rocket blast-off. They show cable scars leading from the launch pads to the bunkers. They show a large reinforced concrete building under construction. A building with a heavy arch may well be intended as the storage area for the nuclear warheads. The installation is not yet complete, and no warheads are yet visible.

The next photograph shows a closer view of the same intermediate-range launch site. You can clearly see one of the pairs of large concrete launch pads, with a concrete building from which launching operations for three pads are controlled. Other details are visible, such as fuel tanks.

And that is only one example, one illustration, of the work being furnished in Cuba on intermediate-range missile bases.

Now, in addition to missiles, the Soviet Union is installing other offensive weapons in Cuba. The next photograph is of an airfield at San Julián in western Cuba. On this field you will see 22 crates designed to transport the fuselages of Soviet Ilyushin-28 bombers. Four of the aircraft are uncrated, and one is partially assembled. These bombers, sometimes known as Beagles, have an operating radius of about 750 miles and are capable of carrying nuclear weapons. At the same field you can see one of the surface-to-air antiaircraft guided missile bases, with six missiles per base, which now ring the entire coastline of Cuba.

Another set of two photographs covers still another area of deployment of medium-range missiles in Cuba. These photographs are on a larger scale than the others and reveal many details of an improved field-type launch site. One photograph provides an overall view of most of the site; you can see clearly three of the four launching pads. The second photograph displays details of two of these pads. Even an eye untrained in photographic interpretation can clearly see the buildings in which the missiles are checked out and maintained ready to fire, a missile trailer, trucks to move missiles out to the launching pad, erectors to raise the missiles to launching position, tank trucks to provide fuel, vans from which the missile firing is controlled, in short, all of the requirements to maintain, load, and fire these terrible weapons. These weapons, gentlemen, these launching pads, these planes—of which we have illustrated only a fragment—are a part of a much larger weapons complex, what is called a weapons system.

To support this build-up, to operate these advanced weapons systems, the Soviet Union has sent a large number of military personnel to Cuba—a force now amounting to several thousand men.

These photographs, as I say, are available to members for detailed examination in the Trusteeship Council room following this meeting. There I will have one of my aides who will gladly explain them to you in such detail as you may require.

I have nothing further to say at this time.

∘⸰◈◈◈⸰∘

After another statement by the Soviet representative, Ambassador Stevenson replied as follows:

Mr President and gentlemen, I won't detain you but one minute.

I have not had a direct answer to my question. The representative of the Soviet Union says that the official answer of the USSR was the TASS statement that they don't need to locate missiles in Cuba. Well, I agree—they don't need to. But the question is, have they missiles in Cuba—and that question remains unanswered. I knew it would be.

As to the authenticity of the photographs, which Mr Zorin has spoken about with such scorn, I wonder if the Soviet Union would ask its Cuban colleague to permit a UN team to go to these sites. If so, I can assure you that we can direct them to the proper places very quickly.

And now I hope that we can get down to business, that we can stop this sparring. We know the facts, and so do you, sir, and we are ready to talk about them. Our job here is not to score debating points. Our job, Mr Zorin, is to save the peace. And if you are ready to try, we are.

Telegram from the Embassy in France to the Department of State representing the views of Turkey on the removal of missiles Paris, October 25, 1962, 9:00 p.m.

CUBA. Secret; Priority. Received at 6:41 p.m. October 25 Eyes only for Secretary. Department may desire repeat Ankara and Rome eyes only ambassadors.

Turkish PermRep here has consistently made it clear that Turks set great store in Jupiters placed in Turkey. He makes very clear that Turkey regards these Jupiters as symbol of Alliance's determination to use atomic weapons against Russian attack on Turkey whether by large conventional or nuclear forces, although Turks have been most reluctant admit presence IRBMs publicly. Fact that Jupiters are obsolescent and vulnerable does not apparently affect present Turkish thinking. My impression is that symbolic importance represents a fixed GOT view, although of course Hare can comment much better than I on this point.

For above reason any arrangement of kind suggested reftel which would not have received prior complete support by GOT would, it seems to us, be most damaging. I emphasize prior consultation, and I think it should be an arrangement freely arrived at by them. My guess is that any arrangement that would not substitute some other considerable kind of atomic capability in Turkey for Jupiters would be rejected by them. See suggestions paras. 8 and 9 below.

In this connection, would appear preferable, since Cuba is by definition outside NATO area, to offer close down some US nuclear-capable base outside NATO area rather than making deal involving Turkey or Italy. Such deal would then be strictly US–USSR trade rather than involving one of our NATO allies in any deal.

I think that we must be fully aware there is real possibility that, outside of any arrangement made in over-all disarmament context, whole Alliance might be dismayed by such a deal which would compromise and invalidate firm US action re Cuba which has received substantial approval from Alliance. As all know, these weapons were put in Europe as result of heads of government decision in 1957 in response to boastful Soviet MRBM threat to Europe, and Alliance might very well conclude that US was willing to weaken nuclear defenses in Europe in order to remove threat in Western Hemisphere. However, cannot discount possibility that some members Alliance might be willing accept Cuba–Turk deal "to avoid nuclear war," i.e., Norwegians, Danes, and maybe even British.

Re question of removal Jupiters accompanied by stationing of Polaris submarines in area, doubt whether mere deployment of Polaris would be attractive to Turks since they really would have no say in use of Polaris in time of crisis and they turned down similar proposal in April 1961. Nevertheless, one might argue Turks really have no say over Jupiter use now because of custodial arrangements, but they feel some assurance in having weapons on their territory and somewhat in their hands. Turkish concern re Polaris substitution might be partially met by consulting them on targeting so as to assure that targets of interest to them are covered by Polaris. Also could point out that three Polaris submarines in area would effectively more than double coverage presently afforded by obsolete Jupiters. Doubt, however, above arrangements would adequately compensate Turks.

Re suggestion reftel concerning some other significant military offset such as NATO seaborne multilateral nuclear force, we believe most expeditious way to do this would be set up small Southern Command Multilateral Seaborne Force on a "pilot basis." If such firm suggestion made this should be acceptable arrangement to Turks to compensate for loss of obsolete Jupiters. Such offer would take form of converting a number of merchant-type vessels to MRBM force, utilizing Polaris A-2 missiles along general lines of US studies and presentation to NAC by Smith on 22 October. Ships could be deployed in eastern Mediterranean and could be manned by Turkish, Italian, and American mixed crews and also possibly Greeks, with appropriate targets of interest to Mediterranean allies covered. Although implementation of this type of force could be realized in short period of time, it would be necessary, as interim step before force comes into being, to station Polaris, as suggested reftel, in eastern Mediterranean. Polaris deployment would then fill gap caused by removal of Jupiters, while Southern Command Multilateral Force was being put together. At same time, rest of Alliance could be investigating possibility of setting up NATO-wide multilateral seaborne force. Southern Command MLF might well serve as model for larger force and could be expanded as other allies indicated desirability to join arrangements this type. To make this whole alternative palatable to Turks and others would require clear US support to implement multilateral seaborne-type force, and if properly presented to Turks and Italians we could highlight flexibility and greater efficiency this type force over Jupiters. Our impression here is that Italians more prone to dismantle Jupiters if proper substitute can be found.

Such pilot arrangement, which would not come into being immediately, could permit us offer Soviets withdrawal obsolete Jupiters as face-saving device for Cuban withdrawal (Polaris deployment would cover in interval). Whether or not this would be acceptable to Soviets, the gesture could be made and might well look good in face of world opinion. Whether or not they accept this type of trade, we believe that in any event strong consideration should be given to withdrawing Jupiters and creating pilot MLF since this would strengthen NATO nuclear capability in eastern Mediterranean. Although Turks didn't agree to stop Jupiter program in 1961, even when faced with facts Jupiters obsolete, of no military value and good Soviet target, they might be willing now to accept substitute in MLF which more effective from all angles.

Memorandum From ABC Correspondent John Scali to the Director of the Bureau of Intelligence and Research (Hilsman)
Washington, undated

Aleksandr S. Fomin, Sov Emby Counselor, at lunch which he sought urgently, asks if State would be interested in settlement of Cuban crisis along these lines:

Bases would be dismantled under United Nations supervision and Castro would pledge not to accept offensive weapons of any kind, ever, in return for US pledge not to invade Cuba.

I said I didn't know but that perhaps this is something that could be talked about. He said if Stevenson pursued this line, Zorin would be interested. Asked that I check with State and let him know. He gave me his home telephone number so I could call him tonight, if necessary.

Fomin claimed that Cuban delegate to UN during Security Council debate asked for such no-invasion assurances in return for dismantling but that he got no reply. I told him I'd followed the UN debate very carefully but could not recall any such remarks on Cuba's part.

Fomin also said Russia had been forced "to make some concessions" to Communist China in order to convince them to stop the fighting against India. He declined to say what under my questioning. But he recalled they hadn't helped the ChiComs with nuclear weapons or conventional weapons in the past, even tanks, and hinted it might be aid in the conventional field.

Scali

OCTOBER 26–28, 1962

Telegram from the Embassy in the Soviet Union to the Department of State
Moscow, October 26, 1962, 7:00 p.m.

Embassy translation follows of letter from Khrushchev to President delivered to Embassy by messenger 4:43 p.m. Moscow time October 26, under cover of letter from Gromyko to me.

Begin text.

Dear Mr President: I have received your letter of October 25. From your letter, I got the feeling that you have some understanding of the situation which has developed and a sense of responsibility. I value this.

Now we have already publicly exchanged our evaluations of the events around Cuba and each of us has set forth his explanation and his understanding of these events. Consequently, I would think that, apparently, a continuation of an exchange of opinions at such a distance, even in the form of secret letters, will hardly add anything to that which one side has already said to the other.

I think you will understand me correctly if you are really concerned about the welfare of the world. Everyone needs peace: both capitalists, if they have not lost their reason, and, still more, Communists, people who know how to value not only their own lives but, more than anything, the lives of the peoples. We, Communists, are against all wars between states in general and have been defending the cause of peace since we came into the world. We have always regarded war as a calamity, and not as a game nor as a means for the attainment of definite goals, nor, all the more, as a goal in itself. Our goals are clear, and the means to attain them is labor. War is our enemy and a calamity for all the peoples.

It is thus that we, Soviet people, and, together with US, other peoples as well, understand the questions of war and peace. I can, in any case, firmly say this for the peoples of the socialist countries, as well as for all progressive people who want peace, happiness, and friendship among peoples.

I see, Mr President, that you too are not devoid of a sense of anxiety for the fate of the world understanding, and of what war entails. What would a war give you? You are threatening us with war. But you well know that the very least which you would receive in reply would be that you would experience the same consequences as those which you sent us. And that must be clear to us, people invested with authority, trust, and responsibility. We must not succumb to intoxication and petty passions, regardless of whether elections are impending in this or that country, or not impending. These are all transient things, but if indeed war should break out, then it would not be in our power to contain or stop it, for such is the logic of war. I have participated in two wars and know that war ends when it has rolled through cities and villages, everywhere sowing death and destruction.

In the name of the Soviet Government and the Soviet people, I assure you that your arguments regarding offensive weapons on Cuba are groundless. It is apparent from what you have written me that our conceptions are different on this score, or rather, we have different definitions for these or those military means, indeed, in reality, the same forms of weapons can have different interpretations.

You are a military man and, I hope, will understand me. Let us take for example a simple cannon. What sort of means is this: offensive or defensive? A cannon is a defensive means if it is set up to defend boundaries or a fortified area. But if one concentrates artillery, and adds to it the necessary number of troops, then the same cannons do become an offensive means, because they prepare and clear the way for infantry to advance. The same happens with missile-nuclear weapons as well, with any type of this weapon.

You are mistaken if you think that any of our means on Cuba are offensive. However, let us not argue now, it is apparent that I will not be able to convince you of this, but I say to you: You, Mr President, are a military man and should understand: can one advance, if one has on one's territory even an enormous quantity of missiles of various effective radiuses and various power, but using only these means. These missiles are a means of extermination and destruction, but one cannot advance with these missiles, even nuclear missiles of a power of 100 megatons because only people, troops, can advance, without people, any means however powerful cannot be offensive.

How can one, consequently, give such a completely incorrect interpretation as you are now giving, to the effect that some sort of means on Cuba are offensive. All the means located there, and I assure you of this, have a defensive character, are on Cuba solely for the purposes of defense, and we have sent them to Cuba at the request of the Cuban Government. You, however, say that these are offensive means.

But, Mr President, do you really seriously think that Cuba can attack the United States and that even we together with Cuba can advance upon you from the territory of Cuba? Can you really think that way? How is it possible? We do not understand this. Has something so new appeared in military strategy that one can think that it is possible to advance thus. I say precisely advance, and not destroy, since barbarians, people who have lost their sense, destroy.

I believe that you have no basis to think this way. You can regard us with distrust, but, in any case, you can be calm in this regard, that we are of sound mind and understand perfectly well that if we attack you, you will respond the same way. But you too will receive the same that you hurl against us. And I think that you also understand this. My conversation with you in Vienna gives me the right to talk to you this way.

This indicates that we are normal people, that we correctly understand and correctly evaluate the situation. Consequently, how can we permit the incorrect actions which you ascribe to us? Only lunatics or suicides, who themselves want to perish and to destroy the whole world before they die, could do this. We, however, want to live and do not at all want to destroy your country. We want something quite different: to compete with your country on a peaceful endeavor. We quarrel with you, we have differences in ideological questions. But our view of the world consists in this, that ideological questions, as well as economic problems, should be solved not by military means, they must be solved on the basis of peaceful competition, i.e., as this is understood in capitalist society, on the basis of competition. We have proceeded and are proceeding from the fact that the peaceful co-existence of the two different social-political systems, now existing in the world, is necessary, that it is necessary to assure a stable peace. That is the sort of principle we hold.

You have now proclaimed piratical measures, which were employed in the Middle Ages, when ships proceeding in international waters were attacked, and you have called this "a quarantine" around Cuba. Our vessels, apparently, will soon enter the zone which your Navy is patrolling. I assure you that these vessels, now bound for Cuba, are carrying the most innocent peaceful cargoes. Do you really think that we only occupy ourselves with the carriage of so-called offensive weapons, atomic and hydrogen bombs? Although perhaps your military people imagine that these (cargoes) are some sort of special type of weapon, I assure you that they are the most ordinary peaceful products.

Consequently, Mr President, let us show good sense. I assure you that on those ships, which are bound for Cuba, there are no weapons at all. The weapons which were necessary for the defense of Cuba are already there. I do not want to say that there were not any shipments of weapons at all. No, there were such shipments. But now Cuba has already received the necessary means of defense.

I don't know whether you can understand me and believe me. But I should like to have you believe in yourself and to agree that one cannot give way to passions; it is necessary to control them. And in what direction are events now developing? If you stop the vessels, then, as you yourself know, that would be piracy. If we started to do that with regard to your ships, then you would also be as indignant as we and the whole world now are. One cannot give another interpretation to such actions, because one cannot legalize lawlessness. If this were permitted, then there would be no peace, there would also be no peaceful co-existence. We should then be forced to put into effect the necessary measures of a defensive character to protect our interest in accordance with international law. Why should this be done? To what would all this lead?

Let us normalize relations. We have received an appeal from the Acting Secretary General of the UN, U Thant, with his proposals. I have already answered him. His proposals come to this, that our side should not transport armaments of any kind to Cuba during a certain period of time, while negotiations are being conducted—and we are ready to enter such negotiations—and the other side should not undertake any sort of piratical actions against vessels engaged in navigation on the high seas. I consider these proposals reasonable. This would be a way out of the situation which has been created, which would give the peoples the possibility of breathing calmly. You have asked what happened, what evoked the delivery of weapons to Cuba? You have spoken about this to our Minister of Foreign Affairs. I will tell you frankly, Mr President, what evoked it.

We were very grieved by the fact—I spoke about it in Vienna—that a landing took place, that an attack on Cuba was committed, as a result of which many Cubans perished. You yourself told me then that this had been a mistake. I respected that explanation. You repeated it to me several times, hinting that not everybody occupying a high position would acknowledge his mistakes as you had done. I value such frankness. For my part, I told you that we too possess no less courage; we also acknowledged those mistakes which had been committed during the history of our state, and not only acknowledged, but sharply condemned them.

If you are really concerned about the peace and welfare of your people, and this is your responsibility as President, then I, as the Chairman of the Council of Ministers, am concerned for my people. Moreover, the preservation of world peace should be our joint concern, since if, under contemporary conditions, war should break out, it would be a war not only between the Soviet Union and the United States which have no contentions between them, but a worldwide cruel and destructive war.

Why have we proceeded to assist Cuba with military and economic aid? The answer is: we have proceeded to do so only for reasons of humanitarianism. At one time, our people itself had a revolution, when Russia was still a backward country, we were attacked then. We were the target of attack by many countries. The USA participated in that adventure. This has been recorded by participants in the aggression against our country. A whole book has been written about this by General Graves, who, at that time, commanded the US Expeditionary Corps. Graves called it "The American Adventure in Siberia."

We know how difficult it is to accomplish a revolution and how difficult it is to reconstruct a country on new foundations. We sincerely sympathize with Cuba and the Cuban people, but we are not interfering in questions of domestic structure, we are not interfering in their affairs. The Soviet Union desires to help the Cubans build their life as they themselves wish and that others should not hinder them.

You once said that the United States was not preparing an invasion. But you also declared that you sympathized with the Cuban counter-revolutionary emigrants, that you support them and would help them to realize their plans against the present Government of Cuba. It is also not a secret to anyone that the threat of armed attack, aggression, has constantly hung, and continues to hang over Cuba. It was only this which impelled us to respond to the request of the Cuban Government to furnish it aid for the strengthening of the defensive capacity of this country.

If assurances were given by the President and the Government of the United States that the USA itself would not participate in an attack on Cuba and would restrain others from actions of this sort, if you would recall your fleet, this would immediately change everything. I am not speaking for Fidel Castro, but I think that he and the Government of Cuba, evidently, would declare demobilization and would appeal to the people to get down to peaceful labor. Then, too, the question of armaments would disappear, since, if there is no threat, then armaments are a burden for every people. Then, too, the question of the destruction, not only of the armaments which you call offensive, but of all other armaments as well, would look different.

I spoke in the name of the Soviet Government in the United Nations and introduced a proposal for the disbandment of all armies and for the destruction of all armaments. How then can I now count on those armaments?

Armaments bring only disasters. When one accumulates them, this damages the economy, and if one puts them to use, then they destroy people on both sides. Consequently, only a madman can believe that armaments are the principal means in the life of society. No, they are an enforced loss of human energy, and what is more are for the destruction of man himself. If people do not show wisdom, then in the final analysis they will come to a clash, like blind moles, and then reciprocal extermination will begin.

Let us therefore show statesmanlike wisdom. I propose: we, for our part, will declare that our ships, bound for Cuba, are not carrying any armaments. You would declare that the United States will not invade Cuba with its forces and will not support any sort of forces which might intend to carry out an invasion of Cuba. Then the necessity for the presence of our military specialists in Cuba would disappear.

Mr President, I appeal to you to weigh well what the aggressive, piratical actions, which you have declared the USA intends to carry out in international waters, would lead to. You yourself know that any sensible man simply cannot agree with this, cannot recognize your right to such actions.

If you did this as the first step toward the unleashing of war, well then, it is evident that nothing else is left to us but to accept this challenge of yours. If, however, you have not lost your self-control and sensibly conceive what this might lead to, then, Mr President, we and you ought not now to pull on the ends of the rope in which you have tied the knot of war, because the more the two of us pull, the tighter that knot will be tied. And a moment may come when that knot will be tied so tight that even he who tied it will not have the strength to untie it, and then it will be necessary to cut that knot. And what that would mean is not for me to explain to you, because you yourself understand perfectly of what terrible forces our countries dispose.

Consequently, if there is no intention to tighten that knot and thereby to doom the world to the catastrophe of thermonuclear war, then let us not only relax the forces pulling on the ends of the rope, let us take measures to untie that knot. We are ready for this.

We welcome all forces which stand on positions of peace. Consequently, I both expressed gratitude to Mr Bertrand Russell, who manifests alarm and concern for the

fate of the world, and readily responded to the appeal of
the Acting Secretary General of the UN, U Thant.

There, Mr President, are my thoughts, which, if you
agreed with them, could put an end to that tense situation
which is disturbing all peoples.

These thoughts are dictated by a sincere desire to relieve
the situation, to remove the threat of war.

Respectfully yours,

N. KHRUSHCHEV

End text.

Original of letter being air pouched today under transmit-
tal slip to Executive Secretariat.

KOHLER

Message from Chairman Khrushchev to President Kennedy
(a second letter)
Moscow, October 27, 1962

A note on the source text indicates a copy was sent to
Acting Secretary General U Thant. Problems of
Communism reports that this message was broadcast over
Moscow radio at 5:00 p.m., the same time the Russian text
was delivered to the Embassy.

Dear Mr President, I have studied with great satisfaction
your reply to Mr Thant concerning measures that should
be taken to avoid contact between our vessels and thereby
avoid irreparable and fatal consequences. This reasonable
step on your part strengthens my belief that you are showing concern for the preservation of peace, which I note
with satisfaction.

I have already said that our people, our Government,
and I personally, as Chairman of the Council of Ministers,
are concerned solely with having our country develop and

occupy a worthy place among all peoples of the world in economic competition, in the development of culture and the arts, and in raising the living standard of the people. This is the most noble and necessary field for competition, and both the victor and the vanquished will derive only benefit from it, because it means peace and an increase in the means by which man lives and finds enjoyment.

In your statement you expressed the opinion that the main aim was not simply to come to an agreement and take measures to prevent contact between our vessels and consequently a deepening of the crisis which could, as a result of such contacts, spark a military conflict, after which all negotiations would be superfluous because other forces and other laws would then come into play—the laws of war. I agree with you that this is only the first step. The main thing that must be done is to normalize and stabilize the state of peace among states and among peoples.

I understand your concern for the security of the United States, Mr President, because this is the primary duty of a President. But we too are disturbed about these same questions; I bear these same obligations as Chairman of the Council of Ministers of the USSR. You have been alarmed by the fact that we have aided Cuba with weapons, in order to strengthen its defense capability— precisely defense capability—because whatever weapons it may possess, Cuba cannot be equated with you since the difference in magnitude is so great, particularly in view of modern means of destruction. Our aim has been and is to help Cuba, and no one can dispute the humanity of our motives, which are oriented toward enabling Cuba to live peacefully and develop in the way its people desire.

You wish to ensure the security of your country, and this is understandable. But Cuba, too, wants the same thing; all countries want to maintain their security. But how are we, the Soviet Union, our Government, to assess your actions which are expressed in the fact that you have surrounded the Soviet Union with military bases; surrounded our allies with military bases; placed military bases literally around our country; and stationed your missile armaments there? This is no secret. Responsible American personages openly declare that it is so. Your missiles are located in Britain, are located in Italy, and are aimed against us. Your missiles are located in Turkey.

You are disturbed over Cuba. You say that this disturbs you because it is 90 miles by sea from the coast of the United States of America. But Turkey adjoins us; our sentries patrol back and forth and see each other. Do you consider, then, that you have the right to demand security for your own country and the removal of the weapons you call offensive, but do not accord the same right to us? You have placed destructive missile weapons, which you call offensive, in Turkey, literally next to us. How then can recognition of our equal military capacities be reconciled with such unequal relations between our great states? This is irreconcilable.

It is good, Mr President, that you have agreed to have our representatives meet and begin talks, apparently through the mediation of U Thant, Acting Secretary General of the United Nations. Consequently, he to some degree has assumed the role of a mediator and we consider that he will be able to cope with this responsible mission, provided, of course, that each party drawn into this controversy displays good will.

I think it would be possible to end the controversy quickly and normalize the situation, and then the people could breathe more easily, considering that statesmen charged with responsibility are of sober mind and have an awareness of their responsibility combined with the ability to solve complex questions and not bring things to a military catastrophe.

I therefore make this proposal: We are willing to remove from Cuba the means which you regard as offensive. We are willing to carry this out and to make this pledge in the United Nations. Your representatives will make a declaration to the effect that the United States, for its part, considering the uneasiness and anxiety of the Soviet State, will remove its analogous means from Turkey. Let us reach agreement as to the period of time needed by you and by us to bring this about. And, after that, persons entrusted by the United Nations Security Council could inspect on the spot the fulfillment of the pledges made. Of course, the permission of the Governments of Cuba and of Turkey is necessary for the entry into those countries of these representatives and for the inspection of the fulfillment of the pledge made by each side. Of course it would be best if these representatives enjoyed the confidence of the Security Council, as well as yours and mine—both the United States and the Soviet Union—and also that of Turkey and Cuba. I do not think it would be difficult to select people who would enjoy the trust and respect of all parties concerned.

We, in making this pledge, in order to give satisfaction and hope to the peoples of Cuba and Turkey and to strengthen their confidence in their security, will make a statement within the framework of the Security Council to the effect that the Soviet Government gives a solemn promise to respect the inviolability of the borders and sovereignty of Turkey, not to interfere in its internal affairs, not to invade Turkey, not to make available our territory as a bridgehead for such an invasion, and that it would also restrain those who contemplate committing aggression against Turkey, either from the territory of the Soviet Union or from the territory of Turkey's other neighboring states.

The United States Government will make a similar statement within the framework of the Security Council regarding Cuba. It will declare that the United States will respect the inviolability of Cuba's borders and its sovereignty, will pledge not to interfere in its internal affairs, not to invade Cuba itself or make its territory available as a bridgehead for such an invasion, and will also restrain those who might contemplate committing aggression against Cuba, either from the territory of the United States or from the territory of Cuba's other neighboring states.

Of course, for this we would have to come to an agreement with you and specify a certain time limit. Let us agree to some period of time, but without unnecessary delay—say within two or three weeks, not longer than a month.

The means situated in Cuba, of which you speak and which disturb you, as you have stated, are in the hands of Soviet officers. Therefore, any accidental use of them to the detriment of the United States is excluded. These means are situated in Cuba at the request of the Cuban Government and are only for defense purposes. Therefore, if there is no invasion of Cuba, or attack on the Soviet Union or any of our other allies, then of course these means are not and will not be a threat to anyone. For they are not for purposes of attack.

If you are agreeable to my proposal, Mr President, then we would send our representatives to New York, to the United Nations, and would give them comprehensive instructions in order that an agreement may be reached more quickly. If you also select your people and give them the corresponding instructions, then this question can be quickly resolved.

Why would I like to do this? Because the whole world is now apprehensive and expects sensible actions of us. The greatest joy for all peoples would be the announcement of our agreement and of the eradication of the controversy that has arisen. I attach great importance to this agreement in so far as it could serve as a good beginning and could in particular make it easier to reach agreement on banning nuclear weapons tests. The question of the tests could be solved in parallel fashion, without connecting one with the other, because these are different issues. However, it is important that agreement be reached on both these issues so as to present humanity with a fine gift, and also to gladden it with the news that agreement has been reached on the cessation of nuclear tests and that consequently the atmosphere will no longer be poisoned. Our position and yours on this issue are very close together.

All of this could possibly serve as a good impetus toward the finding of mutually acceptable agreements on other controversial issues on which you and I have been exchanging views. These views have so far not been resolved, but they are awaiting urgent solution, which would clear up the international atmosphere. We are prepared for this.

These are my proposals, Mr President.

Respectfully yours,
N. KHRUSHCHEV

Memorandum from S. P. Ivanov to Comrade N. S. Khrushchev
October 28, 1962

TOP SECRET
CC CPSU

I am reporting:
27 October 1962 a U-2 aircraft entered the territory of Cuba at an altitude of 16,000 meters at 17:00 hours Moscow time with the objective of photographing the

combat disposition of troops, and in the course of 1 hour 21 minutes proceeded along a flight route over Yaguajay–Ciego de Avila–Camagüey–Manzanillo–San Luis–Guantánamo–Preston.

With the aim of not permitting the photographs to fall into US hands, at 18:20 Moscow time this aircraft was shot down by two antiaircraft missiles of the 507th Antiaircraft Missile Regiment at an altitude of 21,000 meters. The aircraft fell in the vicinity of Antilla; a search has been organized.

On the same day there were eight violations of Cuban airspace by US aircraft.

R. MALINOVSKY
28 *October* 1962, 10:45
No. 80819

Attested: Colonel General
S.P. IVANOV
28 *October* 1962

Message from Chairman Khrushchev to President Kennedy
Moscow, October 28, 1962

This message was broadcast over Moscow radio at 5:00 p.m. and a copy delivered to the Embassy in Moscow at 5:10.

Dear Mr President: I have received your message of October 27. I express my satisfaction and thank you for the sense of proportion you have displayed and for realization of the responsibility which now devolves on you for the preservation of the peace of the world.

I regard with great understanding your concern and the concern of the United States people in connection with the fact that the weapons you describe as offensive are formidable weapons indeed. Both you and we understand what kind of weapons these are.

In order to eliminate as rapidly as possible the conflict which endangers the cause of peace, to give an assurance to all people who crave peace, and to reassure the American people, who, I am certain, also want peace, as do the people of the Soviet Union, the Soviet Government, in addition to earlier instructions on the discontinuation of further work on weapons construction sites, has given a new order to dismantle the arms which you described as offensive, and to crate and return them to the Soviet Union.

Mr President, I should like to repeat what I had already written to you in my earlier messages—that the Soviet Government has given economic assistance to the Republic of Cuba, as well as arms, because Cuba and the Cuban people were constantly under the continuous threat of an invasion of Cuba.

A piratic vessel had shelled Havana. They say that this shelling was done by irresponsible Cuban émigrés. Perhaps so, however, the question is from where did they shoot. It is a fact that these Cubans have no territory, they are fugitives from their country, and they have no means to conduct military operations.

This means that someone put into their hands these weapons for shelling Havana and for piracy in the Caribbean in Cuban territorial waters. It is impossible in our time not to notice a piratic ship, considering the concentration in the Caribbean of American ships from which everything can be seen and observed.

In these conditions, pirate ships freely roam around and shell Cuba and make piratic attacks on peaceful cargo ships. It is known that they even shelled a British cargo ship. In a word, Cuba was under the continuous threat of aggressive forces, which did not conceal their intention to invade its territory.

The Cuban people want to build their life in their own interests without external interference. This is their right, and they cannot be blamed for wanting to be masters of their own country and disposing of the fruits of their own labor.

The threat of invasion of Cuba and all other schemes for creating tension over Cuba are designed to strike the Cuban people with a sense of insecurity, intimidate them, and prevent them from peacefully building their new life.

Mr President, I should like to say clearly once more that we could not remain indifferent to this. The Soviet Government decided to render assistance to Cuba with the means of defense against aggression—only with means for defense purposes. We have supplied the defense means which you describe as offensive means. We have supplied them to prevent an attack on Cuba—to prevent rash acts.

I regard with respect and trust the statement you made in your message of October 27, 1962, that there would be no attack, no invasion of Cuba, and not only on the part of the United States, but also on the part of other nations of the Western Hemisphere, as you said in your same message. Then the motives which induced us to render assistance of such a kind to Cuba disappear.

It is for this reason that we instructed our officers—these means as I had already informed you earlier are in the hands of the Soviet officers—to take appropriate measures to discontinue construction of the aforementioned facilities, to dismantle them, and to return them to the Soviet Union. As I had informed you in the letter of October 27, we are prepared to reach agreement to enable United Nations Representatives to verify the dismantling of these means.

Thus in view of the assurances you have given and our instructions on dismantling, there is every condition for eliminating the present conflict.

I note with satisfaction that you have responded to the desire I expressed with regard to elimination of the afore-mentioned dangerous situation, as well as with regard to providing conditions for a more thoughtful appraisal of the international situation, fraught as it is with great dangers in our age of thermonuclear weapons, rocketry, spaceships, global rockets, and other deadly weapons. All people are interested in insuring peace.

Therefore, vested with trust and great responsibility, we must not allow the situation to become aggravated and must stamp out the centers where a dangerous situation fraught with grave consequences to the cause of peace has arisen. If we, together with you, and with the assistance of other people of good will, succeed in eliminating this tense atmosphere, we should also make certain that no other dangerous conflicts which could lead to a world nuclear catastrophe would arise.

In conclusion, I should like to say something about a detente between NATO and the Warsaw Treaty countries that you have mentioned. We have spoken about this long since and are prepared to continue to exchange views on this question with you and to find a reasonable solution.

We should like to continue the exchange of views on the prohibition of atomic and thermonuclear weapons, general disarmament, and other problems relating to the relaxation of international tension.

Although I trust your statement, Mr President, there are irresponsible people who would like to invade Cuba now and thus touch off a war. If we do take practical steps and proclaim the dismantling and evacuation of the means in question from Cuba, in so doing we, at the same time, want the Cuban people to be certain that we are with them and are not absolving ourselves of responsibility for rendering assistance to the Cuban people.

We are confident that the people of all countries, like you, Mr President, will understand me correctly. We are not threatening. We want nothing but peace. Our country is now on the upsurge.

Our people are enjoying the fruits of their peaceful labor. They have achieved tremendous successes since the October Revolution, and created the greatest material, spiritual, and cultural values. Our people are enjoying these values; they want to continue developing their achievements and insure their further development on the way of peace and social progress by their persistent labor.

I should like to remind you, Mr President, that military reconnaissance planes have violated the borders of the Soviet Union. In connection with this there have been conflicts between us and notes exchanged. In 1960 we shot down your U-2 plane, whose reconnaissance flight over the USSR wrecked the summit meeting in Paris. At that time, you took a correct position and denounced that criminal act of the former US Administration.

But during your term of office as President another violation of our border has occurred, by an American U-2 plane in the Sakhalin area. We wrote you about that violation on August 30. At that time you replied that that violation had occurred as a result of poor weather, and gave assurances that this would not be repeated. We trusted your assurances, because the weather was indeed poor in that area at that time.

But had not your planes been ordered to fly about our territory, even poor weather could not have brought an American plane into our airspace. Hence, the conclusion that this is being done with the knowledge of the Pentagon, which tramples on international norms and violates the borders of other states.

A still more dangerous case occurred on October 28, when one of your reconnaissance planes intruded over Soviet borders in the Chukotka Peninsula area in the north and flew over our territory. The question is, Mr President: How should we regard this? What is this: A provocation? One of your planes violates our frontier during this anxious time we are both experiencing, when everything has been put into combat readiness. Is it not a fact that an intruding American plane could be easily taken for a nuclear bomber, which might push us to a fateful step? And all the more so since the US Government and Pentagon long ago declared that you are maintaining a continuous nuclear bomber patrol.

Therefore, you can imagine the responsibility you are assuming, especially now, when we are living through such anxious times.

I should like to express the following wish; it concerns the Cuban people. You do not have diplomatic relations. But through my officers in Cuba, I have reports that American planes are making flights over Cuba.

We are interested that there should be no war in the world, and that the Cuban people should live in peace. And besides, Mr President, it is no secret that we have our people in Cuba. Under such a treaty with the Cuban Government we have sent there officers, instructors, mostly plain people: specialists, agronomists, zoo technicians, irrigators, land reclamation specialists, plain workers, tractor drivers, and others. We are concerned about them.

I should like you to consider, Mr President, that violation of Cuban airspace by American planes could also lead to dangerous consequences. And if you do not want this to happen, it would be better if no cause is given for a dangerous situation to arise.

We must be careful now and refrain from any steps which would not be useful to the defense of the states involved in the conflict, which could only cause irritation and even serve as a provocation for a fateful step. Therefore, we must display sanity, reason, and refrain from such steps.

We value peace perhaps even more than other peoples because we went through a terrible war with Hitler. But our people will not falter in the face of any test. Our people trust their Government, and we assure our people and world public opinion that the Soviet Government will not allow itself to be provoked. But if the provocateurs unleash a war, they will not evade responsibility and the grave consequences a war would bring upon them. But we are confident that reason will triumph, that war will not be unleashed and peace and the security of the peoples will be insured.

In connection with the current negotiations between Acting Secretary General U Thant and representatives of the Soviet Union, the United States, and the Republic of Cuba, the Soviet Government has sent First Deputy Foreign Minister V.V. Kuznetsov to New York to help U Thant in his noble efforts aimed at eliminating the present dangerous situation.

Respectfully yours,
N. Khrushchev

Letter from Chairman Khrushchev to President Kennedy
Moscow, October 28, 1962

Dear Mr President, Ambassador Dobrynin has apprised me of his conversation with Robert Kennedy which took place on October 27. In this conversation Robert Kennedy said that it is somewhat difficult for you at the present time to publicly discuss the question of eliminating the US missile bases in Turkey because of the fact that the stationing of those bases in Turkey was formalized through a NATO Council decision.

Readiness to agree on this issue that I raised in my message to you of October 27 was also emphasized. In this context Robert Kennedy said that removal of those bases from Turkey would take four to five months. Furthermore, a wish was expressed that exchanges of views on this matter between you and I should continue through Robert Kennedy and the Soviet ambassador, and that these exchanges should be considered confidential.

I feel I must state to you that I do understand the delicacy involved for you in an open consideration of the issue of eliminating the US missile bases in Turkey. I take into account the complexity of this issue and I believe you are right about not wishing to publicly discuss it. I agree that our discussion of this subject be pursued confidentially through Robert Kennedy and the Soviet ambassador in Washington. You may have noticed that in my message to you on October 28, which was to be published immediately, I did not raise this question—precisely because I was mindful of your wish conveyed through Robert Kennedy. But all the proposals that I presented in that message took into account the fact that you had agreed to resolve the matter of your missile bases in Turkey consistent with what I had said in my message of October 27 and what you stated through Robert Kennedy in his meeting with Ambassador Dobrynin on the same day.

I express my great appreciation to you for having instructed your brother R. Kennedy to convey those thoughts.

I hope, Mr President, that agreement on this matter, too, shall be a no small step advancing the cause of relaxation of international tensions and the tensions between our two powers. And that in turn can provide a good impetus to resolving other issues concerning both the security of Europe and the international situation as a whole.

Mr President, the crisis that we have gone through may repeat again. This means that we need to address the issues which contain too much explosive material. Not right away, of course. Apparently, it will take some time for the passions to cool down. But we cannot delay the solution to these issues, for continuation of this situation is frought [sic] with many uncertainties and dangers.

Sincerely

N. KHRUSHCHEV

Telegram from the Department of State to the Embassy in the Soviet Union
Washington, October 28, 1962, 5:03 p.m.

Following is text President's reply to Khrushchev letter of October 28 for delivery to highest available Soviet official. Text has been handed to Soviet Embassy and released by White House at 4:35 p.m.

Begin text.

Dear Mr Chairman: I am replying at once to your broadcast message of October 28 even though the official text has not yet reached me because of the great importance I attach to moving forward promptly to the settlement of the Cuban crisis. I think that you and I, with our heavy responsibilities for the maintenance of peace, were aware that developments were approaching a point where events could have become unmanageable. So I welcome this message and consider it an important contribution to peace.

The distinguished efforts of Acting Secretary General U Thant have greatly facilitated both our tasks. I consider my letter to you of October 27th and your reply of today as firm undertakings on the part of both our governments which should be promptly carried out. I hope that the necessary measures can at once be taken through the United Nations as your message says, so that the United States in turn can remove the quarantine measures now in effect. I have already made arrangements to report all these matters to the Organization of American States, whose members share a deep interest in a genuine peace in the Caribbean area.

You referred in your letter to a violation of your frontier by an American aircraft in the area of the Chukotsk Peninsula. I have learned that this plane, without arms or photographic equipment, was engaged in an air sampling mission in connection with your nuclear tests. Its course was direct from Eielson Air Force Base in Alaska to the North Pole and return. In turning south, the pilot made a serious navigational error which carried him over Soviet territory. He immediately made an emergency call on open radio for navigational assistance and was guided back to his home base by the most direct route. I regret this incident and will see to it that every precaution is taken to prevent recurrence.

Mr Chairman, both of our countries have great unfinished tasks and I know that your people as well as those of the United States can ask for nothing better than to pursue them free from the fear of war. Modern science and technology have given us the possibility of making labor fruitful beyond anything that could have been dreamed of a few decades ago.

I agree with you that we must devote urgent attention to the problem of disarmament, as it relates to the whole world and also to critical areas. Perhaps now, as we step back from danger, we can together make real progress in this vital field. I think we should give priority to questions relating to the proliferation of nuclear weapons, on earth and in outer space, and to the great effort for a nuclear test ban. But we should also work hard to see if wider measures of disarmament can be agreed and put into operation at an early date. The United States Government will be prepared to discuss these questions urgently, and in a constructive spirit, at Geneva or elsewhere.

John F. Kennedy

RUSK

POSTSCRIPT

Cuban record of conversation, Mikoyan and Cuban leadership
Havana, 4 November 1962

Meeting of the Secretariat of the CRI with Mikoyan at the National Palace

Preamble by Mikoyan:

He says he has come to Cuba to discuss their differences with the Cuban Companeros [comrades] and not to [discuss] what has been stated by the imperialists. They trust us as much as they trust themselves. He is willing to discuss for as long as it takes to solve the differences. The interests of the Soviet Union are common to ours in the defense of the principles of Marxism–Leninism and in all the other interests.

Fidel: Summarizes our differences in terms of the procedures used to deal with this crisis.

Dorticos: Asks whether Mikoyan considers that they have obtained the guarantees that President Kennedy offered.

Carlos: Asks whether the victory mentioned by the Soviets has been attained.

Mikoyan: Says he will respond to the questions, and asks to be excused for he will speak for a long time. He says he will start with the doubts expressed by Fidel in order to explain them.

He thinks that the main problem consists in explaining why they have sent troops and strategic weapons. If this is not understood, it is very difficult to understand the whole situation. He did not think we had doubts about this. He said that the fate of the Cuban revolution is a permanent preoccupation of ours, especially since its socialist character was declared. When the imperialists were defeated in Giron [Beach at the Bay of Pigs], we congratulated ourselves, but we also worried. The *yanquis* did a stupid thing but we knew they would continue harassing because Cuba is an example that they could not tolerate. Our assessment was that they had two parallel plans; the first one consisted of the economic strangulation of Cuba in order to bring down the regime without a military intervention. The second one consisted of an intervention organized by Latin American governments and their support, as an alternative to the other plan.

We consider the victory of the Cuban revolution as an enormous contribution to Marxism–Leninism. Its defeat would be an irreparable damage to Marxism and to other revolutionary movements in other countries. Such a defeat would mean the preponderance of imperialism over socialism in the world. Such a defeat would mean a terrible blow against the world revolution. It would break the correlation of forces. It is our duty to do everything possible to defend Cuba.

Our comrades told us that the economic situation in Cuba had worsened due to the *yanquis'* pressure and the enormous military expenses. This worried us for it coincided with the plans of the *yanquis*. We had a discussion about the economic decline and we have helped without you requesting it. You are very modest in your requests and we try to help you. We decided to give you weapons for free and donated equipment for 100,000 men. In addition, in our commercial negotiations, we have looked at all the possibilities and we have tried to provide everything you needed without payments in kind. We have given you 180 million roubles in order to help you. This is a second phase of help because before that there were commercial and credit agreements but these last deliveries have been in aid.

When Khrushchev visited Bulgaria [on 14–20 May 1962] he expressed many things to us, he said "Although I was in Bulgaria, I was always thinking of Cuba. I fear the *yanquis* will attack Cuba, directly or indirectly, and imagine of the effect on us of the defeat of the Cuban revolution. We cannot allow this to happen. Although the plan is very risky for us, it is a big responsibility for it exposes us to a war. Cuba must be saved[.]" They thought it over for three days and later all the members of the Central Committee expressed their opinions. We have to think a lot about this action in order to save Cuba and not to provoke a nuclear war. He ordered the military to develop the Plan and to consult with the Cubans. He told us that the main condition was to carry out the Plan secretly. Our military told us that four months were needed for the preparations. We thought the enemy would learn about it right in the middle of the plan and we anticipated what to do. We thought the plan would not be carried out to the end, but this was an advantage, for the troops would already be in the Island. We foresaw that, in order not to provoke a war, we could use the UNO and the public opinion. We thought the Plan would not provoke a war but a blockade against weapons and fuel instead. How to solve this—your lack of fuel? Considering the geographic situation of the Island, it has been very difficult to avoid the blockade. If you were closer we could have used our Air Force and our Fleet, but we could not. The *yanquis* do have bases surrounding us in Turkey and blocking the Black Sea. Given the situation, we cannot strike back. Okinawa is too far away too. The only possibility was to cut the communications with West Berlin. In Berlin this is possible.

We have not thought of building a Soviet Base on the Island to operate against the North Americans. In general, we consider that the policy of bases is not a correct one. We only have bases in [East] Germany, first because of the right we have as an invading country, and after that due to the Warsaw Treaty. (Stalin did have bases abroad.) In the past, we have had them in Finland and in China too (Port Arthur)—those bases we have abandoned. We only have troops in Hungary and Poland, to protect the troops in Germany and the communications with Austria.

We do not need bases to destroy the United States because we can attack with the missiles deployed in our territory. We do not have a plan to conquer North America. The only thing we need to do is to launch a counter strike, but that will serve to destroy them without having to send in our troops.

We have sent the troops and strategic missiles only to protect the Island's defense. It was a plan of containment [*contension*] so that the *yanquis* could not provoke an explosion in Cuba. If the missiles are well camouflaged and the *yanquis* do not know where they are deployed, then they can help to contain them. The military told us that they could be well hidden in the palm forests of Cuba. The *yanquis* were not going to locate them. They could not destroy them. During July and August, they did not find anything, it was not until October that they have been found. We were surprised that Kennedy only made reference to technicians and not to our troops. At first, it seems that that is what he thought. Later we learned that he knew more than he was saying, but he was not revealing it not to hinder the electoral campaign. We let the *yanquis* know that we were going to solve the Berlin problem, in order to distract their attention from the other problem. We did not intend to act on Berlin. I can explain this later. It was known through diplomatic channels that Kennedy did not want to make matters more serious and asked us not to move on the issue of Berlin before the elections. We told him that we agreed to this. We would please him and we would solve it later. We thought it was convenient to please him. In addition, we had not thought of bringing up this problem.

When the North Americans learned about the transports to Cuba, they also concentrated their campaign on Berlin. Both sides had their principal interest in Cuba, but appeared as if concentrated on Berlin. In the middle of October, they [the North Americans] learned about it through Cuba, via the West Germany information service who passed it to the CIA, they first learned about the missiles. They took aerial pictures and located them. Khrushchev ordered that the missiles be laid down during the day and that they be raised only during the night. Evidently, this order was never carried out. Kennedy did not want to talk about the missiles until the end of the elections. But two Republican Senators learned the news and they had no alternative but to act. We did not know what Kennedy would do and we worried about the preparations or maneuvers of Vieti—an operation named after Castro but backwards. When Kennedy talked about the blockade, we did not have data showing whether it was a maneuver or a preparation for aggression. On the morning of the 28th we received the news confirming that it was an aggression. Although it was announced that the maneuvers were suspended due to a storm, the storm was over and the maneuvers were not carried out. In the meantime, the concentration continued. Khrushchev has strongly criticized Kennedy's words about the blockade. They did not approve of the kind of weapons that Cuba should own and thus they organized a direct aggression. Their plan consisted of two parts: using missiles with conventional loads to destroy the nuclear missiles and then landing and destroying the resistance.

In case of the latter, we would be forced to respond because it is an attack against Cuba and against us too—because our troops were here and this was the unleashing of the World War. We would destroy North America. They would inflict huge loses on us; but they would make every effort to destroy Cuba completely. All the measures we took were taken to protect Cuba. What would have been the result if the plan of the *yanquis* was carried out? Lose Cuba, inflict enormous damages upon the Socialist countries with a nuclear war? While we were in the midst of our discussions, we received a cable from Fidel that coincided with other information in the same vein. After that, 10 to 12 hours were left. Given that such a short time was left, we used diplomatic channels. Because when policymakers want to avoid a war, they have to use diplomatic means. It's important to underscore that Kennedy says now that he was not against the presence of troops here and that he accepts ground-to-air missiles. But once known, the strategic weapons, were not useful anymore.

The withdrawal of the missiles was a concession on our part. But Kennedy also makes a concession by permitting the Soviet weapons [to remain in Cuba], in addition, declaring that they will not attack Cuba nor permit that it be attacked. In assessing the outcome, we have gained, because they will not attack Cuba and there will be no war.

In normal conditions, it would be natural that we send you a project [*draft*] for you to study and you could then publish it. But that can be done only in normal conditions. An invasion was expected within the next 24 hours. When Fidel sent his cable, there were only 10 to 12 hours left. If a cable was sent it had to be encrypted, that would take more than 10 to 12 hours. Consultations would have been appropriate, but Cuba would not exist and the world would be enveloped in a war. After the attack, they would have never accepted a truce, due to the warmongers of the Pentagon. Our attitude has produced difficulties, but in making an overall evaluation, in spite of the psychological defects, we can see that the advantages are undeniable.

Com[panero] Dorticos asks: What guarantees offered by Kennedy have really been obtained? We consider that all agreements cannot be rejected in a nihilistic fashion. Although agreements can be breached, they are important for they are useful for a certain period of time.

In addition, a problem arose with the Turkey issue. [Mikoyan said:] Why did we include the problem of Turkey and the bases? We did not have in our plans to discuss Turkey; but while we were discussing that issue, we received an article from [US journalist Walter] Lip[p]man[n] saying that the Russians will discuss that, [and] that is why we included it. The bases in Turkey are of no importance because in case of war they would be destroyed. There are also bases in England that could damage all the bases anywhere in the world.

Fidel asks whether there were in fact two letters [from Khrushchev to Kennedy], one that mentioned the issue of Turkey, which was broadcast on Radio Moscow, and another in which the issue was not mentioned.

[Mikoyan replied:] We sent two letters, one on the 26th that was not published, and another one on the 27th. The issue of Turkey was not included at the beginning, we included it later. But we can describe all that in more detail through a reviewing of the documents. We have had discussions about your question whether the dismantling of the base at Guantánamo is better. That would be better for Cuba, but from a military point of view of the interest of Cuba, it is not possible. If we decided to withdraw all the weapons from Cuba, then we could demand the withdrawal from Guantánamo, Guantánamo has no importance in military terms. That would be more dangerous, and that is important from a political perspective. Concerning the inspection: if we said we reject any inspection, the enemy could interpret that as an attempt to trick them. All it is about is seeing the sites, where the weapons were and their shipping for a few days. Cuba is in the hands of the Cubans. But because we were the owners of those weapons . . . (paragraph missing). [*notation in original*] We thought that you, after the consultations, you would accept the inspection. But we never thought of deciding anything for you. Why did we think that we could accept a verification of the dismantling by neutrals, without infringement of the Cuban sovereignty? It was understood that no State would accept an infringement of your sovereignty. In very particular cases, a State can . . . [*ellipsis in document*] its acts, by agreement and not due to pressures from abroad—the territory of the Embassy within a sovereign State for example. When discussing the problem of Indo-China and Vietnam in Geneva [in 1954], an agreement was reached to create an International Control Commission.

∘⊸◦◈◦⊷∘

We spoke about the problem of dismantling with [US negotiator John J.] McCloy in New York. He said that "given that Cuba is opposed to the North American inspection, he did not insist on this formula—for them to verify that the weapons will not be kept hidden in the forest. [*no close quotation marks in original*]

I talked to them about the aerial photographic inspection, but I responded that Cuba has the right to its air space. I told them that their planes have flown over Cuba and they were convinced that the dismantling is being carried out. They admitted that, but pointed that not everything is finished. We told them that this is nearly completed and he did not talk further about it. [McCloy said:] We have to be sure that they are not going to hide them in the forest. We do not want data pertaining to your military secrets; but we need assurances that the missiles will go.

We can provide the pictures of the dismantled weapons and how they are loaded. Nor will we oppose that you observe the ships on the high seas, at a particular distance. They (or you) will see something on the decks. I did not tell them that, but that is our opinion and we will provide them with the materials to convince them that we have withdrawn the missiles. So we will not contradict your [Cuban] declaration, against the inspection or the aerial verification.

They feared that the Cubans would not allow us to withdraw the missiles, given that they have 140,000 and you only have 10,000 men. I did not talk about these numbers. He said that the U–2 that was shot down here, was shot at with Russian missiles and probably operated by Russians. Although they think there may be Cubans who are able to operate those weapons. We kept on insisting that they lift the quarantine immediately. I told them that if they wanted the missiles withdrawn faster, they should lift the blockade. Because the ships that are now in Cuba are not able to take those missiles out. I told them they should issue instructions so that the inspection of the ships be carried out without anybody boarding the ships. It would rather be carried out in a symbolic manner, asking by radio, as it was done with the tanker *Bucharest*.

Stevenson said they will accept the proposals of U Thant. We reproached him that he proposed not to bring weapons to Cuba and to lift the blockade. We have complied with this and they continue.

We have losses because the ships wait on the high seas. The losses are considerable, that is why we have allowed the control of the Red Cross. The Red Cross is better because it is not a political institution, nor a governmental institution. U Thant proposed two inspections, one at the shipping harbors and another on the high seas. Not wanting to hurt his feelings, we responded that we accept the inspection on the high seas and not at the shipping harbors. U Thant, when returning from Cuba, told me that you did not agree, although this verification is easier at the harbors. U Thant is ready, he is choosing the personnel and has already two ships. I do not know more about it, for it is [Soviet Deputy Foreign Minister V. V.] Kuznetsov who deals with this issue.

In this situation, Thant has played a good role. You cannot ask more, given his situation, he even seems to have a little sympathy for our position. While in Moscow, we received a plan of guarantees. We thought this plan seemed interesting and useful for Cuba.

Why: If the inspection of Cuba, the southern coast of the US and other countries in the Caribbean will be approved (Central America[)] because this way you deprive the aggressor of the possibility to carry out its goals. Of course, this can be circumvented, however. I have been interested in this variant from another point of view. There is an OAS, and it is the US who profits from it instead of using the UN. But if this plan is approved, it is the UNO that will deal with this part of the American Continent, this constitutes a blow to the Monroe Doctrine. U Thant said that the representatives from Latin American countries agree with this plan, the North Americans avoid responding to it. I asked McCloy and he said at the beginning (as did Stevenson) that the U Thant Plan does not exist. But afterward they discarded the US inspection and they said they can give their word that in Latin America all the camps [of anti-Castro Cuban exiles] are liquidated. I asked him if all were, and he avoided the question. They said that Cuba was a revolutionary infection, he said that the Latin American countries fear Cuba. A formula can be searched in which Cuba will abandon the clandestine work in exchange for their not attacking.

Fidel was right when he said that it's easier for the USSR to maneuver and maintain a flexible policy than it is for Cuba, all the more as the *yanqui* radio reaches Cuba easily. It is not just to say that we are more liberal. The Cuban revolution cannot be lost. You have to maneuver to save the Revolution by being flexible.

In retrospect the question that arises is whether it was a mistake to send the missiles and then withdraw them from the Island. Our Central Committee says that this is not a mistake. We consider that the missiles did their job by making Cuba the focus of the world diplomacy. After they were captured in photos, they cannot accomplish their role of containment.

In Latin America no country has the power that Cuba has. No Latin American bloc can defeat Cuba.

In order to understand on what victory rests, you may compare the situation of Cuba now and four months ago (in July). The first advantage is that the North Americans stopped talking about the Monroe Doctrine and before, the whole basis for their policy toward Latin America was that doctrine.

Before, they declared they would not tolerate the existence of a Marxist–Leninist regime in Latin America, now they declare that they will not attack Cuba. Before they did not tolerate a country from abroad in the Caribbean and now they know of the existence of Soviet specialists and do not say a thing.

Before, you could not have any action of the UN in favor of Cuba and now it is working in that sense, all the peoples are mobilized.

The prestige of the Socialist Camp has grown because it defended peace. Although the United States brought the world to the brink of a war, the USSR, by pacific means, was able to save Cuba and the [world] peace.

Peace has been secured for several years and Cuba must be consolidated for it to continue building socialism and continue being the Lighthouse for Latin America.

The prestige of Cuba has grown as a consequence of these events.

∞⚬⚭⚬∞

Fidel asks whether he [Mikoyan] will speak about the Soviet policy in Berlin. Mikoyan agrees to do so in a later interview.

Conversation between the Cuban Secretariat and Mikoyan
Havana, Monday, November 5, 1962, 3:00 p.m.

After hearing Mikoyan, Fidel says: We consider that the intentions of the Soviet Government cannot be determined only by the analysis of what happened in face of an unforeseen situation. Instead, they should be analyzed taking into account the set of agreements we have reached—the weapons were brought under those precepts. One of them is the military agreement that was to be published once all the weapons were brought in and once the Elections were held in the United States. These agreements represent a firm desire of the Soviet Union.

That is why this has to be analyzed under the light of what we intended to do and not under the light of what happened.

If all the steps were carried out, we have no doubt that they would have served as a containment to the plans of the North Americans to attack our country. And the objectives of the Soviet Government and Cuba would have been attained.

At the same time, we knew that the deployment of missiles in Cuba had in sight the defense of the Socialist Camp. They were important not only in military terms, but also from a psychological and political point of view. Besides serving the interests of Cuba, they served the interests of the Socialist Camp as a whole, and we evidently agreed with that. That is how we have understood the step taken, and we also understand it was a step in the right direction. We also agree with the need that a war be avoided and we do not oppose that. In this case, all the measures oriented to attain the two objectives were undertaken. We are in absolute agreement with the goals sought by the Soviet Union, the misunderstandings arise as a result of the way they were attained. We also understand that the circumstances were compelling. They were not one hundred percent normal.

In assessing how the events occurred, we think they could have been dealt with differently. For instance, one thing discussed is the impact that my letter had on the

Soviet Government's decision of the [October] 28th. And it is evident that my letter had nothing to do with the course of the events—given the messages that were exchanged between the Soviet and North American Governments on the 26th and 27th. My letter's only goal was to inform the Soviet Government of the imminent attack, and it did not contain any hesitation on our part. Furthermore, we expressed that we did not expect an invasion. We expressed that the invasion was possible, but we understood that it was the least probable variant. The most probable event was an aerial attack to destroy the strategic weapons.

The Soviet Government's decision on the 28th, is based on the letter to Kennedy and the response on the 27th. The real basis for the 28th decision lies within these two documents. Kennedy's letter on the 28th was an agreement to the proposals Khrushchev sent on the 26th—in the sense that he [Krushchev] was willing to resolve the issue of all the weapons if the US ceased the aggression. The aggression was the only reason for the military strengthening of Cuba.

Once Kennedy accepted this proposal—which we did not know of—the conditions were set to carry it out starting with a declaration by the Soviets stating that their side was on board and that they would proceed to discuss it with the Cuban Government.

I think that such a declaration, instead of communicating an order to withdraw the Strategic Weapons, would have decreased the tension and would have allowed to carry the discussions in better terms.

But this is a mere analysis of what happened, it does not matter now. What matters now is simply to know what to do and how to attain the main goals that are to stop the aggression and to secure the peace at the same time. If a true and effective peace are attained in the near future, then—under the light of the recent events—we will be able to judge better the steps taken. The future outcome—for which we need to struggle—will either credit or discredit the value of the acts of the present. It is evident that attaining that outcome does not depend so much on us. We are very grateful for all the explanations given and of the effort made for us to understand the things that occurred. We know they happened in abnormal circumstances. There is no question in our minds about the respect of the Soviet Union toward us, the respect of the Soviet Union for our sovereignty, and, the help of the Soviet Union. That is why what is important to discuss is what are the steps to take in the future. We want to reaffirm our trust in the Soviet Union.

New titles in this series

The War Facsimiles

The War Facsimiles are exact reproductions of illustrated books that were published during the war years. They were produced by the British government to inform people about the progress of the war and the home-defence operations.

The Battle of Britain, August–October 1940

On 8 August 1940, the Germans launched the first of a series of mass air attacks on Britain in broad daylight. For almost three months, British and German aircraft were locked in fierce and prolonged combat in what has become known as the Battle of Britain. In 1941 the government published *The Battle of Britain* to explain the strategy and tactics behind the fighting that had taken place high in the sky over London and south-east England. Such was the public interest in this document, with its graphic maps and photographs, that sales had reached two million by the end of the war.

ISBN 0 11 702536 4   Price £4.99 US $8.95

The Battle of Egypt, 1942

Often referred to as the Battle of El Alamein, this battle was one of the major turning points for the Allies in World War II. The British, commanded by General Montgomery, were defending Egypt while the Germans under Rommel were attacking. This was a campaign the British could not afford to lose, because not only would it leave Egypt wide open for invasion, but it would also mean the loss of the Suez Canal and the oil fields. First published in 1943, *The Battle of Egypt* is an astonishing contemporary report of one of the most famous military victories in British history.

ISBN 0 11 702542 9   Price £5.99 US $10.95

Bomber Command: the Air Ministry account of Bomber Command's offensive against the Axis, September 1939–July 1941

Churchill declared on 22 June 1941: "We shall bomb Germany by day as well as by night in ever-increasing measure." Bomber Command of the RAF was to translate those words into action, beginning its attacks on Germany in May 1940, and steadily increasing its efforts as the war progressed. Published in 1941 at the height of World War II, *Bomber Command* tells the story of this fighting force during those early years.

ISBN 0 11 702540 2   Price £5.99 US $11.95

East of Malta, West of Suez: the Admiralty account of the naval war in the eastern Mediterranean, September 1939 to March 1941

This is the story of the British Navy in action in the eastern Mediterranean from September 1939 to March 1941 and their bid to seize control. During this time British supremacy was vigorously asserted at Taranto and Matapan. This facsimile edition contains contemporary maps, air reconnaissance photographs of the fleets and photographs of them in action.

ISBN 0 11 702538 0   Price £4.99 US $8.95

Fleet Air Arm: the Admiralty account of naval air operations, 1943

The Fleet Air Arm was established in 1939 as the Royal Navy's own flying branch. With its vast aircraft carriers bearing squadrons of fighter pilots, its main role was to protect a fleet or convoy from attack, or to escort an air striking force into battle. In *Fleet Air Arm*, published in 1943, the public could read for the first time of the expeditions of these great ships as they pursued and sank enemy warships such as the *Bismarck*.

ISBN 0 11 702539 9   Price £5.99 US $11.95

Land at War: the official story of British farming
1939–1944

Land at War was published by the Ministry of Information in 1945 as a tribute to those who had contributed to the war effort at home. It explains how 300,000 farms, pinpointed by an extensive farm survey, had been expected to increase their production dramatically, putting an extra 6.5 million acres of grassland under the plough. This is a book not just about rural life, but of the determination of a people to survive the rigours of war.

ISBN 0 11 702537 2   Price £5.99 US $11.95

Ocean Front: the story of the war in the Pacific,
1941–44

Ocean Front tells the story of the Allies' war against Japan in the central and western Pacific. Starting with Pearl Harbor in December 1941, this fascinating book recounts the Allies' counter-offensive, from the battles of the Coral Sea and Midway, to the recapture of the Aleutian Islands and the final invasion of the Philippines. Illustrated throughout with amazing photographs of land and sea warfare, *Ocean Front* provides a unique record of the American, Australian and New Zealand fighting forces in action.

ISBN 0 11 702543 7   Price £5.99 US $11.95

Roof over Britain: the official story of Britain's
anti-aircraft defences, 1939–1942

Largely untold, *Roof over Britain* is the story of Britain's ground defences against the attacks of the German air force during the Battle of Britain in the autumn of 1940. First published in 1943, it describes how the static defences – the AA guns, searchlights and balloons – were organised, manned and supplied in order to support the work of the RAF.

ISBN 0 11 702541 0   Price £5.99 US $11.95

Uncovered editions: how to order

FOR CUSTOMERS IN THE UK
Ordering is easy. Simply follow one of these five ways:

Online
Visit www.clicktso.com

By telephone
Please call 0870 600 5522, with book details to hand.

By fax
Fax details of the books you wish to order (title, ISBN, quantity and price) to: 0870 600 5533.
Please include details of your credit/debit card plus expiry date, your name and address and telephone number, and expect a handling charge of £3.00.

By post
Post the details listed above (under 'By fax') to:
The Stationery Office
PO Box 29
Norwich NR3 1GN
You can send a cheque if you prefer by this method (made payable to The Stationery Office). Please include a handling charge of £3 on the final amount.

TSO bookshops
Visit your local TSO bookshop (or any good bookshop).

FOR CUSTOMERS IN THE UNITED STATES
Uncovered editions are available through all major wholesalers and bookstores, and are distributed to the trade by Midpoint Trade Books.
Phone 913 831 2233 for single copy prepaid orders which can be fulfilled on the spot, or simply for more information.
Fax 913 362 7401